90 0963688 8

D1756129

...URE IN
..., 1559 – 1...

The Huguenots formed a privileged minority within early modern France. During the second half of the sixteenth century they fought for freedom of worship in the French 'wars of religion', which culminated in the Edict of Nantes in 1598. The community was protected by the terms of the edict for eighty-seven years until Louis XIV revoked it in 1685. The Huguenots therefore constitute a minority group tolerated by one of the strongest nations in early modern Europe, a country more often associated with the absolute power of the crown – in particular that of Louis XIV.

This collection of essays explores the character and identity of the Huguenot movement by examining their culture and institutions, their patterns of belief and worship, and their interaction with the French state and society. The volume draws upon recent research by leading historians and new specialists from across Europe and North America.

RAYMOND A. MENTZER holds the Daniel J. Krumm Family Chair in Reformation Studies, University of Iowa.

ANDREW SPICER is a Research Fellow in the Department of History, University of Exeter.

SOCIETY AND CULTURE IN THE HUGUENOT WORLD
1559–1685

EDITED BY

RAYMOND A. MENTZER

AND

ANDREW SPICER

CAMBRIDGE
UNIVERSITY PRESS

CAMBRIDGE UNIVERSITY PRESS
Cambridge, New York, Melbourne, Madrid, Cape Town, Singapore, São Paulo

Cambridge University Press
The Edinburgh Building, Cambridge CB2 8RU, UK

Published in the United States of America by Cambridge University Press, New York

www.cambridge.org
Information on this title: www.cambridge.org/9780521773249

First published 2002
Reprinted 2003
This digitally printed version 2007

A catalogue record for this publication is available from the British Library

Library of Congress Cataloguing in Publication data

Society and culture in the Huguenot world, 1559–1685 / edited by Raymond A. Mentzer.
p.   cm.
Includes bibliographical references and index.
ISBN 0 521 77324 5
1. Huguenots – France – History – 16th century.   2. Huguenots – France – History –
17th century.   I. Mentzer, Raymond A.   II. Spicer, Andrew.
BX9454.3 .S63   2002   305.6′45044 – dc21   2001037547

ISBN 978-0-521-77324-9 hardback
ISBN 978-0-521-03788-4 paperback

Contents

Illustrations

Tables

Notes on contributors

PHILIP BENEDICT is Professor of History at Brown University. His books include *Rouen during the Wars of Religion* (1981) and *The Faith and Fortunes of France's Huguenots* (2001). He is also the editor of *Cities and Social Change in Early Modern France* (1989) and *Reformation, Revolt, and Civil War in France and the Netherlands, 1555–1585* (1999).

MARTIN DINGES is Deputy Director of the Institute for the History of Medicine of the Robert Bosch Foundation, Stuttgart, Germany and Adjunct Professor of Early Modern and Modern History at the University of Mannheim. He has written a number of articles and essays on medical history and is the author of *Stadtarmut in Bordeaux (1525–1675) – Alltag, Politik, Mentalitäten* (1988) and editor of *Hausväter, Priester, Kastraten. Zur Konstruktion von Männlichkeit in Spätmittelalter und Früher Neuzeit* (1998).

AMANDA EURICH is the author of *The Economics of Power: The Private Fortunes of the House of Foix-Navarre-Albret during the Religious Wars* (1994) and has written a number of articles on the contours of confessional identity and community in early modern France. She is researching a case study of Béarn and Orange entitled *Confessional Identity and Community: The Politics and Practice of Religious Co-existence in Early Modern France.* She is Associate Professor of History, Western Washington University, Bellingham.

MARK GREENGRASS has a personal chair in History, University of Sheffield. He has published extensively on sixteenth-century French history and seventeenth-century intellectual history. His recent books include: *France in the Age of Henri IV: the struggle for stability* (2nd edition, 1994) and *The Longman Companion to the European Reformation, c. 1500–1618* (1998). He is currently engaged in writing a book on the reform of the state endeavoured by the last Valois king, Henri III.

ALAN JAMES is a lecturer at the University of Manchester and is the author of *The Ship of State: Naval Affairs in Early Modern France, 1572–1661* (2002).

KARIN MAAG is Director of the H. Henry Meeter Center for Calvin Studies at Calvin College and Calvin Theological Seminary in Grand Rapids, Michigan in the United States. She is also Associate Professor of History at Calvin College. She is the author of *Seminary or University? The Genevan Academy and Reformed Higher Education, 1560–1620* (1995) and editor of *The Reformation in Eastern and Central Europe* (1997) and of *Melanchthon in Europe: His Work and Influence Beyond Wittenberg* (1999).

RAYMOND A. MENTZER holds the Daniel J. Krumm Family Chair in Reformation Studies, School of Religion, University of Iowa. He was previously Professor of History, Montana State University. He is the author of *Heresy Proceedings in Languedoc, 1500–1560* (1984), *Blood and Belief: Family Survival and Confessional Identity among the Provincial Huguenot Nobility* (1994) and *La construction de l'identité des Réformés aux 16e et 17e siècles: le rôle des consistoires* (forthcoming). He has edited *Sin and the Calvinists: Morals Control and the Consistory in the Reformed Tradition* (1994) and is currently preparing a study of moral and social discipline among French Protestants during the sixteenth and seventeenth centuries.

LUC RACAUT is a lecturer at the University of Glasgow, Crichton Campus. He is the author of several articles and his monograph, *Hatred in Print: Catholic Polemic and Protestant Identity during the French Wars of Religion*, is to be published in 2002.

PENNY ROBERTS is Lecturer in History at the University of Warwick. Her publications include *A City in Conflict: Troyes during the French Wars of Religion* (1996), *Fear in Early Modern Society* (coeditor, 1997), *The Massacre in History* (coeditor, 1999), *The Adventure of Religious Pluralism in Early Modern France* (coeditor, 2000), as well as a number of articles and essays on the religious and social history of sixteenth-century France. She is currently completing a monograph, *Brokering the Peace: The Pacification of France, 1561–1598* and also writing *The Wars of Religion and the French People*.

BERNARD ROUSSEL is Directeur d'Études à la Section des Sciences religieuses de l'École Pratique des Hautes Études in Paris and holds the chair of 'Réformes et protestantismes dans l'Europe moderne'. His research has focused on French Protestantism and on the translation, interpretation and use of the Scriptures in the sixteenth and seventeenth centuries. He has published a number of articles on French protestantism and most recently has coedited *Coexister dans l'Intolérance: l'Édit de Nantes (1598)* (1998) and *Entrer en Matière. Les Prologues* (1998).

ANDREW SPICER is a research fellow in History at the University of Exeter. He is the author of *The French-speaking Reformed Community and their Church in Southampton* (1997) and a number of articles on exile communities. He is currently writing a monograph, *The Reformation Church: Architecture and Society*, and has published essays on the impact of the Reformation upon church architecture.

TIMOTHY WATSON is Lecturer in History at the University of Newcastle. He completed his thesis, 'The Lyon City Council c.1525–1575: Politics, Culture, Religion', at the University of Oxford. He has published articles on city council administration and on the development of the Huguenot government in Lyon during the early years of the wars of religion.

Preface

Historians and their readers might well view French Protestantism under the *ancien régime* with considerable professional relish. The field of study is tightly defined, above all by strict chronological limits. The phenomenon unfolded tangibly and publicly in 1534 with the 'Affair of the Placards' and the repression that ensued, and closed in 1685 with the proscription of Reformed churches and worship within the kingdom. These 150 years represent, drawing an analogy with geology, a cross-section of time sufficient for significant stratigraphy without the need to sink into the impermeable and impenetrable geological strata. At the same time, providential reference points suitably structure this middling span. The first national synod of the Reformed churches opened in 1559; the final synod concluded exactly a century later. In between, the St Bartholomew's Day massacre, the Edict of Nantes and the Peace of Alès regularly and unmistakably punctuated the collective fate of the Huguenots until their official proscription with the Revocation.

The historiographic advantages of a legally recognized and tolerated Protestantism do not end here. Its implantation and continuing presence was soon concentrated in several relatively limited areas, which offer the additional pleasure of being largely south of the Loire in a region that is exceptionally inviting in terms of climate and countryside, historical patrimony and gastronomy. It would not be an excessively hazardous presumption to find here a related motive for the passion among many Anglo-Saxon historians for our Protestant past! On a more serious note, the community or collectivity, while not always collective, of Huguenots possesses comfortable dimensions, neither too large nor too small for those who wish to understand it. They were perhaps 15 per cent of the kingdom's population and maintained a stability wholly remarkable from the end of Henri II's reign until the middle of that of Louis XIV. In short, they constituted an undeniable minority in terms of mass, space and time. Accordingly, this appealingly pure minority has been, for the past half century, the chosen territory, the exquisite field for the historian of culture and society.

After having toured the deeply esteemed object, having determined the reference marks and offered the definitions, the moment comes to enter into the reality of things and to explore the terrain patiently and profoundly. What was the unique character and singularity of these populations, these groups, and these individuals whom the law and various institutions designated special or unusual without being foreign or unfamiliar? How did they feel about themselves? How were they recognized by others, especially when they were not worshipping in their temples or singing the psalms in their homes? Even the most fervent, who were undoubtedly not the most numerous, could not spend their entire lives in these pious activities. It is not always the distinctive nature of war, repression, massacres, or even petitions and remonstrances that allows us to see clearly. Faced with the etiquette of being Protestant under a monarchy ever more absolutist and Catholic, the historian's eye joins with that of the anthropologist.

This double vision, which leads us to read in fresh ways materials already examined and to gather and explore previously ignored sources, makes all the more valuable the project designed and executed by Professors Mentzer and Spicer. The dozen original essays gathered here have the common purpose of responding with nuance and variety, all the while avoiding excessive complexity, to a question put very simply, almost as if it has never been posed. What did it mean to be Protestant in France during the sixteenth and seventeenth centuries, for them, among them, for others, and for the powerful Catholic majority, which was both close by and typically hostile? How do we provide a concrete response to the two fundamental points raised by the prince de Condé in his 1563 letter to the king: 'this is to say, the unequal treatment of your subjects and the liberty to live among themselves without fear of being sought out for reason of their conscience'?

Leaving aside these general ideas, upon which French historians have written prodigiously and with which their foreign colleagues are well acquainted, the scholars at hand depart with near-missionary zeal to flush out, wherever they find – at worship, at school, in the army, at home, among friends, confronted by adversaries, at work, in midst of destitution, even as far as the cemetery – Protestants in their normal course of speaking, thinking, writing, calculating, organizing themselves, acting and, above all, simply existing in expansive and delightful as well as constrained circumstances and the small worries that formed the fabric of their daily lives. The internal and external sociability of a minority and frequently bullied community, whose shared faith does not guarantee homogeneity, requires, for precise description or, better yet, reconstitution, enormous tact in the approach as well as a fresh spirit. People in any society do not always tell us what they are doing, and the Huguenots are no different. The normative texts, whose interpretation is never simple, often serve as a screen or pretext for practices which are very different in either the letter or the spirit, as demonstrated by family or professional strategies revealed through private correspondence. In addition, spiritual and ecclesiastical issues are mixed with material, social and cultural considerations, which complicate matters and intensify their meaning.

In the presence of this Huguenot world and of the mass of documentation that it has produced, our colleagues, however familiar they may be with the subject, come almost entirely from a cultural universe that is external to Protestant France. In most cases, French and especially its Huguenot variant is not their mother tongue. Accordingly, they reflect on matters that no longer attract our attention. They see and discover things that we no longer recognize because we are too close. The horizon of truth is never clearer than in advancing pure vistas and multiplying the perspectives.

All of this explains why I, as the president of the Société de l'Histoire du Protestantisme Français, honoured by the request to write this preface, and cognizant that the Society's Library and its many publications are integral to the work of the contributors, find it entirely in keeping with my position to celebrate the present volume, whose learned commentary does not exclude clarity of tone, as the admirable result of shared labour conceived essentially beyond the Channel and the Atlantic. In truth, the international network of skills and friendships present in this collection witnesses the unique and multiple interest elicited by the 'French Protestant' to whom this volume confers a presumption of an additional and particularly convincing existence.

LAURENT THEIS
President, Société de l'Histoire du Protestantisme Français

Acknowledgements

The completion of an edited volume inevitably incurs a number of debts and the editors would like to thank the contributors for their enthusiastic support. They are also grateful to Montana State University and the University of Exeter for continuing their encouragement. Professor Mentzer, in addition, wishes to acknowledge well-received assistance from the American Council of Learned Societies and the National Endowment for the Humanities. Finally, the editors take this opportunity to thank Beth Mentzer for her assistance and comments in the final editorial stages of this project.

Abbreviations

AC	Archives Communales
AD	Archives Départementales
AM	Archives Municipales
AN	Archives Nationales, Paris
ARG	*Archiv für Reformationsgeschichte*
Aymon	J. Aymon, *Tous les synodes nationaux des églises réformées de France*, 2 vols. (The Hague, 1710)
BHR	*Bibliothèque d'Humanisme et Renaissance*
BN	Bibliothèque Nationale, Paris
BSHPF	*Bulletin de la Société de l'Histoire du Protestantisme Français*
CO	G. Baum, E. Cunitz and E. Reuss (eds.), *Joannis Calvini opera quae supersunt omnia*, 59 vols. (Brunswick, 1863–1900)
MS	Manuscripts/Manuscrits
MS Fr	Manuscrits Français
SHPF	Société de l'Histoire du Protestantisme Français
SCJ	*Sixteenth Century Journal*

1. Introduction: Être protestant

Raymond A. Mentzer and Andrew Spicer

What did it mean to be Protestant in France during the sixteenth and seventeenth centuries?[1] How did the Huguenots understand and articulate the character of their community? What were the social, cultural and institutional dynamics of the movement between the 1550s, when Reformed churches first set roots in the French kingdom, and the proscription of Protestantism that occurred after 1685? In responding to these and related queries, the present collection draws upon important new and innovative research from leading European and American historians as well as younger, extremely promising scholars. Together, they examine a series of critical subjects ranging from Protestant self-image, forms of religious expression and the construction of identity to processes of petitioning the royalist state and communicating among one another. Other essays explore pacification efforts following the religious wars, the emergence of Huguenot elites, the meaning of physical structures for worship, the nature of ritual, and the institutional frameworks for education, poor relief and military preparedness. Each constitutes an important element in the overall development of the Huguenot world. Who were these French Protestants? What were their collective achievements and frustrations? How does the movement's past continue to resonate, even at the beginning of the twenty-first century?

Already in the early 1960s, Emile Léonard viewed Jean Calvin's Genevan reform as leading to the creation of a new human type, the *réformé*.[2] More recently, Janine Garrisson's survey of French Protestantism from its sixteenth-century origins to the present addressed anew the issue of Protestant identity. The book's very title, *L'Homme protestant*, reveals her purpose – an attempt to define the meaning of 'being Protestant' in France. No more than a third of Garrisson's study dwells on French

---

[1] The title is drawn from J. Garrisson, *L'Homme protestant* (Brussels, 1986).
[2] E. G. Léonard, *Histoire générale du protestantisme*, 3 vols. (Paris, 1961), I, p. 307.

Protestantism's historical chronology: the violent sixteenth century, gradual suffocation in the decades following the Edict of Nantes (1598), the traumatic 'lost' years after the Edict's Revocation (1685) and a reawakening in the late eighteenth century. The bulk of her analysis focuses instead on matters of the Reformed understanding of the divine, the imposition of moral discipline, the role assigned to women in Protestant society, educational aspirations, provisions for social welfare and the ongoing ambivalent Huguenot relationship with the French state. By way of conclusion, she underscores enduring pressure, if not persecution. French Protestants were, and are, a minority that has constantly sought and pursued strategies for survival in a hostile environment. This reality has indelibly marked and shaped the community.[3]

By confining the analysis to the earlier part of their history, the sixteenth and seventeenth centuries, what can be seen as being the defining characteristics of the Huguenots? What distinguished the *homme protestant* from the mass of the French population? First and foremost the Huguenots were identified by their religion, its beliefs and forms of worship. They rejected the traditions of Catholicism, did not attend Mass and failed to recognize Catholic holy days or celebrate feasts such as Candlemas and Corpus Christi. The simplicity of their services contrasted with the ceremonial of Catholic worship; the temple differed in its architectural precepts from those of the parish church. Prohibited in certain cities and relegated from the centres of others, Reformed worship was set apart spatially from the mainstream by being confined to designated places, often in the suburbs or more remote locations.[4]

Underlying the visual distinction between the Catholic and the Protestant was the Huguenots' understanding of the church and its relationship with God. As early as 1536, in his *Institutes of the Christian Religion*, published shortly after he had fled France, Calvin carefully defined this relationship between God and humanity. The church was a single entity, the Body of Christ, which united those 'who live together in one faith, hope and love, and in the same spirit of God'.[5] Scripture provided the means by which it was possible to identify fellow members of this church:

all who profess with us the same God and Christ by confession of faith, example of life and participation in the sacraments, ought by some sort of judgment of

---

3 Garrisson, *L'Homme protestant*.
4 See P. Roberts, 'The Most Crucial Battle of the Wars of Religion? The Conflict over Sites of Reformed Worship in Sixteenth-century France', *ARG* 89 (1998), 247–50, 257–62; see also A. Spicer, '"Qui est de Dieu, oit la Parole de Dieu": The Huguenots and their Temples', below.
5 John Calvin, *Institutes of the Christian Religion (1536 edition)*, ed. by F. L. Battles (Grand Rapids, 1975), p. 58.

love be deemed elect and members of the church . . . For by these marks and traits Scripture delineates for us the elect of God, the children of God, the people of God, the church of God . . . But those who either do not agree with us on the same faith or, even though they have confession on their lips, still deny by their actions the God whom they confess with their mouth . . . all of this sort show themselves by their traits that they are not members at present of the church.[6]

This assurance of their relationship with God was not an abstruse theological statement but was a belief that served to reassure the persecuted during the dark days of the wars of religion and was a concept which was recognized and asserted by the faithful. Fellow believers greeted each other as brothers in Christ in their letters; on their temples and homes, inscriptions such as 'Die[u] est avec nous, qui sera contre nous' or 'La paix de Dieu soit en cette méson' openly proclaimed their faith.[7]

The temple was 'La Maison de Dieu' where the Reformed community, through the minister's sermons, heard the Word of God several times a week; four times a year they joined together as the Body of Christ for the Lord's Supper. Their services not only rejected the traditional forms of Catholic worship but reasserted the Calvinist understanding of the Reformed churches. Apart from the Eucharistic differences between the two communities, it was perhaps in their attitudes towards the dying that the two faiths diverged the most in their forms of worship. The honest simplicity of Reformed burial sat in marked contrast to the extensive services and customs that commemorated the Catholic departed. Death was the culmination of the ritual sequence of French Protestantism stretching back to the promise of union of the immortal soul with Christ made in the administration of the Lord's Supper. While not physically present, the departed remained a member of the Body of Christ. However, for Catholics, death was only the beginning of the travails of purgatory and of the journey to achieve salvation. The clear theological distinctions were reflected in these contrasting funeral liturgies, which, of necessity, partly took place outside the church or temple in full view of the local community.[8]

This religious identity was not confined to the temple and worship; it pervaded their lives, for the Huguenots were the children of God. Worship and the way in which they lived could not be divorced as only the

---

[6] *Ibid.*, p. 61.

[7] H. Gelin, 'Inscriptions Huguenotes (Poitou, Aunis, Saintonge)', *BSHPF* 42 (1893), 585; 'Inscriptions concernant l'histoire de protestantisme', *BSHPF* 79 (1930), 484. See also Spicer, '"Qui est de Dieu"' and M. Greengrass, 'Informal Networks in Sixteenth-century French Protestantism', below.

[8] See B. Roussel, '"Enselevir honnestement les corps": Funeral Corteges and Huguenot Culture'.

worthy were permitted to participate in the administration of the Lord's
Supper. The consistory – a supervisory and administrative body composed of pastors, elders and deacons – maintained a keen watch over the
community, investigating and discussing in its weekly meetings all aspects
of an individual's behaviour in the public sphere and at home, even in the
bedchamber. It had responsibility for financial affairs, poor relief and,
most conspicuously, the maintenance of moral standards within each
local church.[9] Such supervision of all aspects of an individual's life set
the Huguenots apart from their Catholic neighbours and made them
accountable to a panel of predominately lay peers.

The willingness to submit regularly to the examination and strictures of
the consistory in an increasingly hostile environment reflects the strength
of the beliefs and commitment of the Reformed community. Remaining
a Huguenot with all the limitations and inconveniences that this caused
became essentially a question of choice.[10] Some have argued that, during the course of the seventeenth century, the exercise of discipline was
effectively emasculated with the end of the national synods, which had
served as the final court of appeal. This reduced the effectiveness of
the consistories, which, in turn, became more indulgent in dealing with
those members of the community whose behaviour fell below the accepted standards.[11] During the 1670s John Locke observed that 'there
was very little piety or religion among their people and that the lives of
the Reformed was [sic] no better than that of the Papists'.[12] None the
less, where the Huguenots still formed the majority of the population,
it was easier to exercise discipline, occasionally with the co-operation
of the civil authorities. Although Elisabeth Labrousse concluded that it
was not their morality but their religious practices which distinguished
the Huguenots from their Catholic compatriots,[13] we should not negate
the significance that discipline had over some communities and what it
contributed to the development of their character and identity.

The consistory's role was not solely as a disciplinary body, it also provided support for the Huguenot community at times of personal crisis.
Through the consistory, the system of poor relief was well organized and

[9] For further explanation of the consistory's role, see: R. A. Mentzer, '"Disciplina nervus
ecclesiae": The Calvinist Reform of Morals at Nîmes', *SCJ* 18 (1987), 91–115.
[10] H. Phillips, *Church and Culture in Seventeenth-century France* (Cambridge, 1997), pp. 206–7.
[11] On the welfare of the community, see M. Dinges, 'Huguenot Poor Relief and Health Care in
the Sixteenth and Seventeenth Centuries'.
[12] J. Lough (ed.), *Locke's Travels in France, 1675–1679* (Cambridge, 1953), p. 94; E. Labrousse,
'Calvinism in France' in M. Prestwich (ed.), *International Calvinism* (Oxford, 1985), p. 291;
E. Labrousse, *Une foi, une loi, un roi? La Révocation de l'Édit de Nantes* (Paris, 1985), p. 80.
[13] Labrousse, *Une foi, une loi, un roi?*, pp. 80–1.

provided assistance for the sick, the indigent and the unemployed. The result was an extensive support network for the Huguenots. The consistory often went to considerable lengths to help members of the community. At L'Albenc, in spite of their financial difficulties, the consistory fought hard and at great length for the interests of a widow and her three daughters. The level of support could also extend beyond the congregation; those travelling between churches were assisted, money was raised for troubled communities further afield.[14] This broad umbrella of moral assistance and social welfare provided by the Reformed churches served to foster further a sense of the movement's identity as well as being part of a much wider community than that based solely on the local congregation.

The consistory was the smallest component of institutional structures that extended through the regional colloquies and provincial synods to the national synods. This organization gave coherence to the religious identity of the movement; it provided an institutional framework that served to distance the Huguenots from the broad religious enthusiasm of a range of discontented elements within French society and developed the distinctive character of the emerging churches in the 1550s.[15] The hierarchy of assemblies also served to place clearly the local congregation within the wider network of the Reformed churches. The regional and national meetings offered a forum for the discussion of theological disputes, matters of discipline and practical concerns about the implementation of Reformed beliefs. With its oversight of the Reformed community, the national synod during the early seventeenth century directed the movement and, until 1644, appointed and then confirmed the *députés généraux*, the Huguenots' representatives to the king at court.[16] Concomitant with this structure was an increasing professionalism in the cadre of ministers; the Reformed academies provided training and the system of assemblies attempted to ensure that unsuitable and disreputable individuals were prevented from working within the churches.[17] The informal contacts that were established at these meetings also served to develop a sense of fellowship and support amongst the ministry.[18] The Reformed churches therefore developed as a distinct organization with their own

---

[14] See Dinges, 'Huguenot Poor Relief'.

[15] See T. Watson, 'Preaching, Printing, Psalm-singing: The Making and Unmaking of the Reformed Church in Lyon 1550–1572', below.

[16] Labrousse, 'Calvinism in France', p. 288.

[17] A. Pettegree, 'The Clergy and the Reformation: From "Devilish Priesthood" to New Professional Elite' in his (ed.), *The Reformation of the Parishes: The Ministry and the Reformation in Town and Country* (Manchester, 1993), pp. 1–21.

[18] See Greengrass, 'Informal Networks'; K. Maag, 'The Huguenot Academies: Preparing for an Uncertain Future', below.

hierarchy and institutions, which were able to define and personify the activities of the movement.

The religious identity of the Huguenot community extended beyond the structures of the Reformed church. In the earliest years of the movement before 1562 and once again in the wake of the Edict of Nantes, there had been a degree of fluidity resulting from the coexistence of both Catholicism and Protestantism within France. During the course of the seventeenth century confessional identities hardened, communities became more endogamous and their dealings with Catholics in both the economic and social spheres changed.[19] The restriction of the professions open to the Huguenots served to isolate further this group within the local community. The contrast between the two confessions can be clearly seen amongst the office-holding elites. While the *chambres de l'Édit* saw the emergence of Huguenot dynasties dedicated to royal service, Catholics resisted open-ended commitment, limited their own tenure on these courts and chose to pursue careers in other administrative and legal arenas that were open to them. While there were similarities between these elites, and individuals might meet together on a social level such as in the academy of Castres, in their professional endeavours they represented distinct groups within French society.[20]

In some ways it is an artificial construct to discuss the religious aspects of Huguenot culture in isolation. From the very beginning, religious beliefs were entwined with the militancy of the movement. The seizure and iconoclastic destruction of ecclesiastical buildings, notably churches and monasteries, during the 1560s engendered alarm and even the opprobrium of Calvin due to the defiance of the political order. The capacity for religious violence was, of course, translated into political violence over the course of the civil wars.[21] It was a militancy and radicalism, which was also seen at polemical level, especially in the wake of the St Bartholomew's Day massacre. Following the massacre, the Huguenots were prepared to think the unthinkable and to develop political theories that, although unpalatable for many, justified tyrannicide.[22] In spite of this, Protestants remained fundamentally loyal to the crown and the

---

[19] See P. Benedict, 'Confessionalization in France? Critical Reflections and New Evidence', below.

[20] A. Eurich, '"Speaking the King's Language": The Huguenot Magistrates of Castres and Pau', below.

[21] See P. Benedict, 'The Dynamics of Protestant Militancy: France, 1555–1563' in P. Benedict, G. Marnef, H. van Nierop and M. Venard (eds.), *Reformation, Revolt and Civil War in France and the Netherlands, 1555–1585* (Amsterdam, 1999), pp. 35–50.

[22] R. M. Kingdon, *Myths about the St Bartholomew's Day Massacres, 1572–1576* (Cambridge, MA, 1988), pp. 166, 173–82.

established order, even if the French monarchical state upheld the authority of a Catholic church to which they were diametrically opposed. It has been argued that the Edict of Nantes successfully institutionalized this dichotomy, and that the Huguenot movement became isolated from the mainstream of European Calvinism and increasingly introspective and conservative.[23] And yet this Huguenot militancy was not stifled in the decades after the Edict of Nantes. In subsequent years those who adhered to the Reformed faith had a clear choice to make between either loyalty to the king or whether to fight for their religious beliefs and community. This led many Huguenots into conflict with the monarchy in the 1620s, to oppose actively the circumscription of their privileges by the crown and ultimately to resist the Revocation of the Edict of Nantes. The Huguenots maintained 'a tenacious instinct for survival' which could at times override their innate conservatism.[24]

The *homme protestant* was also defined by the stance taken by confessional opponents. From the very outset, Reformed Protestants sought to respond to Catholic persecution in France by portraying themselves as martyrs of the True Church oppressed for their religious beliefs. As the nature of the persecution changed, so the Huguenots were forced to reassess their self-image. Gradually the movement came to see itself as the victim not just of the Gallican church but of Roman Catholicism as a whole. In doing so it came to place French Reformed Protestantism within the tradition of resistance to the papacy, appropriating the history of the Albigensians as the proto-martyrs of the True Church.[25] However, this representation of Huguenot identity was not confined to polemical debates. From as early as the 1560s, the crown had described the movement as the *Religion Prétendue Réformée* and in 1576 the Edict of Beaulieu ordered that the term was to be used to describe French Protestants in all edicts and legal documents. The Edict of Nantes employed this language and not only did the nomenclature continue into the seventeenth century, it was even more keenly enforced.[26] The term directly challenged the Huguenots' view of themselves as the *Églises Réformées de France*.

It was not merely the name of the movement that was defined by terms of the law; Protestant rights and privileges were all carefully delineated

[23] M. Wolfe, 'Protestant Reactions to the Conversion of Henry IV' in his *Changing Identities in Early Modern France* (London, 1997), pp. 384, 389–90.
[24] See A. James, 'Huguenot Militancy and the Seventeenth-century Wars of Religion', below.
[25] L. Racaut, 'Religious Polemic and Huguenot Self-perception and Identity, 1554–1619', below.
[26] A. Stegmann (ed.), *Edits des Guerres de Religion* (Paris, 1979), pp. 53, 101; J. Garrisson (ed.), *L'Édit de Nantes* (Biarritz, 1997); see below, P. Benedict, 'Confessionalization in France?'

through royal edicts. The privileged status of the Reformed dated to 1562 when they had been granted freedom of worship, a concession which although defined in different ways was repeated in all but three of the edicts during the course of the religious wars.[27] None the less, these were concessions that carefully prescribed the places where Protestants could and could not worship, and sought to demarcate their relationship with the Catholic church and the state. The Edict of Nantes and its associated documents provided a further definition of the rights and privileges accorded Protestants and institutionalized their legal existence. Commissions of pacification and *chambres de l'Édit*, in which both Huguenots and Catholics participated, sought to implement these measures.[28] This legal identity was not simply something imposed upon Protestants, it also provided a framework within which the two confessions interacted. The Huguenots from the earliest stages of the movement were prepared to use the law to handle disputes, seek compensation and generally maintain the guarantes of security which they believed were contained in the royal edicts and subsequently the Edict of Nantes.[29] They were prepared to bring cases before the *chambres de l'Édit* and to provide the personnel for them to function properly. This legal system also served to define the basis of the relationship between the crown and the Huguenots, encouraging a sense of conservatism and loyalty to the monarch within the movement. Yet it was this very legal system that served as the means to undermine the Reformed churches and their adherents. The reintroduction of Catholicism into Béarn, the encouragement of bipartisan government and education in the Protestant south as well as the more precise and painful definition of their rights, exploited the legal system ultimately to the detriment of Huguenot interests.

The *homme protestant* of the sixteenth and seventeenth centuries was therefore a complex and contradictory character: at times violent and driven to direct action, on other occasions prepared to work within the legal system; militant, and yet innately conservative and loyal to the crown; the persecuted victim of the papacy and Roman Catholicism but a member of the Body of Christ. These character traits can be traced from the earliest days of French Protestantism and can be discerned in a number

[27] P. Benedict, '*Un Roi, une Loi, deux Fois*: Parameters for the History of Catholic–Reformed Co-existence in France, 1555–1685' in O. P. Grell and B. Scribner (eds.), *Tolerance and Intolerance in the European Reformation* (Cambridge, 1996), p. 75.

[28] R. A. Mentzer, 'The Edict of Nantes and its Institutions', below.

[29] P. Roberts, 'Huguenot Petitioning during the Wars of Religion', below.

of facets of Reformed society and culture. In their examination of the salient institutions and features of the Huguenot world, these essays help to provide a greater understanding of French Protestantism in this period. Although they only represented a minority of the overall population and came to be geographically confined to the south and west of the kingdom, the Huguenots were a significant element in French society. In 1562 France was the first powerful nation state to concede freedom to a religious minority. The terms of the Edict of Nantes of 1598 technically remained in force for eighty-seven years. By exploring what defined and shaped the Huguenot existence and identity, and the movement's relationship with the crown, this volume contributes to the wider analysis of the development of the *ancien régime* as well as to an understanding of persecution and tolerance in the early modern period.

2. Preaching, printing, psalm-singing: the making and unmaking of the Reformed church in Lyon, 1550–1572

Timothy Watson

The rise and fall of the Huguenot movement in Lyon, as conventionally told, presents one of the most spectacular stories of the early French Reformation. In the decades leading up to 1562, it has been estimated that more than a third of the city's population of 60,000 converted to the new faith – yet just ten years later, after the bloody 'Lyon Vespers' massacre of early October 1572, the Huguenot church of Lyon had effectively been stamped out.[1] Looked at more critically, however, the failure of the nascent Huguenot movement to establish itself in Lyon on the base of its apparently remarkable early success raises a number of problems which call into question our whole view of the early history of the French Reformation. What motivated these supposed conversions, and how complete were they? How does one define a potential 'Huguenot' *circa* 1550? How meaningful is such a definition, and does it still hold ten or twenty years later?

The question of definition is complicated by the fact that confessional allegiances in the sixteenth century were fluid and protean. Partly because of this fluidity of context, and partly because of the inscrutability of individual religious choices, historians' attempts to construct models to explain why people converted to a new confession in the sixteenth century have generally proved unsatisfactory – the most convincing analyses generally being the most sceptical with regard to grand theories.[2] Case studies of the religious motivations offered by individuals for conversion, though often extremely illuminating in their own right, tend by their very complexity to evade easy categorization;[3] whereas studies that seek

---

[1] The standard accounts are A. Kleinclausz (ed.), *Histoire de Lyon*, 2 vols. (Lyon, 1939), I, 'Livre 5: le seizième siècle', and R. Gascon, *Grand commerce et vie urbaine. Lyon et ses marchands*, 2 vols. (Paris, 1971), II, pp. 459–535.

[2] See E. Cameron's discussion in *The European Reformation* (Oxford, 1991), chap. 17: 'Motives for Establishing the Reformation?'

[3] A particularly enlightening double conversion tale is told by Robert Kingdon, 'Problems of Religious Choice for Sixteenth-century Frenchmen', *Journal of Religious History* 4 (1966), 105–12. For

to explain religious decisions with reference to social or economic factors, while occasionally shedding light on intriguing questions of local or group identity, are less convincing when woven together into a general theory of religious change.[4]

Perhaps, then, it is more productive to focus in the first instance not on the motives for conversion, but on the mechanics: not on why people converted to the new religion, but on how the Reformed message was spread. Protestant movements, at least in their first stages, are quintessentially proselytizing movements: the process of spreading the evangel, the good news of the gospel, is an inherent part of radical evangelical belief. Such proselytizing activity has both a utilitarian and a symbolic function: it both articulates the way in which a movement will spread and defines the kind of movement that it will be. But the transition from the first to the second stage is not always easy. The institutionalization of the Huguenot movement, and the transformation of its leaders from subversive radicals to respectable leaders (a transformation recently described by Heiko Oberman as the 'Arafat process'[5]), was to have significant implications for the manner in which the new church presented itself. Attempts by Huguenot religious and civil authorities to regulate their community by prescribing – and proscribing – cultural modes of expression were an important aspect of the shift from a diverse popular movement with no clear focus into something that was identifiably a Huguenot church. But this process of 'confessionalization without the state' equally had implications for the success or failure of the Reformation in France, as the Huguenots' confessional opponents responded to the challenge with their own process of redefinition and began to spread their own message in new and effective ways.[6]

It is also important to emphasize the extent to which in the early years of the French Reformation, before the coming into existence of a definably Huguenot church, French heterodoxy was fluid and ill defined.

a more general discussion, see J. Pollmann, 'A Different Road to God? The Protestant Experience of Conversion in the Sixteenth Century' in P. van der Veer (ed.), *Conversion to Modernities: The Globalisation of Christianity* (London, 1996), pp. 47–64.

[4] See the classic articles by N. Z. Davis, 'Strikes and Salvation at Lyon', reprinted as chapter 1 of her *Society and Culture in Early Modern France* (Stanford, 1975), and M. Holt, 'Wine, the Community and the Reformation in Burgundy', *Past & Present* (1993). For the problems with taking this approach to extremes, see the illuminating exchange between Mack Holt and Henry Heller in *French Historical Studies* 19 (1994).

[5] In a paper entitled 'Calvin and Farel' delivered to a conference organized by the Société de l'Histoire du Protestantisme Français, 'Calvin et ses Contemporains', in Paris in October 1995.

[6] See the discussion of confessionalization as a process of self-definition in R. C. Head, 'Catholics and Protestants in Graubünden: Confessional Discipline and Confessional Identities without an Early Modern State?', *German History* 17 (1999), 321–45.

The problems of definition are exacerbated by problems of evidence: the covert nature of early Protestant activity means that historians are forced to rely on later sources with their own confessional agendas. Genevan writers such as Jean Crespin were not trying to present an objective historical account, but rather to edify the Reformed faithful and warn them of the dangers of Nicodemism; works such as the *Histoire des Martyrs* or the *Histoire Ecclésiastique* thus tend to overemphasize the doctrinal coherence of the early Reform movement.[7] For their part, Catholic historians such as the Lyonnais Claude de Rubys display an equal and opposite tendency, presenting the early Reformers as well-organized conspirators in order to play down the popular appeal of their message.[8] Setting these biased sources to one side, we are left only with the glimpses of heterodox activity to be found in council minutes, court records and private correspondence. As might be expected, these documents tend to underemphasize the coherence of early Reformed activity; but the confused picture they paint of the expansionist phase of the French Reformation arguably provides a better sense of how contemporaries actually experienced this disturbing and unprecedented turn of events.

Reformed ideas were spread in the first instance by preachers: charismatic individuals, often well educated and theologically sophisticated, who formed the ideological core of the early Reform movement. The activity of such figures needs, however, to be seen within a pre-existing tradition. Recent work has highlighted the diversity and nonconformity of popular religious discourse during the first half of the sixteenth century, and emphasized the need to take these individuals separately on their merits.[9] Two early examples illustrate the point. Aimé Meigret, a Dominican, was accused of 'Lutheranism' for preaching Lenten sermons in Lyon and Grenoble in 1524. Meigret claimed in his defence not to have been inspired by Luther, and indeed his sermon seems to be an attack on ecclesiastical authority rather than traditional doctrine; his case illustrates the danger of taking such polemical labels at face value.[10] Ten years later, in 1534, Baudichon de la Maisonneuve, a merchant

---

[7] J.-F. Gilmont, *Jean Crespin. Un éditeur réformé du XVIe siècle* (Geneva, 1981), pp. 147, 187–90; M. Greengrass, *The French Reformation* (Oxford, 1987), p. 36.

[8] On Claude de Rubys, see F.-Z. Collombet, *Études sur les historiens du Lyonnais*, 2 vols. (Lyon, 1839–44; repr. Geneva, 1969), I, pp. 50–68.

[9] L. Taylor, *Soldiers of Christ. Preaching in Late Mediaeval and Reformation France* (Oxford, 1992), pp. 10, 181–8.

[10] H. Hours, 'Procès d'hérésie contre Aimé Meigret', *BHR* 19 (1957), 14–43; Taylor, *Soldiers of Christ*, pp. 207–8.

from Berne, was arrested for publicly criticizing the Mass while drinking in one of the city's taverns. The Swiss merchant's personal connections with heterodox circles was easier to establish – he was carrying a letter from Guillaume Farel – but his punishment was simply to be sent back to Berne, a town with which Lyon had a valuable trading relationship that the city's council was anxious not to compromise.[11] These two cases illustrate how traditionalist perceptions of heterodoxy in the early years of the French Reformation combined an uneasy mix of old and new elements.

The origins of more identifiably proto-Protestant missionary activity in Lyon are necessarily obscure, but the *Histoire Ecclésiastique* records the presence of ministers operating underground from about 1546, serving a small congregation of perhaps thirty worshippers.[12] It was relatively easy for such men to operate undetected, finding work as schoolteachers or in the city's print shops. Lyon's geographical situation, as the gateway not only to the Midi but also to Geneva, made it a staging-post for many early refugees.[13] Crucial to the success – or indeed the survival – of such men was the attitude of the authorities. The promotion of heterodoxy was a dangerous business under Henri II, and a number of preachers were arrested and put to death in Lyon in the 1550s, notably Claude Monier in 1551, and most famously the 'five scholars of Lausanne' in May 1553. But the small number of such cases bears witness to the *laissez-faire* policy of the city authorities, compared with towns such as Paris or Toulouse where the presence of a university or a *parlement* provided a focus for repression.[14] This is exemplified by the attitude of the city council, whose willingness to employ pedagogues of questionable religious views at the city's Collège de la Trinité created a Nicodemitical environment in which difficult questions about orthodoxy remained generally unasked.[15]

The oral transmission of the Word was complemented by its communication in more durable form. The crucial importance of the printed

[11] W. G. Naphy, 'Catholic Perceptions of Early French Protestantism: The Heresy Trial of Baudichon de la Maisonneuve in Lyon, 1534', *French History* 9 (1995), 451–77.

[12] *Histoire Ecclésiastique des églises reformées au Royaume de France*, ed. by G. Baum, E. Cunitz and R. Reuss, 3 vols. (Paris, 1883–9), I, pp. 72–3.

[13] For example, Claude Baduel, an elderly pedagogue escaping from Nîmes under a cloud of religious suspicion, spent some time correcting proofs for Sébastien Gryphius in the summer of 1551 while acting as pastor to a small community of Reformed believers, before moving on to Geneva at the end of the year. M.-J. Gaufrès, *Claude Baduel et la réforme des études* (Paris, 1880), pp. 257–9, 273–6.

[14] For an overview, see Kleinclausz, *Histoire de Lyon*, I, pp. 402–8.

[15] G. de Groër, *Réforme et contre-réforme en France. Le Collège de la Trinité au XVIe siècle à Lyon* (Paris, 1995), pp. 51–67.

book to the spread of Protestant ideas has long been recognized.[16] The
dangers of heterodox publications were seen most clearly by the opponents of reform:

> The malicious desire of the heretics to deceive the faithful is nowhere more
> evident than in the production of books full of heresy, for by them they preach
> and dogmatize even in places from which they are absent or which are forbidden
> to them, and imprint in the memory thoughts which time or sound teaching
> would make them forget, and in a more eloquent, attractive and memorable
> style than the spoken word.[17]

The impression given by such sources that most heterodox books were
produced to a coherent ideological agenda should, however, not be taken
too readily at face value. A variety of factors – notably the diversity of
reader response, the demands of the market and the fluid boundary
between orthodoxy and heterodoxy – worked against the promotion of
a coherent Protestant programme, even as they hampered attempts at
effective censorship.

    The printing or importing of dangerous material was, of course, of-
ficially forbidden – but it was profitable; there was a growing market
for evangelical books in France in the 1550s, and Lyon, besides being
itself a printing centre of considerable importance, was on a number
of important trade routes. The city's black market in heterodox publications attracted particular attention in the Edict of Châteaubriant in
1551, which brought in a number of repressive measures. A royal letter to the *sénéchaussée* in 1557 explained how this commerce was carried
out:

> We have heard that the inhabitants of Geneva, under cover of sending to Lyon
> books on the humanities and other matters, put in their bales and packets an
> infinite number of books of forbidden doctrine, and that recently ten or twelve
> such bales have been discovered, carried by poor carters whose letters of carriage
> describe them as cloth or paper, and always addressed to an unknown name,
> by which means the carters make the excuse that they do not know what they
> are carrying.[18]

Case studies show that even when these *colporteurs* could be apprehended,
it was not necessarily easy to pursue the real culprits. In August 1560 the

---

[16] See most recently F. Higman, *Piety and the People: Religious Printing in France 1511–1551* (Aldershot,
     1996). A survey of French religious publishing is currently being undertaken by the Reformation
     Studies Institute, University of St Andrews.
[17] AD Rhône, BP 9339, no. 1 (c. 1560): letter of a cathedral canon to the lieutenants of the
     sénéchaussée.
[18] AD Rhône, BP 2640, Livre du Roi, fos. 370v–371 (8 Apr. 1557).

lieutenant governor of Lyonnais, Antoine d'Albon, reported the arrest of an artisan who had in his possession three heterodox pamphlets bearing the demonstrably false imprint 'En Avignon, Chez Trophime des Rives'. The unfortunate man claimed to be illiterate, saying that the books had been given to him by an acquaintance to help him to learn to read, and the investigation petered out for lack of further evidence.[19]

Once again the inability of the local authorities to agree on a strategy of repression was crucial in enabling this commerce to continue. Instructions to search bales for contraband ran directly counter to Lyon's commercial privileges, under the terms of which foreign merchants were simply required to sign a declaration that they were not importing forbidden material and could then proceed unmolested – a privilege renewed by the king in 1553, apparently in direct contradiction of his own 1551 edict.[20] The incoherence of royal policy-making exasperated the city's cathedral canons, one of whom wrote to the lieutenants of the *sénéchaussée* complaining that he had been appointed by the cathedral to inspect the city's print shops for heretical publications but was being prevented from so doing by the city council.[21] Such reluctance is understandable in view of the fact that a number of the city councillors had business interests in Geneva, at a time when this was evidently not seen as particularly problematic. Some of these men may well have had an ideological agenda; others simply prized free trade over doctrinal purity, or preferred not to mix religion and politics: 'delaissant theologie aux theologiens', as one put it.[22]

Here, too, it is crucial to note that in the 1550s the boundary between acceptable and unacceptable publications was fluid. Many of Lyon's printers were producing popular devotional literature in the vernacular, meeting a widespread demand among the laity for such material. Printers such as Guillaume Rouillé had considerable success not only with vernacular Bibles but also with cheaper and more accessible publications such as biblical emblem books composed of verse paraphrases of Scripture illustrated with striking woodcuts of biblical scenes. Editions in Italian, Spanish and even English bear witness to the commercial potential of such volumes.[23] Rather than jump to the conclusion that such

---

[19] Letter printed in M. Droin-Bridel, 'Vingt-sept pamphlets huguenots (1560–1562) provenant de la Bibliothèque Tronchin', *Mémoires et documents publiés par la Société d'Histoire et d'Archéologie de Genève* 48 (1979), 238–40.

[20] Barthélemy Aneau (ed.), *Ordonnances et privileges des foires de Lyon* (Lyon, 1560), fo. 98v.

[21] AD Rhône, BP 9339, no. 1.

[22] Symphorien Champier, *Cy Commence ung petit livre de lantiquite origine et noblesse de la tresantique cite de Lyon* (Lyon, 1529), fo. 26v.

[23] For Rouillé's output, see Baudrier, *Bibliographie lyonnaise*, 13 vols. (Lyon, 1895–1921), IX, pp. 13–411.

printers were flirting with 'Protestantism', it might be more prudent to suggest that publications of this kind – evangelical in the broadest sense of the word – were both uncontroversial and a good business proposition at this time. More surprisingly, certain kinds of vernacular literature which would later be thought of as typically 'Protestant' were still being published with official approval right up until the outbreak of armed conflict. As late as the autumn of 1561 Antoine Vincent obtained a royal privilege for an edition of the psalms in a French translation to be printed with accompanying music; the privilege (duly registered in December by the *sénéchaussée* of Lyon) describes this publication as 'necessary because of the edification that these psalms can bring to our people'.[24] Vincent would go on to do more than flirt with Protestantism: by 1560 he was already running a printing press in Geneva, and he would go on to be a stalwart member of the Reformed church.[25] His success in obtaining a royal privilege for his psalter on the eve of the wars is surely evidence that the boundaries between the old and the new religion were still too ill defined to allow a successful policy of repression.

Reformed ideas, implanted by preachers and printed texts, took root and grew within a concealed community, which would come together in secret to study and to worship. Identifying such communities and describing their evolution is problematic, not only because Genevan accounts with their neat categories of 'églises dressées' and 'plantées' need to be treated with caution in the absence of reliable corroborating evidence, but also because degrees of commitment are difficult to establish retrospectively.[26] What can be said, however, is that pre-existing patterns of sociability provided an environment within which such ideas could circulate. For example, many of Lyon's artisans already had a tradition of meeting together in secret: they lived within a closed world, with a system of neighbourhood clubs and rituals and passwords and various forms of communal recreation.[27] And the better-educated Lyonnais had their own networks: the younger sons of local families slowly climbing the educational ladder into office-holding met with local authors and educators to read and write poetry or to discuss the latest Renaissance

[24] AD Rhône, BP 3642 (Livre du Roy), fo. 102v.
[25] E. Droz, 'Antoine Vincent. La Propagande Protestante par le Psautier' in G. Berthoud *et al.*, *Aspects de la propagande religieuse* (Geneva, 1957), pp. 276–93.
[26] For an overview, see Gascon, *Grand commerce*, II, pp. 473–7. Compare Guido Marnef's analysis of Calvinist recruitment in a city not unlike Lyon: 'Calvinism in Antwerp 1558–1585' in A. Pettegree, A. Duke and G. Lewis (eds.), *Calvinism in Europe 1540–1620* (Cambridge, 1994), pp. 143–59.
[27] Davis, 'Strikes and Salvation', pp. 3–5.

ideas, leaving evidence of their attachments in the emblem books that are such a feature of the intellectual life of the city.[28] Without being too specific as to dates of conversion, it is reasonable to suppose that the representatives of these groups who 'came out' as Huguenots in 1561 or 1562 would have first encountered Reformed ideas in these contexts. This was certainly the view of Catholic critics such as Claude de Rubys, who saw the root of the corruption of the 'good houses of Lyon' in the informal circles around the city college.[29]

Social networks of this kind allowed for the spreading of new ideas, but they also worked against the coalescing of these ideas into an identifiable 'church' or 'movement' that crossed pre-existing social boundaries. Nor was such activity tolerated when it crossed the boundaries of acceptable behaviour. The consequent lack of cohesion of the embryonic Reformed community is apparent from the most striking example of public proto-Protestant worship in the 1550s: the bands of artisans and *menu peuple* who took to marching through the city centre in the summer of 1551 bearing arms, shouting insults against the clergy and singing the psalms in French in a loud and offensive manner. The reaction from the city's more conservative Reform-minded inhabitants was severe: notably, pastor Claude Baduel who accused the psalm singers of being irresponsible, and forbade his own more modest worshippers from getting involved.[30] Just as interesting is the attitude of the city council, which in its deliberations for 23 June decided upon a two-pronged strategy: despatching the city watch to suppress the marchers, while simultaneously briefing its agent at court to play down the problem and if possible to deny its existence.[31] The repression of 1551 does appear to have successfully deterred the city's Protestants from indulging in public displays of this kind, and there are no reports of similar disturbances in the city until well after the death of Henri II. In Lyon, then, the official attitude seems to have been largely one of 'don't ask, don't tell'.

Lyon's early Reform movement was therefore defined by the very diverse ways by which it came into existence. Charismatic individuals dedicated to the cause; printers anxious to make some profit from a growing market; educated readers interested in the new ideas; artisans

---

[28] A typical emblem book, written by a tutor at the city's college, is C. Fontaine, *Les Ruisseaux de Fontaine* (Lyon, 1555); for a general overview, the starting point remains V.-L. Saulnier, *Maurice Scève*, 2 vols. (Paris, 1948).

[29] Claude de Rubys, *Histoire véritable de la ville de Lyon* (Lyon, 1604), p. 389.

[30] N. Z. Davis, 'The Protestant Printing Workers of Lyons in 1551' in Berthoud *et al.*, *Aspects de la propagande*, pp. 246–8.

[31] AM Lyon, BB 72, fos. 47v–48.

enjoying a spirit of comradeship: all were linked by a common religious
enthusiasm in a broad coalition of different interests. But it is important
to note that the coalition was a loose one. There was as yet no rite of reception, no church discipline, no real way of telling who was (or might be)
a Huguenot and who was not. This is not to say that Lyon was undivided
on religious matters – far from it – but rather that the many social, political and cultural divisions that did exist prevented the formation of a clear
religious party. Paradoxically perhaps, this very lack of cohesion made
the 'movement' impossible to repress, both because there was no clear
target to aim at, and because the consequent lack of consensus among
the city authorities prevented any coherent policy of enforcement. In this
context one can endorse and even extend Mark Greengrass's suggestion
that 'in the years between 1557 and 1562 it may well have been the sense
of gathering numbers and imminent victory . . . that created a national
French church, rather than either Genevan initiative or the uniting force
of a Calvinist church constitution'.[32] In Lyon at least, certainly until 1560
and arguably until the autumn of 1561, there may have been a sense of
'gathering numbers', but the conditions for any 'victory' were so uncertain and the interests of the various parties so diverse that to talk of a
'church' at all at this stage is rather misleading, implying an institutional
coherence that was not yet there.

It was only after the death of Henri II that the various forms of heterodoxy within France began to coalesce into anything resembling a national
movement, as the noble supporters of radical reform and their ministerial allies in Geneva and elsewhere entered into a series of negotiations
with the crown, and as local groups began to grow in confidence and
self-assertion. The legal recognition of the Reformed church in the Edict
of January 1562 was thus little more than an acceptance of a *fait accompli*.
But the search for respectability during this time saw what had been a
loose underground coalition take on a new and significantly different
form, a process that helped to determine how the Huguenot movement
would integrate – or fail to integrate – the diverse elements of its early
promise.
    Paradoxically crucial to the toleration of heterodox activity at a local
level were the terms in which royal concerns were voiced. This is exemplified by a royal letter to the Lyon city council written in the spring of
1560, in the immediate aftermath of the failed 'Conspiracy of Amboise'.

---

[32] Greengrass, *French Reformation*, p. 41.

The noble conspirators are accused of having taken advantage of:

various preachers of new doctrine dispersed throughout our kingdom, who after having dogmatized in secret assemblies and conventicles forbidden by all laws, seeing many people imbued by the new doctrine and desiring religious change, persuaded those who listened to them to rise up from throughout our kingdom with the intention of presenting their request to us in person.[33]

Significantly, the letter goes on to accept the validity of such calls for religious reform, while condemning the treasonous intentions of the plotters. By emphasizing the concern with sedition rather than with heresy per se, this kind of royal rhetoric left a space within which Reformed spokesmen could plausibly argue their loyalty to the crown, while awaiting the verdict of a hoped-for council of the French church on wider questions of religious reform.[34]

From 1560, therefore, voices within Lyon's Protestant community bear witness to a new concern to control the words and deeds by which the message was spread, not seeking to win new converts so much as to control the behaviour of old ones.[35] This position is explored eloquently in an anonymous pamphlet published in Lyon in 1561, which echoes the royal concern to separate religious reform and political radicalism:

Live all of you religiously in your Christian faith, revere your various preachers and ministers, but if the Roman preacher or the Protestant minister spreads words in his sermons which encourage sedition, punish him so grievously that the people, intimidated, will learn from his example not to be so immodest.[36]

The peaceable nature of the Reform-minded is contrasted with the evil designs of the young king's councillors (the Guise):

If you wish to count the Protestant among those who disobey, at least do not let it be said in the future that our little prince will have learned from his childhood at your instigation to bloody his hands with the blood of his people, who desire nothing other than to give him their entire obedience.[37]

---

[33] AM Lyon, GG 77, no. 1 (31 Mar. 1560), p. 4.

[34] See the protestations of Protestant preachers to the city council in October 1561, AM Lyon, BB 82, fo. 79v.

[35] Henri Hauser comments that from this point Huguenot publications become increasingly concerned with swinging public opinion behind the 'cause', rather than with stimulating evangelical interest: *Les sources de l'histoire de France. XVIe siècle (1494–1610). III. Les guerres de religion (1559–1589)* (Paris, 1912), p. 14.

[36] *Exhortation aux princes et seigneurs du conseil privé du Roy. Pour obvier aux seditions qui occultement semblent nous menacer pour le fait de la religion* (1561), p. 30.

[37] *Ibid.*, p. 45.

This pamphlet is evidence of how prominent voices in Lyon's Protestant community had begun to appreciate the need to stress the conservative and conformist nature of their movement. But in its emphasis on listening critically to the right sort of preacher, it is also evidence of a new concern to establish what the 'Reformed message' actually was. A second anonymous pamphlet of 1561 makes the point more explicitly in its title: 'A Warning to the Faithful Dispersed throughout the Kingdom of France, to Watch out for those who without a Legitimate Vocation are Interfering with the Ministry of the Gospel'.

The respectability of the Huguenot cause received a considerable boost with news of the Colloquy of Poissy in September 1561. It was no coincidence that in October 1561 Lyon's Reformed community at last took the decisive step of meeting publicly for services outside the city walls. This exposed for the first time the breadth of the Reformed coalition: notably, conservative councillors were shocked to note the presence of some of their former colleagues at these assemblies. But the news of Poissy also muddied the water by raising hopes of a wider reconciliation between the various parties – a hope shared by the city's agent at court in his report of the proceedings: 'dieu veuille tout conduire en bonne paix'.[38] An assembly of city notables, which met in October to discuss the new situation, was therefore understandably unsure of what action to take. There were, of course, a number of traditionalists who argued that public Huguenot activity was unacceptable and should be forcibly repressed; but the majority took a more sympathetic line, accepting the assurances of the more respectable worshippers that they were loyal subjects who prayed daily for the health of the young king and the stability of his realm.[39] The council therefore compromised for the moment on a policy of toleration, in the meantime ordering the supporters of both sides to desist from 'insulting each other under the names of papists and Huguenots', an order that one may suspect was hard to enforce, but which represents a continuation of the council's longstanding *laissez-faire* policy.[40]

Against a background of increasing popular violence, the willingness of the council to accept the Protestants' good faith is striking, and a meeting between the elders of the Huguenot community and the city council in December revealed a surprising amount of common ground between the two.[41] The councillors' primary concern was that tensions between

---

[38] AM Lyon, AA 32, no. 84 (21 Aug. 1561).   [39] AM Lyon, BB 82, fo. 79 (18 Oct. 1561).
[40] AM Lyon, BB 82, fo. 93 (7 Nov. 1561).   [41] AM Lyon, BB 82, fo. 115 (29 Dec. 1561).

Huguenots and traditionalists would bring down a royal army on the city; for their part, the elders – all respectable citizens, including some former councillors – promised to contain the popular enthusiasm for 'pure and simple evangelical doctrine' as best they could, while regretting that their more unruly co-religionists did not always do as they were told. The tone of the discussion, which is unexpectedly moderate, illustrates the assumption (in both senses, and on both sides) of collective responsibility: the Huguenot burghers endeavouring to take responsibility for the behaviour of their newly visible community, and the councillors expecting that such responsibility will be taken seriously. Seen in this light, the royal edicts recognizing the Huguenot church in the early months of 1562 seem to be designed as much in an effort to contain the enthusiasms of the populace as to permit their exercise of the new religion. In particular, by specifically requiring Huguenot notables and ministers to take responsibility for the moral conduct of their worshippers, and to seek royal permission for their 'synods and consistories', the crown was encouraging the Reformed movement to develop structures sufficiently robust to bear the burden of discipline which its prominent spokesmen had assumed.[42]

The transformation from loose coalition to hierarchical institution was swiftly brought to completion by the outbreak of the first war of religion at the end of April 1562, when the city fell to a Protestant army in one of the first military actions of the war. The immediate consequence was the rapid polarization of the city elite into two confessional alliances. A substantial minority stayed in the city and formed the core of a new Protestant administration – the rest abandoned their positions and chose to go into exile. A Reformed church consistory was set up, Huguenot notables were elected to the council to replace their departed brethren, and within weeks Lyon had effectively become a 'second Geneva', a state of affairs that persisted until the end of the first war in the spring of the following year.

The rapid institutionalization of Lyon's Reformed church, paradoxically perhaps, marked the limit of the Huguenots' success in the city, because it changed the conditions under which the movement had been doing so well. The earlier looseness of the Reform-minded coalition had created conditions ideal for growth; but the events of 1561–2, in bringing the movement out into the open, forced it into a rigid frame, which

---

[42] *Edict du Roy, Charles neufiesme de ce nom . . . sur les moyens les plus propres d'appaiser les troubles et seditions survenus pour le fait de la religion* (Lyon, 1562), fos. Biiv, Dv.

exposed its fragility. The Huguenot burghers who had taken over the city council found themselves pulled in two directions at once, committed both to establishing control over the behaviour of their rowdier co-religionists and to defending themselves from their Catholic opponents. Lyon's Huguenots were further hampered by their continuing need to present themselves as a moderate and law-abiding movement, when the contradiction between rhetoric and reality was so apparent. The rebukes (by no less than Calvin) addressed to a particularly troublesome minister, Jacques Ruffy, for bearing arms during the early days of the occupation could not obscure the fact that such actions had confirmed the link between heresy and sedition in the minds of Catholic critics, thus removing the grounds on which they had previously been tolerated.[43]

The proselytizing techniques, which had been used to such effect during the expansionist phase of the Huguenot movement, were therefore turned inwards during the period of Protestant occupation, to serve the new ends of social control and damage limitation. Pierre Viret, the city's most charismatic preacher, was detailed to preach to the occupying troops in an effort to restrain their violent and destructive impulses.[44] The printed material of the occupation became an elaborate exercise in self-justification, designed to defend the new regime by downplaying its radical implications. The most characteristic pamphlet produced by the new regime, *La juste et saincte Defense de la Ville de Lyon*, is a political manifesto justifying the military takeover as necessary to protect the citizens from the murderous designs of Catholic extremists, while carefully demonstrating social and religious conservatism by calling for the punishment of Anabaptists.[45] The concern of the Reformed consistory with regulating behaviour also took a conservative form: schoolteachers working in the city were now required to submit to a doctrinal examination before receiving a licence to teach, while Natalie Davis has shown how the city's printing workers (who had been early partisans of the Reform) began to chafe under its more rigid discipline.[46]

It would be unreasonable to call the social conservatism of the Huguenot leadership an error of judgement, particularly as more socially and politically radical Reformations had not proved a conspicuous success elsewhere in Europe. Rather, the rapid process of confessionalization forced on Lyon's Reform-minded communities by the outbreak

43 J. Bonnet (ed.), *Lettres françaises de Jean Calvin*, 2 vols. (Paris, 1854), II, p. 466.
44 Archives d'État de Genève, PH 1719 (18 Nov. 1562): letter from the Lyon council and consistory to the Genevan city council.
45 (Lyon, 1563).   46 AM Lyon, BB 83, fo. 73; Davis, 'Strikes and Salvation', pp. 10–14.

of armed conflict exposed the inherent contradictions within the nascent Huguenot movement, and removed much of the energy which had driven the earlier expansion. If this was a 'blind alley', as some have suggested, it was an unavoidable one.[47] For Lyon's Catholics, on the other hand, the experience of exile was to prove a source of strength, forcing them to unite in the face of a greater common foe. The city fathers who had remained loyal to the old church swallowed their pride and began to work together with the local clergy and with sympathetic figures in the royal administration, forming a power bloc which was much more effective at representing their interests on the ground. This formation of a local Catholic party uniting political and religious interests was to set the pattern for an effective challenge to the Huguenots' earlier monopoly on religious enthusiasm.

The return of Lyon to royal control in the spring and early summer of 1563 marked the beginning of a five-year period of uneasy coexistence. The city was henceforth to be governed by a bipartisan city council consisting of royal nominees, six from each confession, under the supervision of a royal military governor – a state of gridlock, which favoured the formation of informal confessional coalitions. The importance of this was noted by the more perspicacious Catholic commentators, aware that in cities such as Lyon where Catholic worship had previously been suppressed, the peace of 1563 opened a window of opportunity that could be exploited.[48] The Reformed church of Lyon consequently found itself under attack from a newly mobilized and energized Catholic party, using evangelistic techniques strikingly similar to those that had favoured the Protestants during their earlier period of expansion, but now targeted against the highly visible Reformed Church.

Lyon's Catholics had long envied the intoxicating power of Protestant preachers[49] – and so to counter the activities of the Huguenot ministers they called upon the Jesuits, whose apostolic ministry placed a special emphasis on the spoken word.[50] The revival in Catholic fortunes after 1563 centred in particular on the person of the Jesuit Emond Auger, known as

---

[47] R. Briggs, *Early Modern France* (Oxford, 1977), p. 16.
[48] M. Venard, 'Catholicism and Resistance to the Reformation in France' in P. Benedict, G. Marnef, H. van Nierop and M. Venard (eds.), *Reformation, Revolt and Civil War in France and the Netherlands, 1555–1585* (Amsterdam, 1999), pp. 136–7.
[49] 'La langue sans frein du ministre les enivre tous': G. Lyasse (ed. and trans.), 'De Tristibus Franciae. Poème latin du XVIe siècle', diplôme d'Etudes Supérieures – Lettres Classiques, Université de Lyon, Faculté des Lettres et Sciences Humaines (s.d.), p. 13.
[50] J. W. O'Malley, *The First Jesuits* (Harvard, 1993), p. 92.

the 'French Chrysostom' for the persuasive power of his oratory.[51] Auger, like Pierre Viret, had proved his abilities in this respect by preaching to the Catholic troops of the duc de Nemours during the military campaigns of 1562–3. His first sermon in Lyon was delivered to a packed audience in the cathedral in July 1563 at a Mass held to mark the return of the Catholic exiles.[52] Auger and his colleagues led a Catholic revival in Lyon, preaching daily throughout the city and debating publicly with the Protestant ministers. Given a firm institutional base from 1565, when a coalition of Catholic councillors, clergy and royal officials arranged for them to take over the running of the city college, the Jesuits became the spearhead of a movement that fits the definitions of both Counter- and Catholic Reformation.[53]

The importance of meeting the popular demand for vernacular publications was also swiftly recognized by the Huguenots' opponents. After 1563 the Catholic return led to an acceleration in the publication of books which both countered the Huguenot message and provided a lively alternative to it. Polemics such as de Rubys's *La Resurrection de la saincte Messe* were rushed out to persuade waverers and to stiffen the resolve of the faithful.[54] On the devotional side, again it was Auger who led the way. His publications, starting in 1563 with an *Apologie ou Defense des bons Chretiens, contre les Ennemis de l'Eglise catholique* and a *Catechisme* (both published by Michel Jove, who was to become the Jesuits' house printer), and following with a flood of works over the coming years, countered the output of successful Protestant apologists such as Pierre Viret on their own ground, besides providing attractive devotional material for a Catholic readership.[55]

Finally, the leaders of Lyon's Catholic revival – like the Protestants – realized the crucial importance of mobilizing lay enthusiasm by encouraging public communal manifestations of traditional piety. The Huguenots were well aware of the significance of this question, which was one of the crucial sticking points in the negotiations for the return of the Catholic exiles in June 1563. They pleaded unsuccessfully that 'the ecclesiastics, in the exercise of their divine service and ceremonies, should not be permitted to march through the city in processions carrying their accustomed relics and idols'.[56] This refusal to countenance such

---

[51] Hauser, *Les sources de l'histoire de France*, III, pp. 126–7.   [52] De Rubys, *Histoire*, p. 400.
[53] Groër, *Réforme et contre-réforme*, pp. 74–88.   [54] De Rubys, *Histoire*, p. 400.
[55] Kleinclausz, *Histoire de Lyon*, I, p. 422; Baudrier, *Bibliographie lyonnaise*, II, pp. 101–5 (for Auger); *ibid.*, II, pp. 293–5 (for Viret's output at this time).
[56] AM Lyon, BB 83, fos. 90ff.

processions was due not only to their reluctance to see their Reformed city space polluted with idolatry, but also surely to a straightforward awareness of the popularity of such processions in Lyon in the past, perhaps simply because they met the longstanding desire of the people to worship alfresco.[57] But this was a vain hope: the public observance of saints' days and other church festivals henceforth became a centre-piece of the Catholic revival, along with a concerted effort to revive pre-existing networks of religious sociability such as *quartier*-based and parish confraternities.[58]

Besides challenging the Huguenot monopoly on religious enthusiasm, the Catholic alliance was now in a position to take more direct action. It was the new visibility of the Huguenot community after 1563 which made this possible: now that the Reformed church had its own buildings, officers and institutions, it could be effectively targeted with a campaign of popular harassment. In 1565 all the Genevan ministers were thrown out of Lyon, the reason given being that they had no right of residence, despite the Reformed church's protests that this was contrary both to the terms of the edict and to the recently renewed French alliance with the cantons of Berne and Fribourg, which guaranteed free passage for their subjects and allies.[59] The combination of positive and negative cam-paigning was strikingly effective. Pierre Viret's complaints about the presence in Lyon of 'déistes', 'épicuriens' and atheists illustrate his frus-tration with the developing situation; his harsh criticism of half-hearted believers, recalling the tone of the anti-Nicodemite polemics of the 1540s, was surely a sign of his increasing despair as his flock slowly drifted back to the old religion.[60] It is easy to imagine how many of the evangeli-cal sympathizers who were caught up in a wave of enthusiasm in 1561 should have now found a re-energized Catholic church more attractive – and safer – than a beleaguered Reformed community. At the same time, a number of the city's more ideologically committed Protestants decided to take refuge in Geneva, taking advantage of that city's proximity.

---

[57] N. Z. Davis, 'The Sacred and the Body Social in Sixteenth-century Lyon', *Past & Present* 90 (1981), 52–7, provides a survey of the city's ritual year; for a particularly elaborate account of a traditional religious festival, see A. Sachet, *Le grand jubilé séculaire de Saint-Jean-de-Lyon. 1451 – 1546 – 1666 – 1734* (Lyon, 1886), pp. 87–180.

[58] De Rubys, *Histoire*, pp. 406 (celebration of St Peter's Day) and 428–9 (foundation of lay confra-ternities); see also P. Hoffman, *Church and Community in the Diocese of Lyon 1500–1789* (New Haven and London, 1984), pp. 30–42.

[59] Archives d'État de Genève, PH 1799 (letter of 28 Aug. 1565).

[60] C. J. Betts, *Early Deism in France* (Nijhoff, 1984), pp. 6–8. See also Pierre Viret's preface to *De l'estat... tant de la vraye que de la fausse Eglise* (Lyon, 1565). I owe the latter reference to Dr Stuart Foster.

The Catholics' hand was then greatly strengthened by the outbreak of the second war of religion in September 1567, at which time they took the opportunity to purge the bipartisan council and take control of the city. The police records kept by the militia in the following months reveal the collapse in numbers of the Huguenot community: of those who had not gone into exile, about half in the poorer *quartiers* – and almost all those in the richer *quartiers* – had now returned to the old faith.[61] De Rubys's account of the spontaneous celebrations in 1567 conveys a sense of justified triumphalism:

From which at once we went to give thanks to God and sing a Te Deum in the cathedral of Saint-Jean, where the people were summoned by the sound of the great bell, which certainly made the Protestants lower their heads, and from then on they spoke only of leaving the town. [62]

The Catholic party was now able to turn its attention to the more efficient repression of heterodox publications, an issue which had long been on the agenda of the city's clergy, but which now found support across a wider coalition of interests. De Rubys, by this time *procureur* to the city council, records approvingly that 'the archbishop arranged for the shops of booksellers and printers to be visited by theologians, who made a search for heretical books, from which were made fine sacrifices to Vulcan on the banks of the rivers'.[63] The willingness of a majority of council members to support this activity, in defiance of the city's commercial privileges and in direct contrast to their *laissez-faire* policy in the 1550s, shows how much had changed.

This formal harassment was accompanied by less-official measures. While Lyon's Huguenots had been bound to peaceful protest by their commitment to the edicts of pacification, the Catholics (who were less concerned about appearing loyal to the crown) could allow their more rumbustious supporters a freer rein. Dossiers of complaints sent by the Reformed church of Lyon to the king as the ultimate arbiter of the edicts of pacification include allegations of assault by the city's gatekeepers on their women and children as they left the city to worship in the countryside, and of more widespread harassment by a self-appointed body of artisans calling themselves 'la Police'. The replies to these complaints are particularly revelatory of the constraints under which the Reformed church now had to work. Generally the crown upheld the letter of the edict, calling on the Catholics to desist from their actions. But on one matter the crown does side with the Catholic critics: the question of acts

---

[61] Gascon, *Grand commerce*, II, pp. 520–1; the police records are at AM Lyon, GG 87.
[62] De Rubys, *Histoire*, p. 412.   [63] *Ibid.*, p. 413.

of worship in private houses, during which the Huguenots are asked to ensure that they do not sing 'with voices so loud that neighbours or passers-by can make of it an occasion for scandal or disorder'.[64] Confined to their homes and forced to lower their voices for the sake of public order: the contrast with the exuberant public assemblies of October 1561 could hardly be greater.

The final act of the tragedy was played out in September 1572, when the remaining hard core of Huguenot believers was eliminated in the massacre of the 'Lyon Vespers'. This bloody event, made possible by a combination of popular hatred and official indifference, provided the opportunity for the settling of scores dating back to the Protestant occupation in April 1562.[65] Yet by the time of the massacre Lyon's small Reformed community no longer posed a real threat to the city. The true turning point in Protestant fortunes was earlier, in 1567 (according to de Rubys) or even in 1563. With the failure of the Reformed church to maintain its numbers even under the relatively favourable conditions of 1563–7, and the resurgence of a renewed Catholicism backed by a coalition of elites and people, it is clear – at least in retrospect – that the end of Protestantism in Lyon was only a matter of time.

The rise and fall of the Reformation in Lyon is a narrative which in its starkness has important implications for our view of the wider French Reform movement. The impression given by the wonder years of 1557–62 has tended to deceive contemporaries and historians alike: the broad, rather fluid coalition of interests which enabled the movement to grow so rapidly was not solid enough to coalesce into a firm party grouping; the enthusiasm which had given a common direction when numbers were growing fast in a *laissez-faire* atmosphere did not survive into the more combative conditions of a religious civil war, when faced with a determined counter-action by a newly energized and enthusiastic Catholic party. The conditions for growth were not necessarily the same as the conditions for maintenance, while the means by which religious enthusiasm could be fostered – preaching, printing and public worship – could be used with striking effectiveness by Catholics as well as by Protestants.

The future character of the French Reformed church was to be defined by this early experience of rapid and buoyant expansion, followed swiftly by conflict, persecution and failure. Its early history has often

---

[64] AM Lyon, GG 77, unnumbered: letter of Charles IX to the royal governor, citing specific grievances of the Reformed church.
[65] Gascon, *Grand commerce*, II, pp. 527–9.

been written in terms of polemical opposites – of light versus darkness, Protestant versus Catholic – because of a desire to bring meaning to an experience of persecution and disappointed hopes, when in reality those hopes rested on a misunderstanding of what was, in its early years at least, a more fluid and complex situation with its own particular logic. The evidence of Lyon would seem to suggest that the French Reformation was not made by the Reformed church; rather, the Reformed church was made – and unmade – by the Reformation.

3. Religious polemic and Huguenot self-perception and identity, 1554–1619

Luc Racaut

Jean Crespin's *Histoire des Martyrs* is perhaps the single most important text for the elaboration of a distinct Huguenot identity. First published in 1554, it went through several editions before the definitive
edition produced by Simon Goulard in 1619. Between those two dates,
the Huguenots had achieved a modicum of political recognition with
the Edict of Nantes of 1598, a precarious end to forty years of civil
war. Crespin's *Histoire des Martyrs* celebrates the exemplary deaths of
French-speaking men and women who suffered persecution under the
Valois monarchy. It relied on the testimony of individuals who flocked
to Geneva to flee from persecution, a phenomenon which has been well
studied. What is perhaps less well understood is the debt the *Histoire des
Martyrs* owes to the Catholic adversary and to the English and Lutheran
traditions. The elaboration of Huguenot self-perception and identity did
not take place in a vacuum. It resulted from a dialectic, often hostile,
between Catholic polemic and Huguenot response. The *Histoire des
Martyrs* resorted to the English and Lutheran traditions to respond to specific arguments that were made by Catholic polemicists. Catholic contributions to the Reformation debate in France have been underestimated
in the historiography. This essay seeks to redress the balance in emphasizing the role that Catholic, English and Lutheran arguments played in the
elaboration of Huguenot identity, as reflected in the *Histoire des Martyrs*.

Before the outbreak of the French wars of religion, the persecution
during the reign of Henri II gave Huguenots the opportunity to draw
comparisons with the early church. To die for one's faith was not in itself
a sign of election and to call those burned at the stake 'martyrs' reflects
a certain ideological standpoint. At their trial, Huguenots were asked to
recant their 'heresy' and return to the bosom of the Roman and Apostolic
church. It was obstinacy, and not heresy as such, that was punishable
by death. For Huguenots, obstinacy was a sign that one was unwilling

to compromise one's faith and to be killed was to be martyred. As Brad Gregory pointed out in *Salvation at Stake*, martyrdom was a cultural representation that depended on one's interpretation of execution.[1]

The Genevan reformer Guillaume Farel was one of the first to write about martyrdom in the French-speaking world.[2] But it was Calvin, by giving it pride of place in his work, who contributed most to the dissemination of the culture of martyrdom. For Calvin, it was preferable to suffer death than to participate in Catholic worship. In his 1543 pamphlet against Nicodemites, Calvin called upon the example of St Cyprian who suffered martyrdom rather than worship idols.[3] Calvin's approach to martyrdom is revealed in his letters written to French prisoners at the height of the persecutions during the reign of Henri II. Calvin urged his co-religionists to remain firm in their faith and maintained that their death was a proof of their election:

> Persecutions are the true combats of Christians to try the constancy and firmness of their faith . . . It has been said of old that the blood of the martyrs is the seed of the Church. If it is a seed from which we derive our origin in Jesus Christ, it should also be a shower to water us that we may grow and make progress, even so as to die well.[4]

The dissemination of the culture of martyrdom did not go unchallenged. Catholics resorted to the dictum found in Augustine that it is not the punishment that makes a martyr but the cause for which he dies.[5] The fact that heretics, such as Arians and Donatists, had also claimed to be martyrs was used to disprove the validity of the Calvinist cause. These arguments were difficult to answer since Calvinists themselves, such as the Walloon Guy de Brès, had used the very same against the Anabaptists.[6] The Polish Cardinal Stanislas Hozius, for example, made the most of this apparent contradiction, and described with a certain irony the 'lust for death' of the Calvinists:

> They have begun to glorify themselves of the number and constancy of their martyrs . . . Calvin must not boast . . . that his followers are poor lambs destined

---

[1] B. S. Gregory, *Salvation at Stake: Christian Martyrdom in Early Modern Europe* (Cambridge, MA, 1999), p. 76.

[2] D. El Kenz, *Les Bûchers du Roi: la Culture protestante des Martyrs (1523–1572)* (Paris, 1997), p. 72.

[3] Jean Calvin, *petit traité montrant que c'est que doit faire un homme fidèle connaissant la Verité de l'Evangile quand il est entre les papistes* in O. Millet (ed.), *Œuvres choisies* (Paris, 1995), pp. 136–7.

[4] J. Bonnet (ed.), *Letters of John Calvin* (Edinburgh, 1980), pp. 219, 223–4.

[5] 'Martyres veros non facit poena, sed causa', quoted in George Witzel, *Discours des Moeurs, tant des anciens heretiques que nouveaux Lutheriens & Calvinistes, auquel leur Resemblance est clerement demonstrée* (Paris, 1567), p. 11.

[6] Guy de Brès, *La racine, source et fondement des Anabaptistes ou rebaptisez de nostre temps* (Lyon, 1565), p. 62.

to be slaughtered: because the Anabaptists . . . have done so for many centuries before anyone had even heard of the sacramentarians . . .[7]

These arguments carried a certain weight given the emphasis placed in martyrologies on the patience with which martyrs suffered death. In place of the Huguenot martyr, the Catholics offered the image of the obstinate heretic. But resort to the stereotypes of heresy fuelled rather than hindered the Huguenot representation of martyrdom. This is nowhere better illustrated than in the polemical exchange that surrounded the 'Affair of the rue Saint Jacques'.

The period that followed the Edict of Compiègnes (1557) marked the crystallization of the Huguenot conception of martyrdom. The discovery of a secret meeting in the rue Saint Jacques in September 1557 was the occasion for the Huguenots to elaborate further on the culture of martyrdom. The incident provoked a lengthy polemical exchange between theologians of the University of Paris and ministers who had witnessed the persecutions in Paris. The most important exchange was between Antoine de Mouchy, a key Catholic figure, and Nicolas des Gallars, minister in Paris at the time of the Affair. Des Gallars was a member of Geneva's Company of Pastors between 1544 and 1554 and volunteered to be minister in Paris between July and September 1557.[8] Following the imprisonment of numerous Huguenots, his *Apologie ou Défense des vrais Chrestiens* was published anonymously. In this work, des Gallars set the tone for the Huguenot response to Catholic accusations. The *Apologie* made the stock comparison with the early church. Although the original edition has not survived, it was reproduced in its entirety by another Parisian minister, Antoine de la Roche Chandieu, in his *Histoire des Persecutions*. Chandieu recounts the reaction that the *Apologie* provoked among Catholic theologians:

This small pamphlet . . . dispelled the bad reputation that many people had of our assemblies and even encouraged others to make deeper inquiries of our doctrine. Some doctors of the Sorbonne attempted to answer it: but the poor beasts, like in any other things, discovered nothing but their own ignorance. One named Mouchi . . . wrote an entire book on the punishment of heretics and showed that they must be burned and dealt with with fire and swords.[9]

[7] Stanislas Hozius, *Des sectes et heresies de nostre temps* (Paris, 1561), pp. 136–7, 142.

[8] W. G. Naphy, *Calvin and the Consolidation of the Genevan Reformation* (Manchester, 1994), pp. 58, 73.

[9] Antoine de la Roche Chandieu, *Histoire des persecutions, et martyrs de l'Église de Paris, depuis l'an 1557. Jusques au temps du Roy Charles neufviesme* (Lyon, 1563), sigs. d1v–d2r.

Antoine de Mouchy had published a response to this first tract in 1558, where he accused Huguenots of taking part in orgies under the cover of darkness.[10] Des Gallars answered de Mouchy directly in a second tract entitled *Seconde Apologie ou Défense des vrais Chrestiens*.[11] It reproduced entire passages of Tertullian's *Apology*, a key text of Christian martyrology.[12] Tertullian's dictum that 'the blood of the martyrs is seed' had been used by Protestants in general, and by Calvin in particular.[13] But Tertullian also reported accusations of sexual improprieties used by Romans against Christians. This enabled des Gallars, and others, to strengthen the comparison with the early church martyrs. Chandieu's *Histoire des Persecutions*, which reports the exchange, was itself used in the first folio edition of Crespin's *Histoire des Martyrs* published in 1564.

It should be noted that the use of the word 'martyr' made the Geneva city council uncomfortable, and Jean Crespin used the ambiguous 'persons who have endured death' and 'witnesses of the truth of the gospel' instead. It was not until the 1580s that these reservations were lifted and the title *Histoire des Martyrs* was used.[14] The stock comparison with the early church implied another between the French crown and the Roman tyrants who had persecuted Christians. This spoke too much of political insurrection for the taste of the Geneva city council that was always wary of its difficult diplomatic position.[15]

Indeed, the culture of martyrdom grew in parallel with a policy of conformity with the laws of the prince, which did not go without a certain ambiguity. At the time of the martyrdom of Cyprian, the cult of the emperors was law, and the refusal of the saint to worship 'idols' was in itself akin to political insurrection. The model of martyrdom held by Calvin was therefore associated with political disobedience. The outbreak of the wars of religion provided Catholic polemicists with further arguments to associate the Huguenot movement with political disobedience.

In the 1560s, Catholic theologians discredited the myth of the Huguenot martyr with accusations of political insurrection. In March 1560, at Amboise, Protestant plotters attempted to rid the court of the Guise's

---

[10] Antoine de Mouchy, *Responce a quelque apologie que les heretiques ces jours passés ont mis en avant sous ce titre: Apologie ou deffence des bons Chrestiens contre les ennemis de l'Eglise catholique* (Paris, 1558).

[11] Nicolas des Gallars, *Seconde apologie ou defense des vrais chrestiens, contre les calomnies impudentes des ennemis de l'Eglise catholique. Ou il est respondu aux diffames redoublez par un nommé Demochares docteur de la Sorbonne* (Geneva, 1559).

[12] Tertullian, *Apologeticus*, ed. by J. E. B. Mayor (Cambridge, 1917), pp. 7, 25, 29, 31.

[13] 'Semen ecclesiae sanguis christianorum': see Gregory, *Salvation at Stake*, p. 150.

[14] J.-F. Gilmont, *Jean Crespin: un éditeur réformé du XVIe siècle* (Geneva, 1981), pp. 169–70.

[15] See P. Chaix, *Recherches sur l'imprimerie à Genève de 1550 à 1564* (Geneva, 1978), p. 80.

influence. The 'Tumult of Amboise' marked the time when French Protestants started to be called 'Huguenots' and were irremediably associated with civil disobedience.[16] In January 1561, Charles IX wrote to Calvin asking him to stop the flow of books from Geneva which were thought to have triggered the conspiracy.[17] In a very carefully worded letter to the king, Calvin denied knowledge of the plot and condemned any Genevan citizens or ministers who may have been involved.[18] In appeasing the king, Calvin was following the recommendations of the Geneva city council that tried at every turn to avoid diplomatic complications with the French crown.[19] In a recent essay, Philip Benedict has shed new light on the discrepancies that lay between Geneva's official support of royal authority and the involvement of Genevan ministers in acts of rebellion. He argues that the image of Calvinism as law-abiding (largely reproduced in the historiography) is the result of careful engineering on the part of the Geneva city council and Calvin himself.[20]

The politicization of the conflict, after Amboise, damaged the image of the Huguenot as an innocent victim, although it was continuously used throughout the wars.[21] Resort to armed rebellion could no longer be squared with the image of the Huguenot martyr that was disseminated by Crespin. Furthermore, the modes of execution of heretics changed from burning to hanging as the theatre of execution increasingly resulted in scenes of violence and disorder. This shift from burning to hanging was motivated by an attempt to prevent spontaneous outbreaks of popular violence, as audiences increasingly wanted to participate in the heretic's death.[22] Whereas the burning of heretics had provided a platform for the 'theatre of martyrdom', hanging (a fate reserved to common criminals) denied the Huguenots their martyrdom. This movement to turn heresy into a political crime went hand in hand with a polemical campaign to portray Huguenots as dangerous agitators and rebels.

[16] Anon., *Complainte au peuple Francois* in [François Hotman], *L'Histoire du Tumulte d'Amboyse advenu au Moys de Mars, MDLX* (s.l., 1560), sig. D2r.

[17] R. Kingdon, *Geneva and the Coming of the Wars of Religion in France, 1555–1563* (Geneva, 1956), pp. 34, 93.

[18] J. Bonnet (ed.), *Letters of Calvin*, 4 vols. (New York, 1972), IV, p. 167.

[19] Chaix, *Recherche sur l'imprimerie à Genève*, p. 80. On Calvin's own views see W. Nijenhuis, 'The Limits of Civil Disobedience in Calvin's Latest Known Sermons: The Development of his Ideas of the Right of Civil Resistance', in W. Nijenhuis (ed.), *'Ecclesia Reformata': Studies on the Reformation*, 2 vols. (New York, 1994), II, pp. 73–97.

[20] P. Benedict, 'The Dynamics of Protestant Militancy: France, 1555–1563' in P. Benedict, G. Marnef, H. van Nierop and M. Venard (eds.), *Reformation, Revolt, and Civil War in France and the Netherlands, 1555–1585* (Amsterdam, 1999), pp. 35–50.

[21] See Penny Roberts's essay in this volume.

[22] D. Nicholls, 'The Theatre of Martyrdom', *Past & Present* 121 (1988), 69.

The death of Henri II marked the emergence of conspiracy theories on both sides of the confessional divide as Huguenot and Catholic factions vied for control at court. In the polemical flood that followed the 'Tumult of Amboise', each faction accused the other of wanting to usurp the throne. The theme of a Huguenot conspiracy began to emerge. François Hotman, one of the instigators of Amboise, provides a good example of the arguments that were used:

Knowing that a great number of Lutherans or Evangelists, as they are called, were involved in the enterprise, the Gospel was blamed for everything. And everywhere in France the news is spread that those who have risen are Lutherans: that their goal was to kill the King, the Queen, the Lords his brothers, and all the Princes: to promote their Religion with sword strokes, to abolish the Monarchy of France, and to reduce it to a kind of Republic.[23]

Although these accusations were a far cry from what was intended at Amboise, they presented a serious challenge to the representation of Huguenots as innocent martyrs. The 'Tumult of Amboise' had irreparably damaged the credibility of the Huguenots who were now on the defensive. After the death of François II, many Huguenot tracts were addressed to the regent, Catherine de Medici, who had managed to restore the balance at court between the vying factions. Augustin Marlorat, in his *Remonstrance a la royne mere du Roy*, attempted to dismiss the conspiracy theory as a clumsy alternative to even more outlandish accusations:

Our adversaries . . . try to convince the King and yourself that our assemblies are nothing but a pretext for a dissolute licence to take part in an orgy . . . But seeing that it is a lie that cannot be proven . . . They find another, that is more easily received, that we meet to plot to kill the King and the nobility . . . and it would be surprising if they could not find, among those that they cruelly put to death, one who could confirm their lies.[24]

Catholics had indeed moved away from accusations of sexual deviance, which had provided the Huguenots with ammunition in their comparison with the early church martyrs. It is clear that this shift to accusations of a political plot to take over the kingdom made Marlorat uneasy. The Huguenot response after Amboise was increasingly defensive and clumsy, often turning accusations around and resorting to petty personal attacks. For example, the fact that the 'Affair of the rue Saint Jacques' coincided with the defeat of St Quentin led Catholics and Huguenots to accuse one

[23] *L'Histoire du Tumulte d'Amboyse*, sig. C1v.

[24] Augustin Marlorat, *Remonstrance a la royne mere du Roy, par ceux qui sont persecutez pour la parole de DIEU. En laquelle ils rendent raison des principaux articles de la Religion, & qui sont aujourdhuy en dispute* (Paris, 1561), sigs. B5v–B6v.

another of having plotted against the kingdom.[25] A pamphlet addressed to Catherine de Medici, *La Maniere d'appaiser les Troubles,* pointed to the Guise as the source of these accusations. Another anonymous work, the *Complainte apologique des Eglises de France,* turned the Catholic accusation on its head and blamed the duc de Guise for the defeat of St Quentin.[26] The *Maniere d'appaiser les Troubles* also attributed the defeat of St Quentin and the death of Henri II to divine providence.[27] The death of François II, which rid the court of the influence of the Guise, had been welcomed by Calvin himself: 'has the death of a king ever been more providential?'[28] Providentialism and the belief that persecutors would die horribly were an important component of Protestant martyrology but it also provided Catholics with arguments for a Huguenot plot.[29]

Although Jean Crespin drew on such polemical material for the compilation of his *Histoire des Martyrs,* any adversarial or political comments were carefully left out. For example, Crespin omitted how de Mouchy and the cardinal de Lorraine had gathered false witnesses to incriminate the Huguenots in the eyes of the queen.[30] This allegation, found in the tracts of Chandieu and Marlorat, was none the less included in the monumental *Histoire Ecclesiastique* (1580).[31] This indicates that the reservations about polemic that had concerned the Genevan authorities in the 1560s had been tempered in the 1580s. This is reflected in the editions of the *Histoire des Martyrs* that appeared from 1582 onwards under the editorship of Simon Goulard.

After 1562 the myth of the innocent Huguenot martyr was losing credibility as the Catholic accusations of civil disobedience took flesh with the revolt of the prince de Condé.[32] Huguenot polemicists understood this well and turned to writing vindictive pamphlets against the Catholic adversary, notably theologians of the University of Paris and the Guise.

---

[25] Chandieu, *Histoire des persecutions,* sig. a1v.
[26] Anon., *Complainte apologique des Eglises de France, au Roy, Royne-mere, Roy de Navarre, & autres du Conseil* (s.l., 1561), sig. E1v.
[27] Anon., *La Maniere d'appaiser les troubles, qui sont maintenant en France, & y pourront estre cy apres: a la Royne Mere du Roy* (Lyon, 1561), sigs. B2r, C1v.
[28] A. Duke, G. Lewis and A. Pettegree (eds.), *Calvinism in Europe 1540–1610: A Collection of Documents* (Manchester, 1992), p. 80.
[29] Gregory, *Salvation at Stake,* p. 326; Theodore de Beza, *Histoire Ecclesiastique des Eglises reformes au royaume de France,* 3 vols. (Antwerp, 1580), I, pp. 234, 236; Lancelot du Voisin de la Popelinière, *L'Histoire de France enrichie des plus notables occurances survenues ez Provinces de l'Europe & pays voisins,* 2 vols. (La Rochelle, 1581), I, fo. 148v.
[30] Chandieu, *Histoire des persecutions,* sigs. x7r–x8r.
[31] Beza, *Histoire Ecclesiastique,* I, p. 228; Popelinière, *L'Histoire de France* I, fo. 147v.
[32] El Kenz, *Les Bûchers du roi,* p. 188.

The massacre of St Bartholomew's Day increased this trend as the Huguenot movement lost all remaining illusions of political obedience to the monarch. In the eyes of the Huguenots, the king had turned into a tyrant who could legitimately be removed by force. It has been argued that the emergence of the Monarchomachs removed all the remaining credit that Huguenot martyrdom might have had.[33] I should like to argue, however, that the massacre of St Bartholomew's Day gave a new lease of life to the theme of Huguenot martyrdom.

The St Bartholomew's Day massacre provoked a transformation of Huguenot self-perception and identity, which is reflected in the subsequent editions of the *Histoire des Martyrs*. Jean Crespin died in 1572, and his work was taken up by Simon Goulard, who published four editions in 1582, 1597, 1608 and 1619. In a section devoted to the massacre, Goulard introduced a distinction between individual and collective martyrdom:

> If we call Martyrs those that were executed one by one by justice, what shall we call so many thousands of excellent figures who were martyred in one fell swoop, not by one executioner, but by a multitude of commoners whose swords were the plaintiffs, witnesses, judges, sentences and executioners of the strangest cruelties that have ever been perpetrated against the Church?[34]

Jean Crespin had primarily been concerned with the individual martyrdom of his contemporary co-religionists whose names figure in the *Histoire des Martyrs*. Simon Goulard extended the status of martyr to medieval heretics who had been persecuted by the thousand. The massacre of St Bartholomew's Day thus opened the door to a comparison with the atrocities that the Catholic church had perpetrated across the ages. Unlike individual martyrs who had died at the hand of the king's justice, medieval heretics had suffered a collective and anonymous martyrdom, sometimes in an open war against temporal and spiritual authority. Their inclusion in the *Histoire des Martyrs* from 1582 onwards marked the beginning of a new militancy perhaps more eloquent than the tracts of the Monarchomachs.

This new militancy was no doubt motivated by the perceived involvement of the papacy in the massacre of St Bartholomew's Day, as reflected in Theodore Beza's own words: 'No one can doubt that these events are the result of a plot worked out at the Council of Trent.'[35] Although it is

---

33 *Ibid.*, pp. 69 n. 3, 237.

34 Jean Crespin, *Histoire des martyrs persecutez et mis a mort pour la verité de l'Evangile, depuis le temps des Apostres jusques à l'an 1574* (Geneva, 1582), fo. 704b.

35 Duke *et al.*, *Calvinism in Europe*, p. 113.

doubtful that the papacy was directly involved in the massacre, this was one of the enduring myths that was identified by Robert Kingdon.[36] As a result, the *Histoire des Martyrs* became a work of anti-papal propaganda following in the tracks of English and Lutheran works that had lambasted the papacy for several decades.[37]

This trend can indeed be found in the Lutheran Matthias Flacius Illyricus's *Catalogus Testium Veritatis* (1556) and the 'Anglican' John Foxe's *Acts and Monuments* (1563). The *Catalogus Testium Veritatis* formed the blueprint for all subsequent Protestant histories of the True Church. It systematically looked for medieval precedents for the reformers' views and literally compiled a 'catalogue of the witnesses of the truth in the face of papal tyranny'.[38] Behind the work of Flacius Illyricus and John Foxe lies the idea of a Protestant 'apostolic succession'. In this light, the medieval persecutions of heretics reflect the suffering of the True Church at the hands of the papal Antichrist.

Despite the attention given to medieval heretics in French Catholic polemic and parallel movements to turn them into martyrs of the True Church, the Huguenots failed to acknowledge their relevance until after 1572. For example, half a dozen distinct histories of the Albigensian Crusade were published by prominent Catholic figures between 1561 and 1590.[39] As early as the 1540s, Bale had argued that papal persecution of the Cathars was provoked by their resistance to the rise of the papal monarchy.[40] John Foxe included an entire chapter on the Albigensian Crusade in the 1570 edition of the *Acts and Monuments*.[41] Yet the Albigensians were not mentioned until the 1582 edition of the *Histoire des Martyrs*. In the words of Simon Goulard, their inclusion was motivated by the fact that they had been enemies of the papacy:

As regards those they call heretics, namely the enemies of the Papacy, they are accused of the most horrid crimes in the world, in order to tarnish their reputation further . . . From the moment the bishop of Rome declared himself to be the universal leader of the Church, there has been people of all kind . . . who have denounced . . . the corporeal and spiritual tyranny of the Popes.[42]

[36] R. M. Kingdon, *Myths about the St Bartholomew's Day Massacres 1572–1576* (London, 1988).
[37] E. Cameron, 'Medieval Heretics as Protestant Martyrs', *Studies in Church History* 30 (1993), 185–207.
[38] Matthias Flacius Illyricus, *Catalogus Testium Veritatis* (Basel, 1556); John Foxe, *Acts and Monuments* (London, 1563).
[39] L. Racaut, 'The Polemical Use of the Albigensian Crusade during the French Wars of Religion', *French History* 13 (1999), 261–79.
[40] H. Christmas (ed.), *Select works of John Bale* (Cambridge, 1849), p. 563.
[41] John Foxe, *Acts and Monuments* (1570), fo. 295.
[42] Crespin, *Histoire des Martyrs* (1582), fo. 25b; *ibid.* (1619), fo. 23.

The fact that these arguments were not used in a French context before points to the differences that existed between the Huguenots and the other Protestant traditions. In Germany and England, anti-papal arguments had been instrumental in rallying the political elite to the Protestant cause. The conflict between pope and secular rulers over the control of church appointments and revenues was central to the Lutheran and English arguments. The arguments concerning the Investiture Contest had no clout in France because of the specificity of the Gallican church, bolstered by the Pragmatic Sanction of 1438 and the Concordat of Bologna in 1516. Whereas the support of secular rulers played a considerable part in the elaboration of Lutheran and 'Anglican' identities, the French monarchy's fluctuating position left the Huguenots to forge their own identity. This might explain why Huguenots clung for so long to the illusion of loyalty to the crown and the striking absence of anti-papal arguments before 1572. With the accession of Henri IV and the Edict of Nantes, the king became the protector of his Huguenot subjects. As it is suggested elsewhere in this volume, this did not provoke the decline of Huguenot militancy, as had previously been thought, but its transformation.[43] 1598 also marks a shift in Huguenot self-perception and identity, which increasingly defined itself in opposition to the Catholic adversary, not within France, but in Rome. This could now be squared with the policies of the monarchy who, short of endorsing the Protestant movement, had recognized its right to exist. The arguments of the Monarchomachs, that had been used with much better results by the Catholic League, were no longer relevant to the Reformation debate. Rome became the convenient other against whom both the monarchy and its Huguenot subjects could unite. This choice was no doubt motivated by the impact that Catholic reform was beginning to have in Europe. This can be shown by the insistence with which the Huguenot movement identified the pope as the Antichrist at the beginning of the seventeenth century.

The Genevan church was at first extremely reluctant to pronounce itself on the Antichrist found in the Revelation of John. Calvin himself had avoided teaching on the Apocalypse and Nicolas Colladon, who published a commentary in 1584, asserted that it was because Calvin himself had not 'fully understood the text'. Theodore Beza was equally cautious in his preface of a commentary on Revelation by Pinet in 1557.[44]

---

43 See Alan James's essay in this volume.
44 I. Backus, *Les sept visions et la fin des temps: les commentaires genevois de l'apocalypse entre 1539 et 1584* (Geneva, 1997).

Geneva Bibles included a cautionary warning against abusive interpretations of Revelation that can be found in six different editions published in Geneva, Saumur, Rouen and La Rochelle.[45] Furthermore, the national synod of Saumur in 1596 forbade pastors from teaching or preaching on the Apocalypse without the advice of the provincial synod.[46]

These warnings, however, were not heeded by Lambert Daneau who published his *Traité de l'Antéchrist* in Geneva in 1577.[47] In this treatise, Daneau argues that Jerome of Prague and Jan Hus were the two witnesses of the True Church described in Revelation, implying that the pope was indeed the Antichrist. The same allegation was made by the Dutch Calvinist Jonius (1545–1602), in his 1592 commentary on Revelation.[48] This commentary was reproduced in subsequent editions of the Geneva Bible and notably in an English edition published in 1607:

And that this was done to very many godly men, by Boniface and others, the histories doe declare, especially since the time that the odious and condemned name amongst the multitude, first of the brethren Waldonenses or Lugdunenses, then also of the Fraticels, was pretended, that good men might with more approbation be massacred.[49]

This indicates that, by the turn of the seventeenth century, the Huguenots had lost their earlier reservations about using the papal Antichrist as a tool of propaganda. This new-found enthusiasm was undoubtedly inspired by Catholic attacks, by Jesuits in general and Robert Bellarmine in particular. In 1599 Philippe de Marnix, in his *Tableau des Differens de la Religion,* made an analogy between the medieval persecutions and Revelation.[50] Flacius Illyricus's *Catalogus Testium Veritatis* was printed in Geneva by Simon Goulard in 1597 and 1608 and was used to add to his editions of the *Histoire des Martyrs.*[51] The seventeenth century saw the Huguenot characterization of the pope as the Antichrist flourish with unprecedented vigour.

---

[45] *Le Nouveau Testament c'est à dire, la nouvelle alliance de nostre seigneur Jesus Christ* (Geneva, 1577), p. 682; *La Bible qui toute la saincte escriture du Vieil & du Nouveau Testament* (Geneva, 1588), fo. 122v.

[46] Aymon, I, p. 203.

[47] C.-G. Dubois, *La conception de l'histoire en France au XVIe siècle, 1560–1610* (Paris, 1977), pp. 501–51.

[48] Fr du Jon, *Apocalypse ou Revelation de S. Jean Apostre Evangeliste de nostre Seigneur Jesus Christ* (Geneva, 1592), p. 208.

[49] Quoted in G. T. Sheppard, 'The Geneva Bible and English Commentary, 1600–1645' in G. T. Sheppard (ed.), *The Geneva Bible* (New York, 1989), pp. i–iv, 1, fo. 129b.

[50] E. Cameron, *The Reformation of the Heretics: The Waldenses of the Alps 1480–1580* (Oxford, 1984), p. 249.

[51] Goulard's two editions of the *Catalogus Testium Veritatis* correspond to his second and third edition of the *Livre des Martyrs,* in 1597 and 1608.

The doctrine of the papal Antichrist was adopted by the national synod of 1603 as an article of the Confession of Faith of the French Reformed churches. This was confirmed at the synod of 1607: 'the article concerning the Antichrist inserted at the synod of Gap, to be the 31st of our Confession of Faith ... has been approved ... to be ... true to what was predicted in the Scriptures'. A commission for the writing of a book on the Antichrist was issued at the same synod: 'Monsieur Vignier is asked to put pen to paper to deal fully with the matter of the Antichrist, & to bring, or to send his work at the next National Synod.'[52]

Nicolas Vignier was the son and namesake of Henri IV's surgeon, and after his father converted back to Catholicism in 1579, he took up his work and published his ecclesiastical history in 1601. This large folio history of the True Church devotes a considerable amount of space to the medieval persecutions of the papal Antichrist in a section comprising no fewer than 167 pages.[53] Vignier was also the author of a defence of the Protestant doctrine of the Antichrist against Cardinal Bellarmine, which was published anonymously in 1606.[54] In 1609, the national synod of Saint Maixent acknowledged the progress of Vignier, whose *Theatre de L'Antechrist* was sent to Saumur where it was printed in 1610.[55] This large folio was clearly intended to be the final word in the matter of the Antichrist and responded directly to Florimond de Raemond's anti-martyrology, François Ribera's commentary on Revelation, and to the works of the Jesuits Pierre Cotton and Cardinal Bellarmine.[56]

In the face of these arguments, Nicolas Vignier argued in *L'Antechrist Romain* that the persecution of the middle ages had been worse than those of the early church:

Since those times have we seen more horrendous butchery and more cruel persecutions exerted against the Saints? It is true that medieval persecutions cannot be compared to those of Nero, Domitian, Decius or Diocletian: Because they were but physical, whereas the former were spiritual as well as physical. The first persecutions were interspersed, and lasted but a few months, or a few years. But the medieval ones continued unabated for several centuries. The first ones took

---

[52] Aymon, I, pp. 258, 303, 313, 316.

[53] Nicolas Vignier, *Recueil de l'histoire de l'Église, depuis le Baptseme de nostre Seigneur Jesus Christ, jusques à ce temps* (Leiden, 1601), pp. 408, 374–541.

[54] *L'Antechrist Romain, Opposé à l'Antechrist Juif du Cardinal de Bellarmin, du Sieur de Remond & autres* (s.l., 1606); Robert Bellarmine, *Disputationes de controversiis Christianae Fidei Adversus Hujus Temporis Haereticos*, 3 vols. (Ingolstadt, 1586–93).

[55] Aymon, I, p. 36; Cameron, *Reformation of the Heretics*, p. 249.

[56] Nicolas Vignier, *Theatre de L'Antechrist Auquel est respondu au Cardinal Bellarmin, au sieur de Remond, à Perenius, Ribera, Viergas, Sanderus et autres qui par leurs Escrits condamnent la doctrine des Eglises Reformees sur ce subiet: Par Nicolas Vignier* (Saumur, 1610).

several thousand martyrs. Whereas the later ones took innumerable multitudes. A chronicler counts 17,000 Christians killed in one month under Diocletian. Bellarmine, while recounting the prowess of the Roman Church, counts 100,000 Albigensians killed in one day under the Papacy of Innocent III.[57]

This marks a striking departure from the earlier period where the representation of martyrdom had hinged on a comparison with the early church martyrs. Vignier's insistence on the hardships of the medieval martyrs of the True Church reflects the new-found impact of anti-popery on French Protestant culture. Vignier resorted to arguments that had been used in the English and Lutheran traditions and gave them a new spin in the context of polemic against the Jesuits.[58]

The specificity of the Huguenot identity is reflected in the special attention that was given to the Albigensians.[59] French Reformed churches in the southern provinces felt a particularly strong kinship with the Albigensians because of the geographical coincidence of the movement with their own. In 1572, the national synod of Montauban issued a commission, which was probably the origin of Jean Chassanion's *Histoire des Albigeois* published in Geneva in 1595.[60] The same national synod that commissioned the *Theatre de L'Antechrist* also commissioned a second history of the Albigensians in 1607.[61] It was completed and published as Jean-Paul Perrin's *Histoire des Albigeois* (1618) and was extensively quoted in the 1619 edition of the *Histoire des Martyrs*.[62]

In the seventeenth century, Huguenot self-perception and identity relied heavily on the production of alternative histories such as the *Histoire des Martyrs* and the *Theatre de L'Antechrist*. It is remarkable that anti-papal arguments that had been available to the French Protestants in the shape of the *Catalogus Testium Veritatis* or the *Acts and Monuments* were not used before. It could be argued that the different political contexts of the Protestant traditions, English, Lutheran and Huguenot, prevented these arguments from being readily used. It is not until the early seventeenth century, when the Catholic Reformation began to have an impact throughout Europe, that the different Protestant traditions made common cause beyond their theological differences.

---

[57] Vignier, *L'Antechrist Romain*, pp. 159–60.
[58] Nicolas Vignier, *Apologie Catholique de la doctrine des Eglises Reformees* (Saumur, 1617).
[59] Racaut, 'Polemical Use of the Albigensian Crusade'.
[60] Jean Chassanion, *Histoire des Albigeois: touchant leur doctrine & religion, contre les faux Bruits qui ont esté semés d'eux, & les ecris dont on les a à tort diffamés: & de la cruelle & longue guerre qui leur a esté faite, pour ravir les terres & seigneuries d'autrui, sous couleur de vouloir extirpé l'hérésie* (Geneva, 1595).
[61] Aymon, II, pp. 123, 316.   [62] Crespin, *Histoire des martyrs* (1619), fo. 22.

The distinctive character of the French Gallican church may explain why anti-papal arguments had to be modified in the Huguenot context. The institutionalization of the Church of England, for example, inten- sified the need for proof of a visible church in the middle ages. The English tradition used the medieval martyrs of the True Church to cre- ate something akin to an apostolic succession of the True Church. This view was elaborated upon by James Ussher, who argued for an unbro- ken historical link between the Apostles and Luther.[63] A 1711 English translation of Perrin's *History of the Albigenses* even argued for an unbroken succession from the middle ages to the sixteenth century: 'And from the Holy Men of that Age the Lamp of pure Doctrine was handed down to Bertram, from him to Peter Bruis to Waldo, from Waldo, to Dulcinus, from him to Marsilius, from him to Wickliff, from him to Hus and Jerom of Prague, and from their Scholars, the Fratres Bohemi, to Luther and Calvin.'[64] This contrasted markedly with the Huguenot use of the medieval martyrs which merely testified to the continuing existence of the True Church at the times of the persecution of the Antichrist. The lack of political patronage, strict opposition to episcopacy, as well as the nature of Gallicanism, made the English arguments unworkable. It was only after the French Reformed churches achieved a degree of political legitimacy with the Edict of Nantes in 1598 that the importance of the English arguments was acknowledged.

Catholics and Huguenots not only fought doctrinally and physically but also created competing narratives and representations of the other. Huguenot self-perception and identity was born of the dialectic between these competing narratives. In the first instance, a comparison with the early church emerged on the eve of the French wars of religion, pro- viding the Huguenots with their best arguments. With the politicization of the conflict, however, the representation of martyrdom became inop- erative as the Huguenots were involved in armed rebellion against the monarch. The St Bartholomew's Day massacre marked the transforma- tion of Huguenot identity in inspiring a comparison with the collective martyrdom of medieval predecessors. Simon Goulard's four editions of the *Histoire des Martyrs* between 1582 and 1619 illustrate this progression as he included more and more material borrowed from the Lutheran and

---

[63] James Ussher, *De Christianorum Ecclesiarum Successione et Statu Historica Explicatio* (London, 1613).
[64] Jean Paul Perrin, *The History of the Old Waldenses and Albigenses; Those Two Glorious Witnesses to the Truth of Christianity: In Opposition to the Antichristianism of Rome, In the several ages preceding the Reformation* (London, 1711), p. 73, note c.

English traditions. At the turn of the seventeenth century, anti-popery became an essential element of Huguenot self-perception and identity, mirroring a similar phenomenon across the Channel.[65]

One can draw some tentative conclusions about the elaboration of a distinct Huguenot identity from this reappraisal of the *Histoire des Martyrs*. The French culture of martyrdom did not flow outwards from Geneva, but was the result of a dialogue with its French outposts. The Huguenot tradition of martyrdom was not monolithic but dynamic, and it followed the events that shaped the history of the movement. The *Histoire des Martyrs* owes a great deal more to the Catholic adversary, and to its Lutheran and English counterparts, than might have been expected. The Huguenot movement was none the less distinct, as it formulated original responses to problems that were specific to the French context. In this regard, the unique position of the crown of France, and the ambiguous approach of the Huguenots to royal power, were determining factors.

---

[65] P. Lake, 'Anti-popery: The Structure of a Prejudice' in R. Cust and A. Hughes (eds.), *Conflict in Early Stuart England: Studies in Religion and Politics, 1603–1642* (London, 1989), p. 82.

4. Confessionalization in France? Critical reflections and new evidence[1]

Philip Benedict

In the past decade, the concept of 'confessionalization' that German historians first began to forge nearly fifty years ago has spread through the international literature on the European Reformation. The word's semantic fortunes received an initial boost outside Germany when R. Po-chia Hsia introduced it to an English-language audience in his 1989 *Social Discipline in the Reformation: Central Europe, 1550–1750*. Its international visibility grew when the authoritative *Handbook of European History 1400–1600* included in 1995 a forceful chapter on 'Confessional Europe' by one of the leading proponents of the confessionalization thesis, Heinz Schilling.[2] In that same year, English-language studies of the Netherlands by Benjamin Kaplan and Jonathan Israel used the theme of confessionalization and its limits to illuminate Dutch religious history in the generations following the Reformation.[3] In France, an ambitious multi-volume history of Christianity involving numerous leading scholars of the subject entitled the volume dealing with the period 1530–1620 'Le temps des confessions'.[4] By 1997, if not before, Italian scholars were also writing of 'confessionalizzazione'.[5]

This is hardly the first time that the terminology and preoccupations of German Reformation scholarship have spread through the international community of those who study the religious history of the early

[1] A preliminary version of this essay was presented to the Équipe de Recherche d'Histoire des Protestantismes in May 1999. I am grateful for critical assistance to those present at this seminar, and also to Marc Foster and Matthew Kadane.
[2] In T. A. Brady Jr, H. Oberman and J. D. Tracy (eds.), *Handbook of European History 1400–1600: Late Middle Ages, Renaissance and Reformation*, 2 vols. (Leiden, 1994–5), II, chap. 21.
[3] B. J. Kaplan, *Calvinists and Libertines: Confession and Community in Utrecht, 1578–1620* (Oxford, 1995); J. I. Israel, *The Dutch Republic: Its Rise, Greatness, and Fall 1477–1806* (Oxford, 1995), chap. 16, 'Protestantization, Catholicization, Confessionalization'.
[4] J.-M. Mayeur *et al.*, *Histoire du Christianisme des origines à nos jours*. VIII. *Le temps des confessions (1530–1620/30)*, ed. Marc Venard (Paris, 1992). See esp. p. 9.
[5] O. di Simplicio, 'Confessionalizzazione e identità collettiva – Il caso italiano: Siena 1575–1800', *ARG* 88 (1997), 380–411.

modern centuries. In preceding decades, the theme of 'the Reformation in the cities' pioneered by Bernd Moeller enjoyed still greater influence; Peter Blickle's idea of 'the communal Reformation', although harder to apply to the Reformation beyond Germany, also has recently sparked international discussion. Nor is it surprising that the history of the European Reformation should so often be written in terms forged in Bielefeld, Göttingen or Berne. Beyond the evident factors of Germany's demographic and economic weight within Europe and its longstanding investment in university research, German scholarship occupies a particularly important place within the international study of the Reformation because the Reformation itself has occupied a particularly central place within German national and historical consciousness since at least the time of Ranke.[6] The venerable *Verein für Reformationgeschichte* and Germany's many Protestant theological faculties provide strong institutional underpinnings for research in the field, while the ties that connect the *Verein* to the American Society for Reformation Research extend the reach of German scholarship across the Atlantic, as does the larger tendency for Reformation scholarship in America to be dominated numerically by specialists in German history.[7] The undeniable inventiveness of German historians in forging ideal-typical interpretative constructs, as well as their high degree of theoretical self-consciousness, also contribute to their strength as exporters of ideas in this field.

Those interested in the Reformation in national contexts other than Germany may wonder if the influence of German historical scholarship is always a blessing. Since the Reformation developed in Germany with a speed and under circumstances that have few parallels elsewhere in Europe, models that illuminate German developments may apply poorly to other national histories. Historians of the French, Dutch, Italian or Scottish Reformations may have more to learn from one another than from looking to the historiography of the German Reformation for inspiration. The current German social history of the Reformation would also appear to be particularly vulnerable to Silvana Seidel Menchi's criticism that the social history of the Reformation is too often a secularized historiography addressed to an audience of agnostics that misses

---

[6] T. A. Brady Jr, 'The Protestant Reformation in German History', *Occasional Paper 22 of the German Historical Institute* (Washington, 1998).

[7] P. Benedict, 'Between Whig Traditions and New Histories: American Historical Writing about Reformation and Early Modern Europe' in A. Molho and G. Wood (eds.), *Imagined Histories: American Historians Interpret the Past* (Princeton, 1998), p. 301.

the *cœur religieux* of its subject.[8] Yet it would be as foolish to reject out of hand the *Begriffen* of *deutsche Geschichte* as it would be to accept them uncritically. The fertility of German historiography offers historians of other countries interpretative models and a conceptual vocabulary with an undeniable potential to generate new questions and insights, as long as these models and concepts are first scrutinized with care. The first part of this essay will attempt to do just that by examining the various ways in which German historians have used the idea of confessionalization, the assumptions associated with their theories and the reception their work has received. The goal here will be to define how confessionalization might most usefully be applied to the religious history of early modern France. The second part of the essay will then suggest how one kind of document found in abundance in French archives, marriage contracts, can be used to shed light on whether or not France in fact experienced a degree of confessionalization as defined in the manner that appears most appropriate.

CRITICAL REFLECTIONS

E. W. Zeeden was the first to articulate the theme of confessionalization. Along with Jean Delumeau in France and H. O. Evennett and John Bossy in England, he was part of that post-war generation of Catholic historians who recognized the ways in which Tridentine Catholicism promoted changes in lay behaviour similar to those long attributed to Protestantism, and who consequently emphasized the parallel consequences of the 'two Reformations'. Attentive to religious life at the parish level as well as to the history of theology, Zeeden also observed in studying the Rhineland that during the later sixteenth century worship in many areas still loyal to Rome contained significant 'Protestant' elements, and that Tridentine orthodoxy often required generations to establish. Like so many other historians of that ecumenical generation, he studied religious traditions beyond his own. This also led him to observe numerous Catholic survivals in post-Reformation Lutheran church orders. An important 1958 article called attention to the process whereby orthodox, self-conscious Catholic, Reformed and Lutheran religious communities emerged from the confused mixture of the early Reformation and deemed this process to constitute one of the most important historical developments of early

[8] S. Menchi, 'Italy' in B. Scribner, R. Porter and M. Teich (eds.), *The Reformation in National Context* (Cambridge, 1994), p. 183.

modern centuries. Zeeden explored this process in greater detail in his
1965 book *Die Entstehung der Konfessionen.* The label he had affixed to it,
Konfessionsbildung, also served as the title of a 1985 collection of essays.[9]

   During the same decades when Zeeden was first exploring *Konfessionsbildung,* Gerhard Oestreich's investigation of early modern political
thought led him to emphasize the importance of 'social disciplining'
(*Sozialdisziplinierung*) for early modern state-building.[10] In Oestreich's
view, the Stoic intellectual legacy was particularly important in teaching Europeans to master their passions and dedicate themselves to the
interests of the state. His ideas inspired two younger historians of the
Reformation era, Wolfgang Reinhard and Heinz Schilling, to see that
confessionalization also contained a good measure of social disciplining
and might thus be said to have served the same function. In a series
of books and articles published between 1980 and 1996, Reinhard and
Schilling argued that it was not simply the establishment of Lutheran
state churches that abetted the power of the territorial princes, as an old
truism of German history asserted.[11] Rulers of all religions embraced
the role of protector of the faith pressed upon them by their theologians, obliged their subjects to participate regularly in church services,

[9] E. W. Zeeden, 'Grundlagen und Wege der Konfessionsbildung in Deutschland im Zeitalter des Glaubenskämpfe', *Historische Zeitschrift* 185 (1958), 249–99, and *Die Entstehung der Konfessionen: Grundlagen und Formen der Konfessionsbildung im Zeitalter des Glaubenskämpfe* (Munich and Vienna, 1965); also his *Konfessionsbildung: Studien zur Reformation, Gegenreformation und katholischen Reform* (Stuttgart, 1985).

[10] Oestreich's most important ideas are usefully collected for English-language readers in *Neostoicism and the Early Modern State* (Cambridge, 1982).

[11] Schilling's *habilitationschrift* was a case study of how one German territorial prince augmented his power by pressing a Reformed state church on Lutheran communities that sought to resist, a situation that reversed the standard associations of Lutheranism with territorial absolutism and Calvinism with democracy. H. Schilling, *Konfessionskonflikt und Staatsbildung: Eine Fallstudie über das Verhältnis von religiösem und sozialem Wandel in der Frühneuzeit am Beispiel der Grafschaft Lippe* (Gütersloh, 1981). For other important statements of these two men's evolving ideas, see W. Reinhard, 'Gegenreformation als Modernisierung? Prolegomena zu einer Theorie des konfessionellen Zeitalters', *ARG* 68 (1977), 226–52, French translation in W. Reinhard, *Papauté, Confessions, Modernité* (Paris, 1998), pp. 155–69, English translation in C. S. Dixon (ed.), *The German Refor-mation: The Essential Readings* (Oxford, 1999), pp. 169–92; 'Konfession und Konfessionalisierung in Europa' in W. Reinhard (ed.), *Bekenntnis und Geschichte. Die Confessio Augustana im historischen Zusammenhang* (Munich, 1981), pp. 165–89; 'Zwang zur Konfessionalisierung? Prolegomena zu einer Theorie des konfessionellen Zeitalters', *Zeitschrift für historische Forschung* 10 (1983), 257–77; 'Reformation, Counter-Reformation, and the Early Modern State: A Reassessment', *Catholic Historical Review* 75 (1989), 383–404; 'Was ist katholische Konfessionalisierung?' in W. Reinhard and H. Schilling (eds.), *Die katholische Konfessionalisierung* (Gütersloh and Münster, 1995), pp. 419–52. H. Schilling, 'Die Konfessionalisierung im Reich – religiöser und gesellschaftlicher Wandel in Deutschland zwischen 1555 und 1620', *Historische Zeitschrift* 246 (1988), 1–25; 'Confessional Europe'; 'Die Konfessionalisierung von Kirche, Staat und Gesellschaft – Profil, Leistung, Defizite und Perspektiven eines Geschichtswissenschaftlichen Paradigmas', in Reinhard and Schilling, *Die katholische Konfessionalisierung,* pp. 1–49.

imposed tests of doctrinal loyalty on the territorial clergy, issued ordinances regulating ever-widening forms of behaviour, and in so doing extended their reach, while at the same time drawing to themselves the strong loyalties that attached people in this era to their faith. At the same time, the various churches also reinforced their oversight of the belief and behaviour of the faithful, whether by visitations, inquisitions or consistories, in so doing moulding disciplined subjects far more powerfully than the writings of a Justus Lipsius could ever hope to do. In thus linking the themes of confessionalization, social disciplining and the growth of the state, Reinhard and Schilling drew inspiration from both Norbert Elias's influential theory of the 'civilizing process' and the older theories of Weber and Troeltsch, shorn of their confession-specific elements. The manner in which their ideas echoed the preoccupations and language of Michel Foucault further facilitated their reception. Three conferences of the *Verein für Reformationsgeschichte*, devoted respectively to Reformed, Lutheran and Catholic confessionalization, were landmarks in their dissemination.[12]

In the passage from the generation of Zeeden to that of Reinhard and Schilling, confessionalization thus took on additional meanings and implications. For analytical purposes, in fact, it is helpful to distinguish between two different versions of the concept. The view formulated by Schilling and Reinhard that links the development of confessional identities to social disciplining and state-building may be called the 'strong theory of confessionalization'. The position first articulated by Zeeden, but also embraced by such recent authors as Gregory Hanlon, may be called the 'weak theory of confessionalization'. This latter view simply defines confessionalization as the process of rivalry and emulation by which the religions that emerged from the upheavals of the Reformation defined and enforced their particular versions of orthodoxy and orthopraxy, demonized their rivals, and built group cohesion and identity. As Hanlon puts it, 'confessionalization can be regarded as the process whereby barricades were erected around each church group'.[13]

Are either of these theories illuminating for the historian of France? An answer to this question might begin by investigating how historians

[12] H. Schilling (ed.), *Die reformierte Konfessionalisierung in Deutschland – das Problem der Zweiten Reformation* (Gütersloh, 1986); H.-C. Rublack (ed.), *Die lutherische Konfessionalisierung in Deutschland* (Gütersloh, 1992); Reinhard and Schilling, *Die katholische Konfessionalisierung*.

[13] G. Hanlon, *Confession and Community in Seventeenth-century France: Catholic and Protestant Coexistence in Aquitaine* (Philadelphia, 1993), p. 193.

of German-speaking Europe have received the arguments of these historians. The strong theory of confessionalization has in fact never been exempt from criticism. Just as enthusiasm for this theory was building in Germany and first spilling over to America, Paula Sutter Fichtner's 1989 *Protestantism and Primogeniture in Early Modern Germany* pointed out one counter-argument to the claim that the Reformation and Counter-Reformation stimulated the emergence of the German territorial state. This slender volume elegantly demonstrated that Luther's criticism of princes who so avidly pursued worldly aggrandizement that they deprived their younger sons of their rightful inheritance slowed the tendency that had begun to develop prior to 1517 for Germany's dukes and counts to turn their possessions into more permanent territorial entities by establishing rules of succession through primogeniture.[14] Several archival studies of church discipline in German-speaking Switzerland then struck at the claim that the Reformation's reinforcement of church discipline abetted the process of state-building. Heinrich Richard Schmidt's study of the discipline exercised by the morals court established in Bernese territory at the moment of the Reformation suggested that this was best understood as an instrument controlled by parish-level notables and used to reinforce pre-existing moral norms, not as an instrument employed by the canton's governors to promote behaviour that enhanced their power.[15] Ulrich Pfister's study of the spread of consistorial discipline throughout the politically decentralized Grisons found that this was promoted more by church synods than by either the communal elites or the political authorities.[16] A 1997 article by Schmidt in the *Historische Zeitschrift* brought together these findings into a frontal attack on the strong theory of confessionalization.[17] Just as the strong theory was gaining wide international visibility, in other words, it was coming under attack within Germany itself. Indeed, Schilling's own recent statements on the question have expressed an open-minded recognition of limitations of the theory.[18] Historians who uncritically embrace it thus run the risk of repeating the experience of so many historians who have attempted interdisciplinary borrowings in the past, that of latching

[14] P. S. Fichtner, *Protestantism and Primogeniture in Early Modern Germany* (New Haven, 1989).
[15] H. R. Schmidt, *Dorf und Religion: reformierte Sittenzucht in Berner Landgemeinden der frühen Neuzeit* (Stuttgart, 1995).
[16] U. Pfister, 'Reformierte Sittenzucht zwischen kommunaler und territorialer Organisation: Graubünden, 16–18. Jahrhundert', *ARG* 87 (1996), 287–333.
[17] H. R. Schmidt, 'Sozialdisziplinierung? Ein Plädoyer für das Ende des Etatismus in der Konfessionalisierungforschung', *Historische Zeitschrift* 265 (1997), 639–82.
[18] Schilling, 'Konfessionalisierung von Kirche'.

enthusiastically on to a concept developed by practitioners of another field of study, just as specialists in that field were turning away from the idea or recognizing its limitations.

The rather heavy-handed functionalism evident in Reinhard and Schilling's linkage of confessionalization with social discipline and state-building provides another reason to be sceptical of the strong theory. Historians of France are particularly likely to think that the association of confessionalization with the growth of the state oversimplifies the extremely unpredictable political consequences that confessional rivalry and religious reform movements could have for state power in early modern Europe. France's wars of religion, after all, illustrate how the division of Christendom into rival confessions could bring even the era's strongest states to the very brink of dissolution. In direct opposition to the Reinhard–Schilling paradigm, recent French historiography has viewed the road to absolutism as passing through the separation of politics from religion, not their association.[19] Where one national historiography views confessionalization as an instrument of state-building and another ties the reinforcement of the state to the secularization of politics, it is legitimate to ask if both are not excessively concerned to relate all developments of the early modern era to the meta-narrative of the growth of the modern state. In any event, the strong theory of confessionalization seems to hold little promise of illuminating French historical experience.

The weak theory of confessionalization is another story. To begin with, it has proven more illuminating and less controversial when applied to German history. Several excellent local studies of German religious life have confirmed and extended Zeeden's insight that the process of building attachment to the practices codified as orthodox by the various churches extended over several generations. R. Po-chia Hsia's excellent study of Münster after the fall of the Anabaptist kingdom revealed a city ruled by a prince-bishop whose inhabitants incorporated such Protestant practices as communion in both kinds and the singing of German hymns into nominally Catholic worship, and who simply defined themselves as 'good Christians' in wills devoid of invocations of the saints or anniversary masses. With time, however, religious life increasingly evolved

---

[19] 'In accelerating the relative distinction between the spheres of religion and politics, the wars of religion facilitated the progress of absolute monarchy': Arlette Jouanna, quoted in O. Christin, 'L'Édit de Nantes. Bilan historiographique', *Revue Historique* 301 (1999), 134. Christin's own *La paix de religion. L'autonomisation de la raison politique au XVIe siècle* (Paris, 1997) advances the same argument.

toward post-Tridentine Catholic orthopraxy, thanks less to political pressure from above than to the Jesuit-led introduction of a new culture.[20] Etienne François's model study of Augsburg after 1648 showed how sharply the religious communities had become divided by the aftermath of the Thirty Years' War. Although the Catholics and Lutherans of that religiously divided city lived peacefully enough with one another, they were so rigidly separated by the 'invisible border' of different religious sensibilities, rituals and historical memories that they virtually never intermarried, changed faith or explored some middle ground between the two orthodoxies.[21] Furthermore, few historians taking the long view not simply of German history, but of the history of Europe as a whole, would deny that the creation of strong loyalties to confessional communities had consequences for political affiliation and personal identity among ordinary Europeans that endured deep into the twentieth century, making this perhaps the most durable long-term consequence of the Reformation.

While the weak theory of confessionalization undoubtedly calls attention to a fundamental set of changes in European culture and society, the historian of France might still question the applicability of one important aspect of this theory to the French case: the corollary that confessionalization was a gradual process extending over several generations. If confessionalization is to be something more than a multisyllabic label for the well-worn observation that the 'magnificent anarchy' of the early Reformation soon gave way to the formulation of creeds, this aspect of *longue durée* would appear to be fundamental. But is it appropriate to speak of a confessionalization process in France, where during just twenty years between 1543 and 1562, the Sorbonne drafted a series of articles that were taken by the law to define Catholic orthodoxy, the proliferation of Reformed churches after 1555 gave structure and doctrinal definition to previously unorganized currents of evangelical dissent, and the rivalry between these two camps precipitated a civil war that so polarized the country that attempts to restore the peace would fail time and again for the next thirty-six years? By the later 1560s, the rival groups of Huguenots and papists were already so sharply defined in many cities that even when Protestantism was outlawed between 1568 and 1570 and former members of the Reformed church brought their infants to

[20] R. P. Hsia, *Society and Religion in Münster, 1535–1618* (New Haven, 1984).
[21] E. François, *Die Unsichtbare Grenze: Protestanten und Katholiken in Augsburg, 1648–1806* (Sigmaringen, 1991), French edn, *Protestants et catholiques en Allemagne: identités et pluralisme, Augsbourg 1648–1806* (Paris, 1993).

the Catholic church for baptism, the parish clergy placed a little 'H' or 'huot' in the margin, indicating that the family continued to be seen, and closely watched, as Huguenot.[22] Choices made for one side or another in a few critical years durably marked people's public identity.

Rather than being marked by a gradual process of confessionalization, France's religious history might best be conceptualized as having been characterized by a brief moment of confessional polarization, followed by a gradual movement toward confessional reconciliation. After the wrenching emergence of divisions between 1540 and 1570, France's violently polarized communities groped their way toward a more stable *convivencia* over the subsequent generations. One can further hypothesize that the situation of relatively stable confessional coexistence established under the provisions of the Edict of Nantes diminished the barriers between Huguenots and Catholics by promoting greater everyday interaction and the slow accumulation of trust.

For all of the plausibility of this scenario, however, two recent books have offered reasons for thinking that the weak theory of confessionalization could apply to France in this period. The first of these is Hanlon's detailed study of the network of social relationships in a single confessionally divided town in Gascony. The second is Bernard Dompnier's wide-angle depiction of the Gallican church's image of Protestantism and its battle to reclaim the lost heretics for the faith.[23] Despite very different approaches, both of these books call attention to corners of early seventeenth-century France, notably the small towns of regions such as Dauphiné and Aquitaine, where a fairly casual everyday coexistence governed relations between Protestants and Catholics at the beginning of the seventeenth century. Both show how, over the course of successive generations, rigourist elements within both churches mounted an ongoing campaign against the customs and social practices that facilitated this trans-confessional co-operation, forbidding the members of one faith from choosing a godparent of the other, and warning them against sending their youngsters to the other's schools.

Far from lessening with time, the degree of suspicion and walls of separation between the two confessions may thus have increased in France over the course of the seventeenth century under the steady drumbeat of

---

[22] AC Rouen, Registre Paroissiaux 172; AD Seine-Maritime, E, parish registers of Saint Godard and Saint Vivien, Rouen (unclassified at the time I consulted them); D. L. Rosenberg, 'Les Registres paroissiaux et les Incidences de la Réaction à la Saint-Barthélémy', *Revue du Nord* 70 (1988), 505.

[23] Hanlon, *Confession and Community*; B. Dompnier, *Le venin de l'hérésie. Image du protestantisme et combat catholique au XVIIIe siècle* (Paris, 1985).

controversial polemics and legal battles over the rights and prerogatives of the Reformed churches. In the current state of our knowledge, it is an open question whether the ongoing process of confessional rivalry raised ever-higher barriers between the two confessions, or whether the experience of stable *convivencia* bred closer interaction with those of the other religion. The weak theory of confessionalization thus poses a very interesting question for historians of France.

NEW EVIDENCE

Many sources could undoubtedly be used to explore confessional identity and possible changes in patterns of interaction between Catholics and Protestants in seventeenth-century France. Here I shall simply report evidence that I encountered about this topic in the course of exploring other issues through a study from a large sample of marriage contracts of the city of Montpellier. Marriage contracts have long been a staple of both legal and social history for what they reveal about the terms of the marriage alliance and the wealth and social origins of the parties agreeing to wed one another. It turns out that they can also shed useful light on confessional identity and interconfessional relations in at least three ways. The sample used here consists of the 1,554 contracts involving at least one resident of Montpellier that survive in the city's archives from the periods 1605–9, 1635–9 and 1665–9.[24]

Montpellier passed from one camp to the other during the religious wars and was more evenly divided in the seventeenth century between Protestants and Catholics than any other major city in France. The Reformed faith grew so rapidly after the first church was organized in 1560 that the Protestants were able to drive out the Mass in October 1561, well before the outbreak of the first civil war. Catholic worship was restored at the end of that conflict, only to suffer again during the second civil war in 1567–8, but after that war the king's lieutenants reasserted crown control over the city and pursued the restoration of Catholic worship with such imperiousness that many Protestants thought it safest to flee. During the third civil war of 1568–70 and again after St Bartholomew's night in 1572, it was the turn of Reformed worship to cease. An uneasy toleration of both faiths reigned between 1570 and 1572 and again during the years between 1574 and 1577, when the duc de Montmorency-Damville

---

[24] Full archival references to the notarial registers consulted and discussion of the representativeness of this sample may be found in my 'Faith, Fortune and Social Structure in Seventeenth-century Montpellier', *Past & Present* 152 (1996), 54–6.

sought to reinforce his power in the region by forging a political alliance between Huguenots and moderate Catholics. When this effort collapsed, the Protestants once again asserted a domination over the city that would endure for the remainder of the wars of religion, although the last decades of the civil wars were less troubled in this corner of Languedoc than else-where in the country, and Catholic worship was allowed to resume in the 1580s and to continue through the period of the League with only a brief interruption. Around 1610, Catholics comprised approximately 40 per cent of the population. When civil war flared up anew in 1621, the Protestants again took control and outlawed Catholicism, but the crown recaptured the city in the following year and restored Catholic worship. Over the subsequent decades, control of the municipality was increasingly transferred to the city's Catholics, while shifting patterns of immigration brought growing numbers of Roman worshippers into the city. In the later 1630s, 60 per cent of all marriages celebrated in the city took place in its Catholic churches. By the 1660s the Catholic share of the population was up to 70 per cent.[25]

The long struggle to control the city produced sharp divisions be-tween the two religious camps, as Jean Philippi's local history admirably illustrates. Philippi was a religious moderate who initially joined the Re-formed church but opposed the more zealous members of the church by seeking to arrange a negotiated peace during the first civil war. He abjured the faith in 1568 in order to retain his seat in the *cour des aides* but remained sufficiently well intentioned to those of both faiths to include in a subsequent will a bequest of 50 *livres* to the city's poor 'without differ-ence of religion'. Despite this moderation, he unambiguously referred to the Protestants as 'the enemies' in the portions of his history written after his return to the Catholic church. He also went back over the early por-tions of the text to insert the phrase 'so-called' into all passages where he had previously spoken of the 'Reformed religion', so that he now called it the 'so-called Reformed religion' (*religion pretendue réformée*).[26] This was the label that the 1576 Edict of Beaulieu ordered be applied to the faith in all public acts and documents, but members of the church naturally detested it and sought to avoid it whenever possible.[27]

---

[25] J. Philippi, 'Histoire des troubles de Languedoc' in L. Guiraud (ed.), *La Réforme à Montpellier. Preuves* (Montpellier, 1918); pp. 1–205; AC Montpellier, GG 1–3; G. Cholvy *et al.*, *Histoire de Montpellier* (Toulouse, 1984), pp. 147–94; P. Benedict, *The Huguenot Population of France, 1600–1685: The Demographic Fate and Customs of a Religious Minority* (Transactions of the American Philosophical Society, 81, 1991), pp. 51–5, 147; Benedict, 'Faith, Fortune and Social Structure', 52–3.

[26] Guiraud (ed.), *Réforme à Montpellier*, esp. pp. 11, 441.

[27] A. Stegmann (ed.), *Édits des guerres de religion* (Paris, 1979), p. 101; E. Benoist, *Histoire de l'Édit de Nantes*, 5 vols. (Delft, 1694–5), I, p. 400, II, pp. 91, 114, 176.

The first way in which Montpellier's marriage contracts shed light on the issue of confessionalization is by revealing what the city's notaries called the two faiths. During the first decade of the seventeenth century, Montpellier's largely Protestant corps of notaries used a surprisingly wide range of designations for the Reformed church. But one – a probable Catholic – used the hated label 'so-called Reformed religion'. Only three others employed the terms 'reformed church' or 'reformed religion'. Instead, Isaac Durand, *notaire royal héréditaire*, wrote that his clients intended to marry in 'the catholic, apostolic, reformed church' (*l'église catholique, apostolique et réformée*), a phrase that claimed for his church the adjectives 'catholic' and 'apostolic' enshrined in the Apostles' Creed. Maître Noel Planque, of uncertain religious affiliation, variously called this church 'the congregation and assembly of those of the religion' or 'the church of God'. Three other notaries also used this latter phrase, whose dissemination may have been fairly broad.[28] Still other documents employed the formulae 'the Christian Reformed church' or 'the Reformed church of God'. Virtually all notaries in this era referred to the Catholic church by the phrase 'catholic, apostolic and roman church', but even here a few notaries were sufficiently inconsistent in the labels they used that it is impossible to determine in which church several dozen marriages were to be celebrated. The very labels attached to the different churches were fluid in this period.[29]

Over the subsequent two generations, this fluidity disappeared, as militant voices within the Catholic church gained the backing of the courts and the crown in imposing use of the phrase 'so-called Reformed religion', on pain of a fine for failure to do so in at least certain regions.[30] Between 1635 and 1639, just two notaries wrote that their clients intended to be married before 'the Christian reformed church', while twelve used the formula '*religion pretendue réformée*', occasionally shortened to 'religion PR' or 'RPR'. Between 1665 and 1669, ten used a variant of this latter formula, while only one supple notary, probably a Catholic, found a way to allow his Protestant clients to avoid using the term by recording that they intended to be married 'in the religion that they profess'. A new consistency of confessional labelling thus triumphed, as the Protestants were forced to include in their legal documents a phrase that

---

[28] See Benoist, *Histoire de l'Édit de Nantes*, III, p. 133.

[29] As they also were in Les Baux (Provence) in the same era. C. Borello, 'Les protestants de la vallée des Baux sous le régime de l'Édit de Nantes (1598–1685)', *Provence Historique* 49 (1999), 625.

[30] A fine of 500 *livres* was imposed throughout the jurisdiction of the *parlement* of Paris in 1634 on those who failed to use this phrase in marriage contracts. A probable native of Languedoc urged a similar measure in 1648. I have not, however, been able to establish if such fines were ever actually instituted in Languedoc. Benoist, *Histoire de l'Édit de Nantes*, II, p. 542, III, p. 133.

expressed the state's disqualification of the fundamental claim of their church.

It is, of course, a sociological truism that the frequency of intermarriage between members of different social groups reveals perhaps more reliably than any other indicator the rigidity or porosity of the barriers between them. Hardly surprisingly, marriage contracts can also illuminate this aspect of the question of confessionalization, although they are harder to use to study the frequency of Catholic–Protestant marriage in seventeenth-century France than might initially be thought. This is because authorities of both churches forbade their members from marrying somebody who was not also a member of the same church. As a result, mixed marriages in seventeenth-century France were generally preceded by the formal conversion of one party or the other, generally the woman, so that both halves of the future couple could qualify as members of the same church at the time of their marriage. This conversion was often purely strategic, and was followed by the convert's return to the church of her upbringing after a decent interval of time had elapsed.[31] Since marriage contracts typically merely specify the church in which the planned marriage was to be celebrated, they provide no direct indication of most cases where the union in question involved two people who had been raised in different faiths. The marriage registers of the two churches likewise mask such cases. A fully reliable statistical study of the frequency of intermarriage during this century would thus require either the extraordinarily time-consuming establishment of complete genealogies for all families within a confessionally mixed community, so that every case where a member of a Protestant family married a member of a Catholic family could be discerned despite the silence of the church registers or marriage contracts on this issue, or the existence for the same confessionally mixed locality of both a full run of marriage records and good registers of abjurations or church receptions that reveal when parties to a marriage had converted shortly before the ceremony, a rare combination of documents. As a result, published evidence about the changing frequency of mixed marriages in seventeenth-century France is scarce, although Dompnier asserts that these fell off sharply after 1663, when the crown made it illegal for Protestant converts to Catholicism to return to their original faith, while figures provided by Hanlon can be recalculated

---

[31] Dompnier, *Venin de l'hérésie*, pp. 154–7; Hanlon, *Confession and Community*, pp. 102–11; R. Sauzet, *Contre-réforme et Réforme catholique en Bas-Languedoc: Le diocèse de Nîmes au XVIIe siècle* (Louvain, 1979), pp. 165–8; E. Labrousse, *'Une foi, une loi, un roi?' La Révocation de l'Édit de Nantes* (Geneva, 1985), pp. 83–4.

to show that mixed marriages fell from 12 per cent of a sample of 130 marriages in Layrac between 1606 and 1636, to 6 per cent of a sample of 86 marriages between 1672 and 1688.[32]

Despite the silence of many marriage contracts about whether or not they concern two individuals raised in different faiths, the sample of contracts examined here can be used to shed some light on the changing frequency of mixed marriages in Montpellier in two ways. First, a few of these contracts contain a clause that established a space for freedom of worship within the household that was about to be formed. After designating that the marriage was to be celebrated in either the Catholic or the Reformed church, these contracts specify that the husband would subsequently allow his future wife to 'live following her conscience' according to the way of the other church 'which she professes'. These clauses show how people negotiated the day-to-day terms of confessional coexistence in a religiously divided city.

Tellingly, the frequency with which such clauses appear in Montpellier marriage contracts diminishes steadily within the sample of contracts examined here. Clauses establishing this sort of contractual claim to freedom of worship within the household appear in 10 of 534 contracts from 1605–9, 4 of 420 contracts from 1635–9, and just 1 of 600 contracts from 1665–9. This would appear to suggest a declining frequency of mixed marriages, although it is impossible to be certain that it does not simply reflect instead a growing sense that such clauses were unnecessary or useless, especially since it seems that these 'religious-liberty clauses' were only written into a fraction of all marriage contracts between people of different religious background.

This last conclusion may be inferred from the second technique for discovering mixed marriages within the sample of marriage contracts. This involves linking together those contracts in the sample that concern the same nuclear family in order to catch instances where siblings or parents and children married in different churches. Of course, even where two siblings married in the same church, one may have made a mixed marriage with a person of the other faith who converted for the purposes of the union. Conversely, cases where siblings or members of successive generations married in different churches may result from sincere conversions, not simply strategic ones made to allow a mixed marriage. None the less, instances where members of the same family married in different churches provide a rough proxy for the frequency

[32] Dompnier, *Venin de l'hérésie*, p. 156; Hanlon, *Confession and Community*, table 4.2, p. 113.

of mixed marriages. Of sixty-seven cases where marriage contracts for
two or more siblings appear in the sample, totalling 144 marriages in all,
brothers or sisters married in different churches seven times. For only
one of these unions does the marriage contract stipulate the right of both
spouses to live according to different faiths. The sample also yields thirty-
seven cases where marriage contracts appear for members of successive
generations of the same family. Eliminating one case where the older
generation had made a mixed marriage, three of the remaining thirty-
six children married in a different church from that of their parents,
none of them with religious-liberty clauses in their contract. With all due
allowance for the approximate character of this measure, it would thus
appear that mixed marriages represented something on the order of 5 to
10 per cent of all Montpellier marriages over the course of this period –
not the 1 per cent of all marriages suggested by the frequency of religious-
liberty clauses. This may be usefully compared with the situation in
Layrac, where mixed marriages made up 10 per cent of all marriages
in the years 1606–36, 1654–63 and 1672–88, and in the Luberon region
of Provence, where the Huguenots were descended from a Waldensian
population that had maintained its distinctiveness over centuries, and
where mixed marriages accounted for 2 per cent of all marriages around
1630.[33]

If marriage across the confessional line was evidently more frequent
than the number of religious-liberty clauses would suggest, it was still
considerably less common than would be expected if the city's residents
chose their spouses without regard to their religion. Given the nearly even
distribution of Montpellier's population between the two faiths over the
periods covered by the sample, it can be calculated that fully 45 per
cent of all marriages would have been mixed had religion been of no
significance in the choice of a spouse. Even if we set the number of mixed
marriages at the upper bound of our estimate of 5 to 10 per cent of all
marriages, this 10 per cent computes to just 23 per cent of the percentage
of mixed marriages that would be expected if religious affiliation were
of no significance. A powerful tendency toward confessional endogamy
clearly marked seventeenth-century Montpellier.

Once again, this tendency also appears to have increased with time.
Four of the cases of siblings who married in different churches come
from 1605–9 (n = 22), one from 1635–9 (n = 10) and two from 1665–9

33 Hanlon, *Confession and Community*, p. 113; G. Audisio, 'Se marier en Luberon: catholiques et
protestants vers 1630' in *Mélanges Robert Mandrou: histoire sociale, sensibilités collectives et mentalités*
(Paris, 1985), p. 243.

(n = 29). All three of the cases of children who celebrated their wedding in a church different from that of their parents involve parents married in 1605–9 and children married in 1635–9.

Marriage, of course, represents a particularly intimate and sustained form of interpersonal interaction. A final way in which Montpellier's marriage contracts can shed light on the extent of the gulf between the two faiths lies in the opportunity they also provide to observe a more casual kind of relationship that linked people across confessional lines – the business relationship between notaries and their clients. A variety of sources enable one to determine the religious affiliation of the majority of the notaries whose surviving registers provide the sample of marriage contracts.[34] Since the marriage contracts contain an indication of the religion of the couples intending to marry, they can be used to determine the frequency with which the city's inhabitants turned to a person of their own faith when seeking a trustworthy notary to handle their contractual affairs. Just as the inhabitants of certain French villages spoke within living memory of 'the Protestant butcher' or 'the Catholic butcher', archivists and researchers will occasionally refer casually to certain notaries as 'Protestant notaries', as if economic transactions followed confessional lines and one could deduce a person's faith from his or her choice of notary. In fact, none of the twenty-seven Montpellier notaries whose religion I was able to determine with confidence did business exclusively with members of his own faith. Since a majority of Montpellier's notaries were Protestant throughout the period examined here, sizeable numbers of Catholics chose to employ the services of Protestant notaries. A smaller number of Protestants likewise opted for Catholic notaries. Still, a fairly clear tendency may be observed for the city's residents to choose notaries of their own religion. Only one notary in the sample, Antoine Comte, was able to win the confidence of so many Catholics that the percentage of marriage contracts in his registers involving members of the Reformed church to which he belonged fell below the percentage of Protestants in the sample population at the time. Most notaries did business disproportionately with co-religionists.

A simple index of integration can be used to gauge the strength of this preference for a notary of the same faith. The procedure utilized here

---

[34] Used for this purpose were: AD l'Hérault, B 22662, 'Emprunt sur les Catholiques 1622/Emprunt sur les habitans de la R Reformee 1622'; the city's Catholic and Protestant parish registers; the registers of the notaries themselves, which sometimes include pious formulae that provide an indication of the notary's faith; and the marriage contracts of notaries that appear in the sample. These sources permitted me to determine with confidence the religion of thirty of the forty-five notaries represented in the sample.

involves first computing from the data collected the number of contracts
that would have been drawn up by a notary of the couple's own faith if
all city residents chose their notary without regard to religious affiliation.
This has been labelled the hypothesis of perfect integration. Next was
computed the hypothesis of perfect segregation: the number of contracts
that would have been drawn up by a notary of the couple's own faith if
everybody did business only with notaries of their own faith. Finally, the
actually observed number of contracts written by notaries of the same
religion was calculated as a percentage of the difference between these
limit hypotheses. This yields what I have called the index of integration.
For the first period this comes out to 56 per cent, for the second to 37 per
cent, and for the third to 46 per cent.[35]

Two conclusions thus emerge. First, the index of integration in all
three periods exceeds the comparable index of 23 per cent that we have
seen to be the upper bound for the strength of the tendency toward
Catholic–Protestant intermarriage. As would be expected, people were
considerably more likely to choose a notary of another religion than a
spouse of another religion. Secondly, the index of integration declined
between the first and the seventh decades of the century, albeit according
to an irregular pattern. Once again, a modest tendency appears that the
two confessions become increasingly self-enclosed communities as the
seventeenth century advanced.

More case studies involving other kinds of localities and additional
means of observation will have to be attempted before it can be stated
with assurance that confessionalization advanced across France as a
whole over the seventeenth century. This admittedly exploratory study
of a single source and a single city none the less clearly suggests that
this is what happened in Montpellier. Even in this city that had been
unusually hotly contested between Protestants and Catholics during the
wars of religion, confessional labels were surprisingly fluid in the first
decade of the seventeenth century, people frequently did business across
confessional lines, and a fraction of the population contractually ensured that two different faiths could be simultaneously practised in the

---

35 Because the sample contained the records of a few very active notaries whose religious affiliation
could not be determined with confidence from other sources, but whose highly skewed clientele
suggested that they were probably of one faith or the other, I calculated this index twice, once with
the uncertain cases included and once with them excluded, to ensure that the decision to use only
those cases where the notary's religion could be established on the basis of independent evidence
about the faith did not affect the results obtained. Reassuringly, these two sets of calculations
yielded virtually identical results, although the pattern of individual cases looked very different
when the uncertain cases were included. The figures provided here are for the sample notaries
whose religion was determined with confidence.

same household. Over time, increasingly tight confessional labels were imposed. Both intermarriage (always fairly rare) and cross-confessional economic interaction (more common) declined in frequency. The thrust toward the separation of the two religious communities generated by the ongoing rivalry between the leading spokesmen of each faith thus seems in the final analysis to have been more powerful than the forces working toward interconfessional co-operation fostered by the establishment of a more stable religious peace after 1598. In this sense, the weak theory of confessionalization would seem to apply fruitfully to France – or, at least, to this one city within it.

5. Huguenot petitioning during the wars of religion

Penny Roberts

From its inception, the Reform movement asserted itself through protestation and remonstrance. Throughout their history as a beleaguered minority the Huguenots continued this approach in their dealings with the French monarchy. Their use of petitioning can be seen as a reformulation of the customary appeals by participants in popular revolts, considered as rebels by their opponents but protesting their unshakeable loyalty to the king and their belief in his justice. Like such groups, the Huguenots couched their demands in the traditional language of supplication and deference and were dependent on the goodwill of the crown in recognizing the validity of their claims. Yet the use of remonstrance by the Huguenots was a reflection of their legitimate rather than rebel status during the religious wars. It is revealing of the conservative rather than radical nature of the movement, for recourse to such appeals was far from being the exclusive preserve of those considered to be rebels, as demonstrated by the *cahiers de doléances* issued by the national and provincial estates. At a time of limited political participation, the right to petition offered aggrieved parties the chance to engage with the established political process of negotiation with the crown. For a previously outlawed group such as the Huguenots, the adoption of this tradition of appeal represented the measure of their recognition and integration within the French polity.

The Reform movement in France is often portrayed as radical in its relationship with the authorities, challenging the status quo and demanding recognition on a par with Catholics. This is reinforced by the approach of Huguenot leaders, such as the prince de Condé, who at various times remonstrated with the crown that they were not being granted their rightful place in government or sought to justify and defend the position which they had adopted.[1] Yet, despite the more radical stance of the Huguenot leadership (and of some regions) at certain times during the wars, there is nothing to compare with the proliferation of calls at the grass-roots level for constitutional change well documented during the English Civil War.[2] Even the development of a doctrine of resistance after the St Bartholomew's Day massacre of 1572 did not have a significant impact outside Huguenot strongholds in the Midi and, arguably, was put to more effective use by the Catholic League later in the wars. On the contrary, keen to shake off the stigma of association with rebellion and to ingratiate themselves with the monarchy, for much of the wars the Huguenots consciously set out to present themselves as obedient and loyal subjects. As a result, their demands often proved to be no more radical than those of their Catholic counterparts, who also used petitioning to draw the crown's attention to their grievances during the conflict. This conservatism is reflected in the majority of surviving Huguenot petitions and can best be explained by the legal status accorded to the Huguenots and their demands.

The right to petition the crown was first explicitly granted to the Huguenots by François II in an edict of March 1560, part of the crown's attempt to defuse the noble-led Conspiracy of Amboise whose participants were disgruntled by the then Guise-dominated regime.[3] Thus, Huguenot petitioning began as a means by which grievances were to be expressed without recourse to arms, a role which it was to continue to play throughout the ensuing wars. The most assertive of the Huguenot petitions, however, preceded the outbreak of war and was submitted by the Reformed churches of France to Charles IX in June 1561. It boldly requested freedom of worship and the provision of temples for the Huguenots, and their case was discussed at the highest level by the royal council and the *parlement* during the so-called *pourparlers* of Paris.[4]

---

[1] Most notably in justifying his taking up of arms in 1562, see A. Stegmann, *Édits des guerres de religion* (Paris, 1979), pp. 25–8; D.-F. Sécousse (ed.), *Mémoires de Condé*, 6 vols. (London, 1743–45), esp. IV, pp. 1–38.

[2] On this and some of the issues discussed here with regard to petitioning traditions, see D. Zaret, 'Petitions and the "Invention" of Public Opinion in the English Revolution', *American Journal of Sociology* 101 (1996), 1497–555. In the French context petitioning remained an essentially conservative act. This has probably to do with the different political structures in the two countries. The petitioning of Parliament as opposed to the monarch (especially at a time of interregnum) encouraged radicalism. The French equivalent of Parliament, the Estates General, met infrequently and did not have the political clout of its English counterpart until the Revolution.

[3] N. M. Sutherland, *The Huguenot Struggle for Recognition* (New Haven and London, 1980), p. 348.

[4] Sécousse, *Mémoires de Condé*, II, pp. 370–2, 396–433.

Whilst this petition, and the seriousness with which it was addressed by the crown, bear vivid testimony to Huguenot strength at this time, like all such documents it was also the product of dissatisfaction with their position. Similarly, the proliferation of petitions during the wars of religion was a direct result of the frustration the Huguenots felt because of the failure to enforce the terms of the edicts of pacification that brought formal hostilities to a close. As a result, the specific target of Huguenot grievances was the violation of their rights as embodied in the articles of the edicts. This reliance on the enforcement of royal legislation meant that, long before the Edict of Nantes of 1598, the Huguenots found themselves dependent on the goodwill of the reigning monarch, who was cast in the role of their protector. The right of appeal direct to the crown, in particular in order to bypass the perceived anti-Huguenot bias of the *parlements*, was forcefully promoted by the Huguenot leadership from an early stage.[5] The Huguenots' call for royal arbitration would allow them to appeal over the head of provincial courts and other local bodies, which they believed were not playing their appointed part in allowing them to benefit from the provisions of, and protection afforded by, the edicts. Petitioning was the means by which the voice of the Huguenot minority could be heard.

However, what is most striking about Huguenot petitions during the wars, in contrast to their position in June 1561, is their concern with local rather than national issues. This was perhaps an inevitable result of the localized basis of the organization both of the Reformed churches and of the enforcement of the edicts of pacification, which confirmed Huguenot rights. Equally, it can be argued that, by offering the Huguenots formal recognition within French society, the edicts curtailed their effectiveness as a national movement. The Huguenot retreat from a position of national vigour to a defensive stance in the local community was a direct result of the impact of war. Petitions can thus act as a barometer of Huguenot fortunes during the wars of religion as well as a guide to the preoccupations of the petitioners.

The patchy survival of sources for the period makes it impossible to know how many Huguenot petitions were presented to the authorities during the wars. However, it is clear that at certain times their numbers were considerable, as can be judged from the registers of the king's

---

5 See C. Stocker, 'The Parlement of Paris and Confessional Politics in the 1560s', *Proceedings of the Western Society for French History* 15 (1988), 43–4. Also the negotiations over the Edict of Amboise of March 1563, the first edict of pacification, in Sécousse, *Mémoires de Condé*, IV, pp. 146–76, esp. pp. 163–4.

council to which contested disputes were appealed.[6] Business was brisk, particularly a year after the publication of the first edict of pacification, that of Amboise, in March 1563. The relative longevity of this edict (some four-and-a-half years) and its application during a favourable period of relative Huguenot strength combined with royal benevolence, allowed it to usher in what was probably the 'golden age' of Huguenot petitioning. It is fair to assume that any community dissatisfied with the enforcement of the edict in their locality during this period petitioned the crown or its representatives, and evidently few were satisfied with the edict's application. The next 'favourable' period was during the enforcement of the Edict of St Germain of 1570, when a flurry of petitions is again evident. However, their production was abruptly cut short by the massacres of 1572. Some detailed examples survive from the 1570s and 1580s, but their appearance is generally quite sporadic until the accession of Henri IV in 1594 revived the Huguenot movement as a national force and the Edict of Nantes brought a fragile end to the wars in 1598. The fortunes of the Huguenot minority during the wars are also reflected in the geographic spread of the petitions. Up to 1572, there are examples of Huguenot appeals from all regions of France; thereafter the pattern is much more localized according to where churches were still able to flourish, largely in the south and west.

Besides their number and regional origin, Huguenot petitions also took a variety of forms according to their representation or constituency. They might come from individuals, social groups such as the nobility, urban communities or the collected churches of whole provinces. Individual petitions were presented before the courts much like any other legal case, with the claimant sometimes represented by a member of the judiciary. Collective petitions were usually more formal, with grievances divided into a number of articles designed to elicit appropriate official responses. Yet they too, once they reached the king's council, were to an extent dependent on judicial representation. Perhaps not surprisingly in view of their concentrations of Huguenot population, most common of all were appeals from the Reformed churches of the larger towns of France. The authorship of such documents, however, can often prove vague with few signatures surviving; references to 'the Reformed church' or, more frequently, 'the inhabitants of the (Reformed) religion' of a particular community were more usual. For instance, the articles of the Reformed

---

[6] BN, MS Fr 18156 (Nov. 1563–May 1567). See also N. Valois, *Le Conseil du Roi aux XIVe, XVe et XVIe siècles* (Paris, 1888), pp. 323–86.

church of Angoulême, dealt with in the king's council on 4 January
1571, began, 'To the King, the inhabitants of Angoulême of the (so-
called) Reformed religion very humbly beseech Your Majesty to provide
them with the articles that follow.'[7] Regardless of their form, the petitions
were traditionally concerned with local and specific grievances experienced directly by the petitioners.[8] Their impact was further inhibited
by their appearance in manuscript rather than printed form, restricting
their potential for circulation and thereby reinforcing the parochial nature of the medium.[9] These documents were, after all, produced as part
of a judicial process, not in order to court popularity or to attract wider
political support. Thus, despite their transmission to the highest level,
Huguenot petitions were intrinsically a localized means to a localized
end, a matter for resolution between the petitioners and the crown.

Closer analysis of a few well-documented and representative cases allows some insight into how Huguenot petitioners chose to portray their
situation as well as the actions of their Catholic opponents. The petitions
of the Huguenot inhabitants of Bordeaux and the *sénéchaussée* of Guyenne
of 1564 represent just one of the numerous appeals to the monarchy made
by Huguenot communities during the progress around the kingdom by
Charles IX and Catherine de Medici, that were generated by the attempts
to enforce the 1563 Edict of Amboise.[10] Typically, the Huguenots did
not wait for the royal party to reach them, but sent their representatives
ahead to catch up with the court at some earlier point in its progress, in
this case the town of Valence in Dauphiné.[11] Their appeal took the form
of twenty-three articles, mostly concerned with safeguarding Huguenot
rights to excuse themselves from participating in Catholic devotions, to
practise their own religion without obstruction, to have access to office
and justice, and to be taxed on a par with Catholics. In general, the
articles sought to ensure that the terms of the edict were observed and
anyone who contravened them (of whatever rank) was punished. What
they reveal most strikingly (if we are to take them at face value) is the degree of non-enforcement and contravention of the recent edict, an impression repeated time and again in such documents.

---

[7] AM Angoulême, AA 5, fo. 62; the 'pretendue' was inserted later.
[8] On petitioning traditions, see Zaret, 'Petitions and the "Invention" of Public Opinion', esp.
    1516–17.
[9] On the significance of printed petitions, see *ibid.*, esp. 1526–35.
[10] Published in April 1565, the articles survive in several copies, including: Sécousse, *Mémoires
    de Condé*, V, pp. 214–22; BN, MS Fr nouvelles acquisitions, 7177, fos. 226–35, 238–9; AD La
    Gironde, 1B 9, fos. 105v–108.
[11] As, for instance, those of the inhabitants of Nantes, submitted at Troyes: BN, MS Fr 15880, fo. 26.

Notably, this picture is reinforced in the exceptionally detailed remonstrances from the Reformed churches of the Lyonnais of 1571.[12] Their grievances included such familiar refrains as the excessive burden of taxation and that the site for worship granted to them was too far away on a route 'fort dangereux et propre à ceulx qui vouldroient commectre ... cruaultez et meurtres'. Furthermore, they were obstructed from (and overcharged for) using the designated site for burial; they continued to be victimized by the authorities and their consciences were restricted; and they were unable to recover confiscated property, or even children, left behind with Catholic relatives when they had fled the recent troubles. Above all, those supposedly responsible for ensuring that they received justice and the full benefit of the most recent edict were prejudiced against them and, as a result, they were 'tellement pressez, vexez et travaillez' that it was 'impossible de plus supporter ung tel et si rigoreux fardeau'. Such language depicts their Catholic oppressors as having acted, not just unlawfully, but callously without regard to the suffering they had inflicted. In contrast, the Huguenots portray themselves as the innocent victims who have done nothing to provoke such cruel treatment. The purpose of such rhetoric is evident, but it is also revealing of Huguenot self-identity. They are the wronged party, the victims of injustice, martyrs to their faith. Such perceptions were only to be reinforced by the aftermath of the St Bartholomew's Day massacre and the continuing struggle for survival of the Reformed churches thereafter, which would continue well into the seventeenth century.

Like these examples from Bordeaux and Lyon, most of the surviving Huguenot petitions are accompanied by official responses to individual articles (often inserted as marginalia). Both the articles and the royal responses to them reveal a remarkable knowledge of the terms of the edicts, and suggest that those who drew up the petitions possessed a degree of legal competence. Those of Lyon, for instance, cite the number of the relevant article of the Edict of St Germain alongside the specific grievance that contravened it. Sometimes reference could be made to several different pieces of legislation, becoming fairly complex later in the wars with the proliferation of such acts. In particular, the decrees emanating from the 1579 conferences at both Nérac and Fleix, along with the subsequent Peace of Fleix of 1580, stimulated such a response.[13] This practice

---

[12] AM Lyon, GG 77, no. 20. Much the same grievances were repeated the following year: GG 78, no. 21.

[13] E.g. the articles of the Huguenot inhabitants of Saintes and Saintonge to the royal commissioners: BN, MS Fr 15564, fos. 81–2 (1581).

served to remind the crown of its responsibility to protect the Huguenots
as embodied in the edicts and other relevant legislation. Furthermore, it
demonstrates the dominance of the role of law in attempts at reconciling
the faiths and pacifying the realm.[14] This was reinforced by the employment of *parlementaires* to ensure the enforcement of the edicts and to judge
contested cases in the localities and on appeal. The principal problem
in this regard was the interpretation of the terms of the edicts, which
were often open to dispute. The resulting disagreements were frequently
reflected in the petitions. In 1571, the king rejected the demands of the
Reformed church at Angoulême for the removal of the town garrison,
use of the communal bell and the replacement of local officials, because
they were judged to be contrary to his most recent edict.[15] Even the
authorities established to enforce the edicts – provincial governors and
royal commissioners (themselves trained in the law) – sometimes struggled to understand exactly what was meant by a particular article and, as
a result, might refer more difficult cases for consideration by the king and
his council. Related to this concern with the application of the law, and
a prominent source of Huguenot anxieties during the first two decades
of the wars, was the perceived success of the *chambres neutres* (established
in the *parlements* in the mid-1560s) and their successors, the *chambres mi-
parties* or *chambres de l'Édit* (established in 1576), in granting Huguenots
equal access to justice.[16] The institution of such bodies reveals the degree to which the Huguenots felt they were not receiving fair treatment
at the hands of the judiciary, as well as the extent to which the crown
was willing to reassure them that it would ensure that they did so. The
establishment of the first *chambres* in the towns of Saintes and Périgueux
in May 1565 was the result of lobbying from the inhabitants of Guyenne,
Saintonge, Périgord and the Agenais.[17] The obstacles that the *chambres*
faced in exercising their duties, notably in the form of obstruction by
the existing judicial bodies in a region, inspired repeated remonstrances
to the crown. This situation ensured the continuing importance to the
Huguenots of the right of petition in securing royal assurances that the
edicts would be enforced.

---

[14] On the concern to stay within the law, see O. Christin, *La paix de religion: l'autonomisation de la raison politique au XVIe siècle* (Paris, 1997), esp. p. 104.
[15] AM Angoulême, AA 5, fo. 62.
[16] On the establishment of a *chambre neutre* in Provence in January 1567, see AD Bouches-du-Rhône, B 3331, fos. 107–10 (420), which mentions their earlier establishment in the jurisdictions of the *parlements* of Paris, Toulouse, Bordeaux and Dijon.
[17] AD La Gironde, 1B 9, fos. 117v–118, 'Lettres patentes d'une chambre de nouveau composee' (May 1565).

The impact of successive edicts of pacification stimulated *remontrances* not only from Huguenots but just as often from Catholics. This was the case not only where Catholics were outnumbered by Huguenots, as at La Rochelle, where the continuing obstruction of Catholic worship was the issue, but also in those communities where they formed the majority due to their concern to restrict Huguenot rights.[18] Catholic appeals were also stimulated by periods of Huguenot control of certain towns, such as Orléans during the 1560s.[19] Furthermore, Huguenot petitions themselves encouraged counter-petitions from local Catholics as both sides vied to present their case to the crown via an extraordinary judicial structure set up specifically to deal with the resolution of confessional disputes. Representations were to be made to the provincial governor (or his lieutenant) and the royal commissioners charged with enforcing the edicts in a given locality. If the matter remained unresolved it could then be forwarded for consideration by the royal council. It is not clear whether the faiths were expected to meet the legal costs themselves. The lack of complaints about the difficulties of meeting the expenses incurred suggests that this was not the case. Despite their differences, Catholics and Huguenots were concerned about similar issues: the provision of sites for worship and burial, the distribution of taxation and the return of confiscated property, appointment to and removal from office, as well as localized concerns such as disruption to trade. In keeping with the judicial character of the enforcement, appeals to the authorities from both faiths were based on legal and practical grounds rather than confessional arguments, although these could also be a feature. However, their approaches were quite different. Huguenots were primarily concerned to ensure the enforcement of the terms of the edicts of pacification since they provided the basis for their legitimacy as a group with rights and privileges. Catholics, on the other hand, tended to oppose the edicts' provisions as granting too much freedom to a group, which, they complained, had already proved itself disruptive and seditious. Catholics often claimed Huguenot forfeiture of the benefits of an edict as the result of local contraventions; Catholic violations of an edict's terms were the usual Huguenot charge. Petitions were a product of confessional conflict and were designed to show the other faith in an unfavourable light. They are a sign that efforts to establish coexistence

[18] For an example of remonstrances from the Catholics of La Rochelle, see BN, MS Fr 15554, fos. 29, 31 (13 Mar. 1572), and the response to them, BN, MS Fr 15558, fos. 36–9 (26 June 1573).
[19] On petitions from the Catholics of Orléans, see Stocker, 'Parlement of Paris', 38–47, and BN, MS Fr 15548, fos. 173–4 (1568).

between the faiths had broken down, in some instances, even before they had begun.[20]

The content of both faiths' petitions, the dominance of particular issues within a community, and the arguments that each side assembled to defend their case, reinforce this view. It was the issue of disarmament that raised confessional hackles in the Loire town of Blois, dominated by the royal château. In October 1563, the crown received a Catholic petition concerning the refusal of local Huguenots to disarm, as well as a Huguenot request to extend the prohibition to the hostile Catholic inhabitants of the nearby village of Mor, designated as their official site of worship.[21] From the Catholic perspective, the continuing prospect of Huguenots in arms posed a serious threat to the town's security; from their side, the Huguenots feared a repeat of earlier acts of violence against them if they were placed in a position from which they could no longer defend themselves against those they perceived to be their enemies. Typically the claims and counter-claims of the faiths on this issue degenerated into general accusations of the contravention of other terms contained in the edict and, conversely, the falsity of the charges laid against them by the other side. Disarmament was to be a contentious issue also in self-styled frontier towns, such as those in Burgundy and Provence, and major ports such as Bordeaux, with the related concerns about how the realm was to be safeguarded from its Protestant enemies if such strategic locations were left exposed.[22] In these circumstances, Catholics requested an exemption for their town from the disarmament article, though this was notably to apply only to 'loyal' Catholic inhabitants. The 'frontier' argument would also be used to attempt to distance sites of Reformed worship and, similarly, to express concerns about the potential disruption to commerce and threat of foreign invasion via the ports. Yet from a Huguenot perspective it was not their activities but those of their Catholic neighbours that posed the greatest threat to commercial prosperity, as argued notably at Nantes and Dieppe.[23] At Dieppe, the Huguenots complained that, following their return after the third war in 1568, they had been terrorized by the soldiers of the local garrison. The soldiers had demanded exactions for releasing their houses as well as charging levies

[20] In contrast, on successful attempts at coexistence, see in particular, O. Christin, 'La coexistence confessionnelle, 1563–1567', *BSHPF* (1995), 483–504.

[21] BN, MS Fr 15878, fos. 151–60, 181–205 (Oct. 1563).

[22] On Provence: BN, MS Fr 15879, fo. 134 and 15880, fos. 228, 276; Bordeaux: BN, MS Fr 15878, fos. 294–5.

[23] Nantes: BN, MS Fr 15881, fos. 373–4; Dieppe: BN, MS Fr 15548, fos. 175, 177.

on their merchandise, as a consequence driving out local merchants and fishermen as well as impoverishing those in the countryside to the detriment not only of the town but also the realm. Both Catholic and Huguenot merchants throughout France would complain of the damage that the wars had done to their livelihoods, chiefly through theft of their merchandise and the expense of ransoms following their capture.[24]

The hotly contested issue of sites for worship was central to confessional disputes at this time, and the available case studies as described in surviving petitions are plentiful.[25] One of the most frequent causes of complaint was the unsuitability of the designated site. Accessibility was a prominent concern, with the Huguenots of Bordeaux requesting somewhere that could be travelled to and from in a day, whilst in the Lyonnais worries were expressed regarding the toll that a long journey would take on newborn babies, women, children and the old.[26] Negotiations over the choice of site were complicated by the differing priorities of both faiths in the locality. A bulky exchange of correspondence took place regarding the provision of a site for the Huguenots of Angers in 1579, involving Henri III and his brother (also the provincial governor), the duc d'Anjou, the local Huguenots, the municipal authorities, the town's governor and the bishop of Angers.[27] The location was still being disputed in 1581.[28] For Huguenots perhaps the most frustrating aspect of such disputes was that the initial designation was often in their favour, since the suburbs of major towns were the usual choice, but Catholic protests frequently resulted in the removal of the location to a much less convenient site.[29] Such is the case with the disputed *prêche* for the Reformed church at Meulan, some twenty-five kilometres from Paris (itself excluded from such provision), and thus in an especially sensitive region from the perspective of both faiths.[30] The Catholic inhabitants were aware that other nearby or similarly distanced towns, such as Melun and Corbeil, were exempt, whilst the Huguenots were alarmed by the further squeezing of

---

[24] E.g. BN, MS Fr 15551, fo. 220r (19 Apr. 1570).
[25] On this issue see P. Roberts, 'The Most Crucial Battle of the Wars of Religion? The Conflict over Sites for Reformed Worship in Sixteenth-century France', *ARG* 89 (1998), 247–67.
[26] For Bordeaux, Sécousse, *Mémoires de Condé*, V, p. 219. For Lyon, AM Lyon, GG 77, no. 20, iii; GG 78, no. 34.
[27] AM Angers, BB 36, fos. 98, 113v–117, 132, 137–8, 141, 148v–149 (Jan.–July 1579).
[28] AM Angers, BB 36, fos. 350–60 (Aug. 1581), as well as a request from the Huguenots of Angers for a place where they could bury their dead.
[29] This could happen even after a designation had been secured direct from the king himself during the royal progress, as the Huguenots of Troyes were to discover: BN, MS Fr 18156, fo. 153v (20 Feb. 1566).
[30] BN, Collection du Vexin, MS 4, pp. 453–5, and MS 26, fo. 156.

the provision of sites for them in the region. Here, as elsewhere, the argument of the remonstrances centred around the much-disputed number of native inhabitants who required access to Reformed worship, and also their social status, as was also the case, to cite just two such instances, at Poitiers and Bordeaux.[31] At Poitiers, the Huguenots claimed that they had 7,000–8,000 adherents at least, mostly 'gens honorables de qualité', and yet had still not been provided with a suitable site for worship.[32] No figure was given for the congregation at Bordeaux, but once again the inclusion of 'la plus grande partie des plus notables familles' of the town was used in mitigation when requesting a more convenient location for services.[33] Whilst Huguenots claimed that their numbers were drawn largely from the upper echelons of local society, Catholics scoffed that those attending Reformed services were mostly from out of town or drawn from socially insignificant groups. Not only was the provision of sites for worship clearly expected to favour the social elite, but also by stressing the social status of their adherents both faiths hoped to lend greater legitimacy to their cause.

A further reflection of the importance of such status in securing sites of worship was the role played by the nobility as intermediaries between Huguenot communities and the crown. During periods of ascendancy, the Huguenot nobility offered petitioners an important channel of communication, and representation, at court. Inevitably, however, this role fluctuated with their political fortunes as, for instance, following their exclusion in 1574. Leading Huguenot nobles also played a pivotal role in the resolution of provincial disputes. In April 1564, in his capacity as provincial governor of Picardy, Louis, prince de Condé, wrote to the sieur d'Humières to request that those Huguenots in his *gouvernement* who were banned from having sites for worship in their respective 'frontier' towns be allowed instead to attend services on the prince's estates.[34] Three months earlier, Henri de Navarre urged the comte du Lude, governor of Poitou, to grant the Huguenots of Poitiers' request to establish a site of worship in the suburbs of the town.[35] Elsewhere it was the members of the Huguenot churches who took the initiative, as at Orléans,

---

[31] On the issue of numbers and the social composition of petitions, see Zaret, 'Petitions and the "Invention" of Public Opinion', 1535–6.

[32] E. de Barthélemy (ed.), 'Lettres historiques du XVIe siècle', *Archives Historiques de la Saintonge et de l'Aunis* 4 (1877), 309–10 (wrongly ascribed to 1559 but clearly dating from after the Edict of Amboise, probably 1563 or 1564).

[33] Sécousse, *Mémoires de Condé*, v, pp. 218–19.   [34] BN, MS Fr 3187, fo. 53.

[35] B. Ledain (ed.), 'Lettres adressées à Jean et Guy de Daillon, Comtes du Lude, Gouverneurs de Poitou de 1543 à 1557 et de 1557 à 1585', *Archives Historiques du Poitou* 12 (1882), 152–3. Cf. similar request from Condé of 8 Sept. 1567: *ibid.*, 174.

addressing their concerns to the marshal de Cossé responsible for the enforcement of the edicts in the region.[36] Other issues contained in petitions were of direct concern to the nobility, in particular the contestation of noble status. Most notably, their right to exercise *haute justice*, crucial for the granting of permission for the exercise of Reformed worship on their estates as specified in successive edicts, was open to dispute. Aside from the satisfaction of noble honour, the value to both faiths of winning such an argument is clear, as shown for instance in the dispute between the Catholic authorities in Nantes and the Protestant seigneur de La Musse, which rumbled on for three decades.[37] Members of the nobility also acted as individual petitioners concerned with safeguarding their property and privileges. A striking feature is the prominent participation of noblewomen in this process, as widows or as estate managers in a husband's absence. Such cases reveal the willingness of women, both Huguenot and Catholic, to make use of the courts, but perhaps more specifically their greater dependence on the implementation of the law if they were to recover property and to pursue compensation for losses which they had incurred during the wars, evident in cases from Toulouse, Mâcon and Bordeaux.[38]

In 1570, Jehanne de Vidal, dame de Miramont and widow of the first president in the *parlement* of Toulouse, protested to Governor Damville against taxes imposed on her and her four children, in view of the expense she had already been put to during the troubles in contributions to municipal defence and the ransoming of her sons. Indeed, she questioned whether she ought to have been taxed at all, and it was also revealed that she had not even been able to afford to pay all of the sum of 2,500 *livres* demanded from her after the previous edict in 1568.[39] Her plea was sympathetically received and she was relieved of paying the outstanding amount and exempted from all future demands. In an earlier case, of April 1563, Barbe de Maupas, widow of the baron de Duras, appealed to the *parlement* at Bordeaux for the restitution of her property in accordance with the recent edict.[40] Her château of Blanquefort had been occupied

---

[36] BN, MS Fr 3189, fo. 8.
[37] AM Nantes, GG 645, nos. 1–28. For further discussion of this case, see Roberts, 'Most Crucial Battle', 263.
[38] This represents in no way a parallel with the activities of women petitioners during the English Civil War; the demands were non-politicized and were more to do with the traditional resolution of personal grievances than radical claims for constitutional change. See, for example, P. Higgins, 'The Reactions of Women, with Special Reference to Women Petitioners' in B. Manning (ed.), *Politics, Religion and the English Civil War* (New York, 1973), pp. 179–224.
[39] AM Toulouse, GG 825.
[40] AD La Gironde, 1B 257, no. 188 (22 Apr. 1563), 1B 262, no. 214 (24 Sept.).

by a local captain who so far had refused to budge and, along with his company, was also guilty of other crimes. The court agreed to support her cause. Nevertheless, in September, the royal commissioner, Anthoine Fumée, was still seeking a resolution to the dame de Duras's problems in co-operation with the *parlement*. Those occupying the château claimed that they had been installed there by Lieutenant-Governor Monluc, who had told them that this was by ordinance of the *parlement*, and they would only leave if the court ordered them to do so. No record was found of the alleged permission for such a garrison being granted, and the *parlement* agreed to assist in evicting the interlopers. In a further case from February 1571, the marshal de Vieilleville approached the royal commissioners for the enforcement in Burgundy of the 1570 Edict of St Germain, regarding the request of Damoiselle Claude Vincent to have exercise of the 'new religion' on her estates in the Mâconnois.[41] This she did, she argued, by virtue of her privilege of *haute justice* through proprietorship of half of the lands she shared with her husband from whom she now sought 'separation de biens' because of his refusal to allow Reformed worship there and his desire to constrain her conscience (which he denied). In Vieilleville's judgement only the lady's family (up to a maximum of ten) were to be allowed to have access to Reformed worship on her estates, thus acceding to her request to be permitted to hold services but not granting her the benefit of *haute justice* that she had claimed.

Besides noblewomen, urban widows are also evident in the courts seeking justice and compensation. In 1565, Antoinette de Puybusque, widow of Councillor de Clapiers, appeared before the commissioners sent to enforce the Edict of Amboise in Languedoc to protest regarding a sum of at least 66 *livres* demanded from her by a (presumably Huguenot) lawyer, Jehan de la Cassaigne, as reimbursement for the money allegedly stolen from him by her late husband during the recent troubles.[42] The widow's claim that the money had been passed on to the city treasurer was upheld, and the commissioners judged that both parties were to be compensated by the said treasurer. More poignantly, other widows sought justice and compensation through the courts for the murder of their head of household as a result of confessional strife, as did nine women from Troyes whose case was heard before the king's council in March and April of 1564.[43] This last example also demonstrates how Huguenots collectively might pursue their claims through the courts quite independently from the more generalized articles of remonstrance

---

[41] AD Saône et Loire, AC Mâcon, GG 123, nos. 14–15.
[42] AM Toulouse, GG 824, fos. 156–66.   [43] BN, MS Fr 18156, fo. 40 (24 Mar. 1564).

presented by the local community as a whole. Petitions such as these generally received a sympathetic hearing from the crown, moved by appeals
regarding familial destitution. Responding to the grievances of whole
communities was more problematic if both faiths were to be appeased.
Enforcing decisions favourable to Huguenots would prove even harder
in the face of local Catholic resistance.

So far this essay has very much emphasized the peculiar conservatism
and parochialism of Huguenot petitions. Yet there is evidence that a
more radical strain emerged in the mid-1570s in those parts of France
where the Huguenots were strong, in the south and west. A petition of
April 1575, for instance, began with a demand for 'the exercise of the
[Reformed] religion by all everywhere in the kingdom, regions, lands
and seigneuries under obedience and protection of the king'.[44] Like the
declarations of the Huguenot leadership, such requests display a more
conscious national awareness than was usual at the time. However, petitioners had always shown some knowledge of developments elsewhere,
as the Reformers of the Lyonnais had regarding events affecting their
co-religionists in the other major cities of Rouen and Paris.[45] This is
not surprising when dealing with a movement many members of which
had spent time abroad in exile during periods of open warfare. The
Lyonnais petitioners, for example, included those who had taken refuge
in Savoy, Switzerland and Geneva.[46] In addition, after 1572, the movement looked to its political assemblies to exert pressure on the crown,
and their negotiations with the monarchy may have replaced petitioning
as a more effective means of ensuring that their grievances were heard.[47]
Nevertheless, these exceptions do not alter the general impression of the
characteristic Huguenot petition. In keeping with the localized nature
of the enforcement of the edicts, local concerns and personal grievances
continued to dominate their demands.

Any assessment of the impact of Huguenot petitioning must be circum-
spect. The reception of the petitions themselves was mixed, depending
on how well they fitted the terms of the edicts as interpreted by the authorities and the existing judgments by commissioners and other judicial
officials. As already argued, even the terms of the edicts were contested
with regard to how they were to be implemented in practice, for instance, whether only what was specifically allowed by an edict should
be observed or only what was specifically prohibited. This was the sort

[44] BN, MS Dupuy 322, fos. 186–8 (Apr. 1575).
[45] AM Lyon, GG 77, no. 20, ii.   [46] AM Lyon, GG 78, no. 34.
[47] J. Garrisson, 'L'Édit de Nantes' in J. Garrisson (ed.), *L'Édit de Nantes* (Paris, 1998), p. 31.

of dispute that divided provincial governors, primarily responsible for regional security, and royal commissioners, charged with upholding the law. It was not always clear whose opinion had precedence if there was no agreement on the way in which to proceed, resulting in further delays in the response to Huguenot appeals. Furthermore, whilst the royal authorities might prove sympathetic to Huguenot grievances, implementing a solution to them in the localities was to prove more problematic in the face of official and popular obstruction of their rights and devotions. This is reflected in the contents of the petitions themselves, revealing Huguenot fears that both their freedom of conscience and the provision of worship would be severely curtailed by local Catholic officials and the hostility of their neighbours in general. However, as so often with the edicts of pacification, gauging which side is in the right on a particular issue often depends on the perspective from which their position is viewed. One individual's defensive stance in retaining arms might be another's act of aggression; confiscated property or office from one perspective might be legitimately purchased from another; the issue of taxation was, as always, fraught with claims of unfairness and corruption. The proliferation of Huguenot petitions was the direct result of such problems of interpretation. They were primarily concerned with questioning the validity of the judgments made with regard to the edicts' implementation, but at the same time they expose Huguenot fears that whatever had been agreed on their behalf at a national level was to be limited in practice by the actions of those who could not accept the concessions granted to them.

Huguenot petitioning was shaped by its function: to gain a sympathetic hearing from the monarchy for Huguenot grievances. As a result, it was conservative and deferential, focusing on the plight of the Reformed churches whose suffering was seen to be contrary to the royal will as embodied in the law. Yet, as Catholic petitioners continually reminded the crown, Huguenot activities during the wars had rendered them suspect. If they were to win the crown over they had to present themselves as the loyal subjects and their opponents as the troublemakers. As a result, Huguenot appeals became somewhat defensive, a stance reinforced by the continuing persecution that they faced in those communities in which they remained a dwindling minority. The Huguenots accepted the crown's role as guarantor of their rights, and petitioning was the means by which they ensured royal awareness of the violation of those rights. They had become dependent on the enforcement of the law to grant recognition and legitimization for their faith, for in most communities they did not have the numerical strength to impose such sanctions by force. In addition, this reliance on royal justice generated the expression of Huguenot grievances and concerns in legalistic terms. [48] None the less, their appeals are characterized by more than an innate conservatism and preoccupation with the law. Descriptions of the cruelties and injustices they faced reveal a much more human side to their plight. The responses of their Catholic neighbours may necessitate questioning the extremity of their position and the innocence of their role in the exacerbation of confessional hostilities, but need not negate their viewpoint. Though slanted by the circumstances that produced them, Huguenot petitions articulate something of the mentality of a persecuted faith, its self-image and preoccupations. Used judiciously, they also shed a more personal light on the world of the Huguenots, their hopes and their fears, during a crucial phase in their history.

---

[48] Not only through the citation of the articles of specific edicts but also through their use of legal language, in particular the terms 'permettre' and 'permission' as early as 1560. See on this point, W. H. Huseman, 'The Expression of the Idea of Toleration in French During the Sixteenth Century', *SCJ* 15 (1984), esp. 306–8.

6. Informal networks in sixteenth-century French Protestantism

Mark Greengrass

French Protestantism was never other than a minority faith in sixteenth-century France. The Huguenot chrysalis grew under the threat of varying but emphatic persecution in the later 1540s and 1550s. At the moment of its metamorphosis into a fully developed ecclesiastical structure and political movement from 1559 to 1562, when French Protestants planted churches in unprecedented numbers and acquired the social geography that was to dominate it for the rest of the century, it also confronted significant, organized Catholic hostility. This was the prelude to the wars of religion in which the movement only enjoyed short periods of somewhat fragile official legitimacy. The life cycle of the Huguenot movement in the sixteenth century created a dominant mentality of defensiveness and stoicism, and the need to rely on its collective resources.

This mentality no doubt also helps to explain the remarkable unity of purpose that characterized the Huguenots in the sixteenth century. This solidarity functioned at formal and public levels. Church structures, notably the Confession and the Discipline that were agreed at the first national synod of Paris in 1559, were essential building blocks. So too were the underlying provincial synods and colloquies. In addition, Protestant political and military organization held up sufficiently well against the monarchy to win the political wing of the Protestant movement some important concessions in successive edicts of pacification. With the protectorship of Henri de Navarre after 1576, 'une église' and 'un parti' were cemented together by 'un roi'.[1] But the scattered churches of this huge kingdom could hardly rely on these instruments alone. The French church was a large and complex one. It had fifteen provinces (sixteen including Béarn) and over fifty colloquies. Some of the colloquies in the south encompassed forty or fifty churches and, although there were fewer churches in northern France, they were more dispersed

---

[1] J. Garrisson, *Les protestants au XVIe siècle* (Paris, 1988), chaps. 7–9.

and required a greater effort to hold together. The national synods only met in peacetime and, even then, only every three years for a week or so. The provincial synods met once a year and the colloquies twice a year. The political assemblies of the Huguenots occurred irregularly and, although we have yet to document the process fully, the king of Navarre's protectorship was only gradually asserted over the movement in the later 1570s and 1580s – and then by the informal channels of patronage and influence rather than through its institutions.

Beyond the formal structure, we must look at how Protestant unity and underlying identity was forged at more informal levels. French Protestantism had an inner fraternalism, a *sociabilité à distance*, that underpinned its institutional framework and political endeavours. This sociability emerges in a variety of contexts. We see it in the shared experience, language and community that was created among the exiles from France. It is evident, at least from the end of the sixteenth century, in the arrows of family fortune delineated by Huguenot genealogists. We stumble across it in the friendships made by students at Calvinist colleges and academies. It is identifiable in studies of Protestant charitable bequests and bursaries in Geneva and elsewhere. When the young church at Montpellier fasted 'because of the great troubles, which are everywhere' in June 1562, it reflected and reinforced the solidarities of the Huguenot movement.[2] When the churches of France rallied to collect money for Geneva, it demonstrated the informal networks that kept French Protestantism intact and strengthened its international affiliations. In a movement whose shared theology emphasized faith as a mutual confidence in God (*fiducia*) through a strong affective and personal liaison with Christ, a faith which was to be firmly distinguished from the working of institutions and the law, we should perhaps not be surprised at the intensity of the informal sociabilities within French Protestantism.[3]

All these various elements are illustrated in the correspondence of French Protestants in the sixteenth century. The transactional history of the Protestant Reformation has long been dominated by the printed book; the manuscript treatise or the letter has not been given comparable attention. Was it not the novel use of the printing press that explained the extraordinary capacity of the Protestant Reformation to transcend established political and geographical boundaries and bring together

---

[2] 'La Réforme en France. Lettres de diverses Églises à Calvin, 1561–1562', *BSHPF* 14 (1865), 325; E. Trocmé, 'L'Église Réformée de La Rochelle jusqu'en 1628', *BSHPF* 98 (1951), 131–99, cited at 152.

[3] See J. Wirth, 'La naissance du concept de croyance (XIIe–XVIIe siècles)', *BHR* 45 (1983), 40.

social groups under the banner of the new faith? Luther referred to the printing press as 'God's highest and most extreme act of grace, whereby the business of the Gospel is driven forward'.[4] Many Protestants concurred that the printed book had been heaven-sent. Manuscripts, by comparison, were disparaged. The pen was 'but as a Rush-Candle to a Torch' in comparison with printed books, said one English Protestant.[5] Manuscripts could, in certain circumstances, symbolize the scholastic learning of the middle ages that had imprisoned God's word for too long. Scholastic theologians were latter-day 'scribes and Pharisees'. Yet there was considerable ambiguity here, represented in the dual use of the word 'scriptura' by Protestant theologians to mean both 'writing' and the 'holy scriptures'. The act of copying and extracting the Bible was a means of prayer, a way of internalizing the Scriptures to enlighten the heart – sentiments that predated the advent of Protestantism.[6] Hence the Protestant fashion – one might say passion – for keeping manuscript scriptural commonplace books. And Protestants played their part in the extraordinary efflorescence of correspondence in sixteenth-century Europe.

We have yet to understand fully the processes at work in the growing use of manuscript letters as a means of communication in the sixteenth century. They were doubtless a complex compendium of the practical and the cultural. Across Western Europe, lay notables were joining the clergy in retreating to their studies for private reading, reflection and the writing of letters. The longer periods of education that were now thought necessary for elites made them fluent writers and readers. Even the growing availability of wax (as opposed to tallow) candles, and the cost of paper, doubtless had its effect on the volume of scribal communication. There was also a slow but significant transformation in the reliability of postal services. Renaissance humanists had also encouraged the manuscript letter, not least in the revival of Ciceronian forms.[7] The popularity of the publication of collections of 'private' letters, especially in sixteenth-century Italy, projected a norm for the attitudes and behaviour of cultivated men of letters that was well known in France by the second half

---

4 Cited in R. G. Cole, 'Reformation Printers: Unsung Heroes', *SCJ* 15 (1984), 328.
5 Cited in P. Beal, *In Praise of Scribes. Manuscripts and their Makers in Seventeenth-century England* (Oxford, 1998), p. 2.
6 They can be found, for example, eloquently put in Johannes Trithemius, *In Praise of Scribes*, ed. by M. S. Batts, trans. by E. Bryson Bongie (Vancouver, 1977), p. 62.
7 E.g. J. R. Henderson, 'Defining the Genre of the Letter: Juan Luis Vives' "De Conscribendis Epistolis"', *Renaissance and Reformation* 7 (1983), 89–105.

of the sixteenth century.[8] The Reformation validated the letter format further and broadened the social constituency. Luther's theology found its roots in the Pauline Epistles and he semi-consciously adapted the forms of the biblical epistle to his correspondence, particularly in his use of Pauline salutations and forms of commendation.[9] Biblical language and epistolary forms quickly inflected Protestant correspondence in the German Reformation a generation before the same process worked within the French Reformation.[10] Fortunately, the means survive to allow the sampling of the correspondence networks of the French Protestant movement through the publication of its surviving epistolary contacts with Geneva.[11] In addition, there are the more fragmentary records of the correspondence received and sent to be found in the martyrology of Jean Crespin, the *Histoire Ecclésiastique* and in the French synods and other church records. These can be supplemented by the letter collections of individual French Protestant pastors and laymen. Although no firm distinction can be sustained between 'private' and 'official' correspondence, these sources illustrate some of the characteristics of the informal networks within French Protestantism in this period.

The significance of correspondence to the vitality of French Protestantism appears at every turn. When, for example, the provincial synod of Montauban was asked by the church in Toulouse to consider the possibility of a blind man 'of good conversation' as a pastor in April 1561, it was rejected on the grounds that 'the ministry does not consist solely in doctrine, but in discipline and administration of the sacraments, for which sight is especially necessary; a person must be able to receive and write

---

[8] G. Fragnito, 'Per lo studio dell'epistolografia volgare del cinquecento: le lettere di Ludovico Beccadelli', *BHR* 43 (1981), 61–87. The first great success of such published collections was apparently Paolo Manuzio's *Lettere volgari* (1542). Montaigne wrote that the Italians were 'grands imprimeurs de lettres' and had hundreds of these volumes on his own shelves (Fragnito, 'Per lo studio dell'epistolografia', 69).

[9] M. Arnold, 'Luther, imitateur de Paul: ses lettres aux communautés évangéliques', *Revue d'Histoire et de Philosophie Religieuses* 72 (1991), 99–112.

[10] R. Bodenmann, 'La Bible et l'Art d'écrire des lettres: pratiques dans l'aire germanique du XVIe siècle', *BSHPF* 141 (1995), 357–82.

[11] These include the 'Thesaurus Epistolicus Calvinianus', the collection of Calvin's correspondence in G. Baum, E. Cunitz and E. Reuss (eds.), *Joannis Calvini opera quae supersunt omnia*, 59 vols. (Brunswick, 1863–1900), henceforth *CO*. I have concentrated on volumes 15–20 for the preparation of this article. See also H. Aubert, F. Aubert, H. Meylan *et al.* (eds.), *Correspondance de Théodore de Bèze* (Geneva, 1960). The relevant seven volumes (to 1599) of J.-F. Bergier *et al.*, *Registres de la Compagnie des Pasteurs* (Geneva, 1964–). Additional publications of the correspondence of the French churches with Geneva, especially 'La Réforme en France', 319–33, 363–8; 'La Réforme en 1561. Lettres des Églises du Vigan, d'Uzès et de Nîmes à la Compagnie de Genève', *BSHPF* 17 (1868), 480–7.

letters, and occasionally deal with matters written in secret letters'.[12] Ten
years previously, the French crown had decreed that anyone caught writing letters to Geneva or found carrying them to Protestant heretics there
would be prosecuted as though he or she was automatically a heretic.[13]
Correspondence for the French Protestants was a potentially dangerous commodity in the 1550s, capable of incriminating individuals. 'I
have put off writing to you until now,' wrote Calvin to the students from
Lausanne imprisoned in Lyon on 10 June 1552, 'fearing that if the letters
had an unfortunate encounter it would be a new excuse for the enemies
to afflict you more harshly.'[14] An elaborate set of aliases was used to dis-
guise the identity both of the individual from whom the letter was sent
and to whom it was addressed. The 'Seelac st' who wrote to Colladon,
secretary of the Company of Pastors on 25 June 1559, was, in reality,
the pastor Lucas Hobé.[15] 'Guy Moranges' signed his letter to 'Monsieur
Despeville' (Jean Calvin) at 'Ville dieu' (Geneva) on 27 June (1561?) but
then thought it prudent to add an alias as well ('La Porte'), different
from the one ('La Garde') that he had used on previous occasions.[16]
Letters were also a vital vehicle for the closet reinforcement of morale,
not merely a means of authenticating their bearers. Jean Crespin's martyrology included substantial letter-collections from and to the martyrs.
The letters and confessions received in Geneva by Calvin from the five
Lausanne students incarcerated by the Lyon authorities must have been
handed over to Crespin. The imprisoned students had apparently been
allowed writing materials so that they could compose their confessions
of faith for submission to the judges, and they took advantage of the concession. This material was the initial stimulus to Crespin's martyrology
and dominated the first edition.[17]

   The tradition of martyrs' letters was expanded in the 'third part' of the
martyrology in 1556 and, by the first folio edition of 1570, there were
well over 100 letters relating to the French martyrs. The letters were
generally written from prison or smuggled into them. They referred to
their awaiting sentence and their lives on the eve of death. The lack of

[12] Bibliothèque de la SHPF, Paris, MS 570(1) fo. 5v; cf. R. M. Kingdon, *Geneva and the Coming of the Wars of Religion in France, 1555–1563* (Geneva, 1956), p. 87.
[13] Edict of Châteaubriant, June 1551: F. A. Isambert, *Recueil des anciennes lois françaises*, 29 vols. (Paris, 1821–33), XIII, pp. 203–4.
[14] *CO*, XIV, 1631.   [15] *CO*, XX, 4194   copy defective.
[16] *CO*, XVIII, 3426; Kingdon, *Geneva and the Coming of the Wars*, p. 38.
[17] G. Truc, 'Calvin et les cinq Prisonniers de Lyon', *Revue des Études historiques* 86 (1920), 43–54; see also preface to Jean Crespin, *Actes des martyrs deduicts en sept livres* (Geneva, 1564).

pens and paper sometimes constrained them: 'I would rather write to you, if I had paper and a writing desk,' said Claude Monier, a prisoner in Lyon.[18] Crespin made something of the letters of the Flemish martyr, Alexandre Deykin, 'written in his own blood, for lack of ink'.[19] 'In the blood of martyrs is the seed of the true church', Tertullian's phrase, became embodied in these epistles in a way that reflected the title to Crespin's work in its 1570 edition. Since we do not have much by way of Crespin's manuscripts to check the veracity of what he printed, we must allow for the possibility of editorial licence. This is not least because in those passages where a prior source can be compared with what Crespin published, there is extensive 'constructive development' of the text.[20] On the other hand, Crespin's well-attested preference for basing himself on a text provided by others should give some confidence that what he printed was likely to have existed in something like the version that he published. He and his collaborators certainly sought such materials and inserted them into later editions, sometimes indicating when new letters had come their way.[21] In doing so, Crespin testified to, but also publicized, the significance of correspondence within the particular circumstances of the emerging French churches.

The majority of the epistles were written by and to the martyrs in vernacular French. They provided a simple but powerful vehicle for the personal expression of religious conviction. A few were addressed from one martyr to another to sustain each other. One of the five prisoners in Lyon, the aptly named Pierre Escrivain – a Gascon 'of lively spirit' and 'a magnificent tongue', from whom an exceptional number of letters survived – wrote letters of consolation to other prisoners.[22] God did not allow useless suffering, he told them. They should take courage under his captaincy and against Satan to the last drop of their blood. They should be patient for their deliverance would come. God would have compassion for them. There were also 'familiar' letters – to wives, brothers, sisters, children – ordinary people of modest background, writing

---

[18] J. Crespin, *Histoire des vrays tesmoins de la verité de l'Evangile, qui de leur sangs l'ont signés depuis Iean Hus iusques au temps present* (Liège: Centre National de Recherches d'Histoire Religieuse, 1570 [1964]), III, fo. 182.
[19] *Ibid.*, VII, fo. 611v.
[20] J.-F. Gilmont, *Jean Crespin. Un éditeur réformé du XVIe siècle* (Geneva, 1981), pp. 182–7.
[21] E.g. the martyr Estienne Gravot, where Crespin notes in the 1570 edition: 'Aux precedentes editions des Martyrs, nous avions fait declaration seulement de la mort d'Estienne le menuisier ... maintenant ... nous donnons certaines lettres qui nous ont esté communiquees, escrites de sa propre main': Crespin, *Histoire des vrays tesmoins*, III, fo. 263.
[22] *Ibid.*, III, fos. 201, 207.

in extraordinary circumstances.[23] Some, like that from Martial Alba, a student from Montauban, were apocalyptic in tone. 'It is the holy Gospel that the angel of the Apocalypse, appearing in the midst of the heavens proclaims and preaches to those who inhabit the earth . . . saying aloud, Fear God and honour him, for the hour of his judgment has come.'[24] Satan was an active, subtle, powerful enemy, present in the minds of most. He 'works as hard as he can, with extreme diligence, to amuse us with the things of this world to make us forget that which we owe God'. Some stressed the distinction between body (bound, imprisoned) and spirit (in true liberty, the seed of the True Church). Others dwelled on the importance of stoic patience and took comfort from the letters of consolation that they received. Martial Naviheres, on the other hand, was probably not alone in finding himself under family pressure to recant. His uncle wrote from Poitiers to tell him sharply of the distress his obduracy was causing his family; 'In the letters that you recently wrote, I see that your extreme confidence persuades you to undertake a reformation of every estate of the church in which we live, a church that belongs above all to God, and to the Magistrate who is charged with its administration.'[25] Above all, they wanted their suffering not to have been in vain. Their letters were to be circulated, read, and used to the greater good of the impending Reformation. Pierre Bergier told his wife: 'So that our children will have a lasting memory of me, I beg you to rescue all the letters that I have sent you, and many others that you wrote to me, of which a great number are in my brother-in-law's possession, and have those to my brother Denis and to others rewritten in a special book. After having had them recopied, you may distribute these letters far and wide, so that they bring great benefit to the church.'[26]

The letters that they wrote to their (generally unnamed) friends or members of the worshipping community were to accomplish the same task. Pierre Escrivain, writing to his 'very dear brother and steadfast friend', spoke of his hopes of deliverance in death. Hearing from one of the 'brethren' who had visited him in prison that 'there were many poor, blind and ignorant people in the town, who are moved and saddened by the death and torments that our enemies prepare for us, and in lamenting and sighing' he was confident that it was 'doubtlessly a sure sign that our death and our blood will be the summons by which God will produce great fruit in his Church'. Some martyrs spoke

---

[23] E.g. the letter from Archambaut Seraphon 'mercier natif du lieu de la moleyre en Bazadois' to his wife (*ibid.*, VI, fo. 451).

[24] *Ibid.*, III, fo. 198.   [25] *Ibid.*, III, fo. 222.   [26] *Ibid.*, III, fo. 236v.

of the unique friendship that had been nurtured by the events that had overtaken them. Denis Peloquin, writing to a female supporter, explained that it was a friendship not like those of the world: 'Lady, sister and good friend in Jesus Christ, there is no one (I mean of regenerated spirit) who cannot easily judge that the friendship which you bear for us and which I discern in your letters, can be but wholly divine and spiritual. In this world, it is not between persons such as us that one seeks earthly friendships and favours, or hopes for some gain or temporal assistance.'[27] Peloquin had experienced a 'conjunction of this Christian friendship' that crossed social and gender boundaries and imitated the moment when Christ welcomed his friends to eat and drink with him.

Some of the letters collected in Crespin's martyrology were, of course, from Calvin and the martyrology certainly commemorated the Genevan component of the French Reformation. But Calvin figures as only one amongst several – Pierre Viret and Guillaume Farel also played their part – of the theologians who developed a distinctive genre of writing letters of persuasion, admonition, consolation and condolence. Although it may reflect patterns of survival more than anything else, the volume of Calvin's surviving correspondence with the communities 'under the cross' in France is not, in fact, significant before 1558. But Calvin's style was, nevertheless, distinctive. He wrote in plain terms, shorn of elaborate courtesies.[28] He wrote 'familiarly' to individuals whom he had typically never met, emphasizing that what he said came from the heart, 'without hypocrisy'. He aimed to replicate 'the ties of the heart' to which all 'good letters' should appeal.[29] He recognized that letters sent and received sustained both parties. They consoled, confirmed and exhorted individuals faced with the persecutions of the Devil who 'contrives to vex us [through] these distresses'.[30] He sent missives to leading French aristocrats either to bolster their convictions or persuade them to support the true faith.[31] Calvin's correspondence became a practical demonstration of God's truth ingrafted in our hearts by means of a Christian community in a dangerous world. It was with theological conviction that he forced himself to maintain his correspondence, despite the migraines that obliged him to put down his pen to recover strength.[32]

---

[27] *Ibid.*, III, fo. 250.
[28] See, for a well-developed example, F. Bonali-Fiquet (ed.), *Jean Calvin. Lettres à Monsieur et Madame de Falais* (Geneva, 1991).
[29] *Ibid.*, p. 38.   [30] *CO*, XIV, 1751.   [31] E.g. *CO*, XVI, 2774; XVII, 2819.
[32] E.g. his letter to Jacques de Bourgogne, sieur de Falais, of March 1546: 'La difficulté est des fascheries et rompemens de teste qui interviennent pour interrompre vingt fois une lettre, ou encor d'advantaige': cited in *CO*, XVI, 81.

The letters of the martyrs, combined with those of the magisterial reformers, helped to create the commonplaces of French Protestant piety that would reverberate through the remainder of the century.

By 1559, however, the institutionalization of the French Protestant church was under way. Communities and individuals had begun to write to Geneva requesting pastors and seeking advice on a variety of matters. Seven thick volumes of manuscripts in Geneva – many hundreds of letters – provide evidence of the significance of correspondence at this critical juncture.[33] Letters were often sent back from the growing numbers of pastors despatched from Geneva.[34] In these cases, they wrote 'for the entire Church' or 'for all' in that particular locality, and sometimes their signatures were accompanied by a selection of those from the elders of the particular church in question. Other missives were sent by deacons or elders in the name of the 'brethren' of the community, especially where there was no serving pastor in place. Occasionally, as at Uzers, a village in the Vivarais where the local population could apparently find no one suitable for writing the necessary letter, they resorted to the services of a deacon at the church of Aubenas to ask Geneva for a pastor so that, having thrown down 'idolotry' they could thereby follow 'la vraie vérité'.[35] Geneva preferred letters to come from the ensemble of the church where one had been established to reinforce 'bon ordre' and 'bonne union' locally; this gradually became the norm in correspondence with Geneva over the 1560s and 1570s. When the pastors of the church at Metz failed to sign their missives along with the elders in 1580, Geneva wrote to ask why and was relieved to learn that it had been an oversight, rather than a sign of dissension in the community: 'by carelessness [and] not by contempt of the good order, which must reign among you . . .'[36]

The forms of salutation in these letters stressed the bonds that drew people together and often reflected, without being particularly slavish towards, the biblical epistolary norms. Crespin had already drawn attention to the significance of the salutation in Christ's name. 'Salut par Jesus Christ nostre Seigneur' or 'Grace et Paix par nostre Seigneur' were the prelude to an address that was fraternal in the case of pastors and respectfully paternal in the cases of those from the laity. When letters were sent from the consistory to Geneva, they were both paternal and

33 Bibliothèque Publique et Universitaire, Geneva, MS Fr 196, 197, 197a: 402, 403; MS Divers 109, 121.
34 Kingdon, *Geneva and the Coming of the Wars*; P. Wilcox, 'L'envoi de pasteurs aux Églises de France. Trois listes établies par Colladon (1561–1562)', *BSHPF* 139 (1993), 347–74.
35 Cited in Garrison, *Les Protestants*, p. 18.   36 Bergier *et al.*, *Registres de la Compagnie*, IV, p. 320.

fraternal ('Messieurs et très honorés pères et frères'). Some pastors were singularly florid. Pierre Fornelet, the minister in Châlons-sur-Marne who confessed to finding it daunting to address Calvin as 'brother', chose instead: 'The grace and peace of our just God and heavenly Father, in the name of Jesus Christ his Son our hope, lives abundantly in our hearts by virtue of the Holy Spirit.'[37] The fraternal and familial greetings that were so distinctive a feature of the epistolary traffic of French Protestants reflected a religion that 'tu-toied' God.

In the letters, the young French churches developed a mature version of the language and imagery utilized by the martyrs in Crespin's letters. The 'moving dialect of Canaan' was a linguistic register with a semi-private resonance, an intense enrichment with implied biblical *loci* for particular purposes.[38] Protestants reserved it for use among themselves; they could abandon it in their correspondence with others. In letters sent to Geneva, the same phraseology recurs in similar contexts. They have great hopes for the 'glory of God and edification of his Church'.[39] 'We hope that within a brief time the great majority of the town will be won over to the reformation of the Gospel, because every day the flock increases, thanks be to God.'[40] The 'flock', the 'vineyard', the 'ship' need protection, cultivation, direction against the wiles of Satan. The community at Uzès saw itself as a 'small flock', growing 'despite Satan and all his followers, who are unceasing in their efforts to hinder the work of the Lord and the benefits of the reign of our Lord Jesus Christ, balking at his spur'. Adrien Duban from the consistory at Is-sur-Tille in Burgundy wrote that 'Satan incites us almost daily to new combat.' From all quarters, the 'wolves' are at their heels: 'wolves and other wild beasts' surround them, as Pierre d'Airebaudouze said from Uzès.[41] Part of the purpose of this correspondence – and that which survives with Geneva must be imagined as a fraction of the informal networks within France itself – was mutual support. They sought to 'advise and strengthen us according to the gifts and grace that you have from God, to support the earliest followers against the assaults of adversaries and to encourage better the others' wrote 'Du Pasquier' (the pseudonym utilized by Augustin Marlorat) from Rouen on 11 July 1561, anticipating the preparations for the Colloquy of Poissy. 'Our brethren at Paris have written to Mr Perron and me', he continued, 'that it would be good for us to travel to Paris to confer with them ... '[42]

---

[37] 'La Réforme en France', 364.   [38] Garrisson, *Les Protestants*, p. 203.
[39] Bergier *et al.*, *Registres de la Compagnie*, II, p. 167.   [40] *CO*, XVII, 2863.
[41] Bergier *et al.*, *Registres de la Compagnie*, III, p. 176.   [42] 'La Réforme en France', 364.

Everywhere, there was 'labour' needed in the vineyard if the 'harvest of the Lord' was to be gathered. But 'there are few workers' and some of them already felt distinctly overwhelmed. 'Certainly, sensing so great a burden, I lost all courage', wrote de Nort from Toulouse in early 1562.[43] They needed half a dozen pastors to minister to this large city at the delicate moment following the 1562 Edict of January, which opened the possibility of a greater degree of public acceptance of the Reformed faith. The need to create and retain a properly trained ministry for the French churches was one of the generators of the informal networks amongst churches, and between them and Geneva. Even relatively modest communities despatched their elders or notables to seek a pastor. Jean Gerard (pseudonym 'Du Gay') was sent from Geneva to the small town of Blaye because 'Letters were received from an assembly of the faithful ... requesting that we send them [someone] to administer the Word of God to them.'[44] In the absence of the ability to satisfy all requests, the Genevan Company of Pastors attempted to fill the most strategically important gaps – which inevitably meant that larger towns were sacrificed to the needs of the rural hinterlands in the short term.[45] They enjoined the French churches to seek to provide for their own pastoral needs through the dispositions of the colloquies and synods. If that would not suffice, they encouraged communities to send and support financially their most promising young men to study in Geneva for the ministry.[46]

The imperative demands to train and deploy an educated ministry inevitably expanded the range of informal contacts that cemented French Protestantism in the critical period of the 1560s and early 1570s. Maintaining students at college and training them for the ministry was time-consuming and expensive. It required sustained financial commitment

43 Bergier *et al.*, *Registres de la Compagnie*, II, p. 261.   44 *Ibid.*, I, p. 71.
45 See the lament of Pierre Fornelet from Châlons-sur-Marne in October 1561. The city itself was provided for, but his trips into the countryside had raised a demand in many villages that could not possibly be satisfied on a regular basis: 'J'ay veu venir les povres gens, de sept et de huit lieues, tant d'hommes que de femmes, ayans seulement oui dire qu'on preschoit l'Evangile. J'ay esté requis quelquefois d'aller en tant de lieux, que j'eusse désiré me pouvoir diviser en plusieurs parties, pour satisfaire au sainct désir de ceux qui me désiroyent'. *BSHPF* 14 (1865), 365.
46 This became a reiterated reply from the Company to informal requests from French churches. So, when Jean de Brunel, seigneur de Saint-Maurice, wrote to Geneva on 15 November 1583, for example, to ask them to provide a pastor for the church near Grenoble where he was a prominent layman, the company replied diplomatically that there was certainly 'belle apparence de grande moisson' but that 'si vous pouviez rencontrer quelques gentz de bonne esperance pour les faire estudier et les voulussiez envoyer par-deça, suivantz en cela l'exemple de plusieurs autres, ce seroit le plus seur, te tiendrons la main à ce qu'ils ne perdissent point leur temps parmi nous et n'espargnerions en sorte quelconque nos peines pour les rendre au plustost propres ...': Bergier *et al.*, *Registres de la Compagnie*, V, p. 268.

and generated considerable paperwork.[47] Not surprisingly, only the major French churches provided bursaries for students at Geneva. Montpellier, Castres, Metz and others wrote initial letters of recommendation for their students. Then they arranged for funds for these students to be transferred to Geneva or for a capital sum to be managed by named individuals in Geneva on their behalf. The local church wanted updates on the student's progress and sometimes engaged him with a written contract to return and become a pastor in their locality. They were often disappointed. Pierre Perron, a student from St Jean d'Angély, who had promised to return to serve there after his studies in 1581, did not live up to their expectations and they sought to recover something of the bursary that had been provided. Sadly, as the Genevan Company informed the French minister, the 'poor young man' had accumulated a host of debts and, because of his 'limited abilities' and a 'natural lack of intellectual weight', he would be unlikely ever to rise to the challenge of pastor at so important a church as St Jean-d'Angély.[48] The student eventually became a pastor in Haute-Savoie.

Sometimes it was the municipality as well as the church that engaged in these delicate negotiations. In late 1593, the lieutenant, consuls and church at Castres joined forces to write to Geneva to ask that its bursary student, Daniel Rafin, return to assist Lambert Daneau in his pastoral duties. At the same time, they took the opportunity to ask about some money that Castres had advanced for the ransom of a Protestant bookseller captured by the League at Lyon and also the administration of a bequest for the French bursary and college at Geneva.[49] The letter is typical of the density of informal contacts that cemented the Protestant communities. Nor should one forget the anxious fathers for whom a letter was the only practical way of finding out how their sons were getting on and ensuring that 'in my absence he does not debauch himself'.[50] It is not surprising that, as the cohorts of French students went through the academy at Geneva, they developed friendships that continued after their formal training, to be resuscitated periodically in colloquies or provincial and national synods. The same must have also been the case for the other Protestant colleges and academies in the French orbit and the two future Protestant universities at Montauban

---

[47] See K. Maag, *Seminary or University? The Genevan Academy and Reformed Higher Education, 1560–1620* (Aldershot, 1995), pp. 105–10.

[48] *Ibid.*, p. 278.   [49] Bergier *et al.*, *Registres de la Compagnie*, VI, p. 314.

[50] Pierre Agard from Châteaudouble in Dauphiné about his son, David (who would, in due course, become a pastor in Dauphiné and the Vivarais): *ibid.*, VII, p. 202.

and Saumur that trained the pastors for France and the principality of Béarn. According to Janine Garrisson, about half the pastors in France between 1559 and 1574 came from these establishments and the proportion rose to three-quarters for the period thereafter.[51] The development is likely to have further concentrated the informal networks within the established pastorate of French Protestantism.

The process of proposing ministers to churches also generated a good deal of informal networking. It can be seen at close quarters in the correspondence of the Company of Pastors at Geneva and we know, especially for the early years, how ministers were trained, examined, and then subsequently recommended and placed in the French churches.[52] The process involved substantial negotiation and mediation. But the role of the Company of Pastors in providing for the French pastorate was, after the first few years, limited. The brokering for ministers continued, instead, at local, regional and sometimes national levels within France as churches sought to provide themselves with the most appropriate ministers. There were delicate negotiations between churches. Ministers were sometimes invited to preach in other churches. They were lent from one church to another. Questions of payment, rarely adequate and often delivered late or not in full, entered into the equation, as did individual domestic circumstances and personal ambitions. They took into account the informal reputations of ministers and their 'bonne conversation'. The brokerage was often carried out by the elders through correspondence or at the meetings of synods. One particularly bitter case involved Etienne Noel, the minister at Grenoble in 1562. He had been the minister in the Savoyard valley of Angrogna before he had arrived, providentially as the consistory of Grenoble saw it, to answer their urgent needs. In 1563, Angrogna sought his return but Grenoble was reluctant to release him until they had found a replacement – and that would depend on the church at Lyon finding them someone appropriate. The Lyon church suggested that it could spare its minister for three months of the year to serve at Grenoble. Etienne Noel pronounced himself willing to serve wherever God put him, but the churches involved, having sent letters fruitlessly between one another, eventually submitted the affair to Geneva. Theodore Beza, writing in the name of the Company, advised that Noel should return to Angrogna but Grenoble refused to listen. Angrogna then sought to use an aristocratic network and wrote to Marguerite de Savoie. She took up the cause and despatched missives to

---

[51] Garrisson, *Les Protestants*, p. 211.
[52] Kingdon, *Geneva and the Coming of the Wars*, esp. chaps. 2–4.

Grenoble and Geneva, stressing the often overlooked needs of the 'infinity of poor people in the valleys of Angrogna, Lucerve and St Martin'.[53] Grenoble seems, eventually, to have released Noel but the case, by no means isolated, is a reminder that the correspondence of the French churches reflects at every turn the equality that was a fundamental feature of their constitution.

Pastors sought to relieve some of the loneliness of their duties in the wider networks of the movement. Simon Goulard, separated from his family in Burgundy in 1583, felt isolated and vulnerable, surrounded by hostile Catholics. He longed to be back in Geneva with its libraries, his friends and a sense of being at the heart of things.[54] Others felt the sudden chill of isolation when under attack from Jesuit critics or malicious libels. Théophile Cassegrain suddenly found himself immersed in 'the thick of my affairs' thanks to a letter that he had supposedly written to the bishop of Evreux, apparently opening up the possibility of his reconciliation with the Catholic church, one that his former 'brother', Victor Palma Cayet ('ce miserable apostat Cahier' as the Genevan pastors called him), had chosen to publish.[55] The ink was hardly dry on the Edict of Nantes when Cassegrain felt the desperate need for support from the wider networks. 'Each is shut up in his own affairs,' he lamented to his brethren in Geneva, 'and so all the poor scattered sheep remain without order and communication with the other provinces, and I can hardly find anyone who can offer me either good counsel or even bad counsel.'[56] Despite being poorly rewarded for their travel and other costs, French ministers regularly attended colloquies and synods. Although they did not meet regularly, the fact that participation was so good suggests that pastors found them rewarding.[57] They recharged their batteries, recovered their sense of purpose and wider community, and revived their informal channels of contact.

Other Huguenot pastors took advantage of the opportunity to serve as chaplains to the French Protestant aristocracy, or to teach at one of the academies. Daniel Chamier had an itinerant Protestant education at Alès, Orange, Nîmes and Geneva before serving as pastor at a

---

[53] T. Heyer, 'Marguerite de France, Duchesse de Savoie. Ses Rapports avec Genève', *Mémoires et documents publiés par la société d'histoire et d'archéologie de Genève* 15 (1865), 143; and also her letter edited in *BSHPF* 28 (1879), p. 306. For the background to the Noel case, see *Registres de la Compagnie*, III, pp. 182–3, 186–91.

[54] Letter of 13/23 March 1583 printed in L. C. Jones, *Simon Goulart, sa vie et son œuvre, 1543–1628* (Geneva, 1917), pp. 367–8.

[55] Bergier *et al.*, *Registres de la Compagnie*, VII, p. 293.

[56] *Ibid.*, VII, p. 300.   [57] Garrisson, *Les Protestants*, p. 216.

succession of churches in the Rhône valley and lower Languedoc. He
was eventually nominated pastor at Montauban and professor at the
university there in 1612. By then, he had become one of the trusted
leaders of the movement, a deputy at the political assemblies leading up
to the Edict of Nantes, a president of the national synod at Gap in 1603
and again at Privas in 1612, and a distinguished controversialist with the
Jesuits in 1600 and 1601.[58] At Gap, he would have certainly met Samuel
Loumeau, the minister from La Rochelle from 1594 to 1629, someone
who had already been a deputy to the assembly at Saumur in 1601 and
who participated in the national synod at Vitré in 1617.[59] Loumeau had
a lower public profile than Chamier and a less mobile career. Still, he
used the informal networks of the Protestant movement to the full. He
was a physician turned pastor who wrote and received letters from the
Protestant deputies at court and the great Huguenot scholar-statesman,
Duplessis-Mornay. He exchanged news about recent publications, political happenings and his great passion in life, botany, with Protestant
friends in the Netherlands and England. Loumeau's correspondence suggests the magnitude of informal networks within French Protestantism
mapped onto a wider continental Calvinism, which provided a far from
exclusive framework for intellectual and scientific communication as well
as theological and political discourse.

The constitution of the Protestant churches required an informal network and the underlying shared attitudes and behaviour that went with
it to function effectively. It was an implied and inevitable consequence of
the consistorial oligarchies that represented and steered French Protestant communities everywhere. The fundamental principle of French
Protestant ecclesiology, enunciated in the Discipline of 1559, and fore-
shadowed in the Articles of Poitiers of 1557, was that 'No church may
pretend to have primacy, or domination, over another.'[60] The principle was reinforced in the early synods with statements about equality
among ministers 'neither one, nor another, especially within the same
church', among elders and deacons in consistory and even among the
deputies sent by the Protestants to represent their affairs at court. They
were all equal under the one Confession and the one Discipline to which
they had committed themselves by oath. Establishing the principle in

---

[58] Details in C. Read, *Daniel Chamier* (Paris, 1858).
[59] Details of his contacts are contained in his diary in *Archives Historiques de Saintonge et Aunis* 15 (1898), 32–97.
[60] B. Roussel and S. Deyon, 'Pour un nouvel "Aymon". Les premiers synodes nationaux des Églises réformées en France (1559–1567)', *BSHPF* 139 (1993), 567.

practice, however, required particular churches to apply the Confession and the Discipline in individual cases, and that raised delicate questions. Channels of communication and consultation within the Protestant community were essential to resolving these questions and to the functioning reality of the churches. The colloquies and provincial synods were particularly important in dealing with a wide variety of business – appointment of pastors, support for students, disciplinary cases, and pensions for the families of deceased ministers. The tasks of their moderators and secretaries were significant and extended beyond the actual meeting of the synod. Summoning a provincial synod required mobilizing the colloquies by means of letters issued at least a month in advance. The colloquies in turn passed the message to the local churches.[61] The provinces generated memoranda and paperwork on particular issues that were then discussed in national synods. The role of the moderator and his assistant at the national synod was, therefore, even more fundamental, requiring a combination of exceptional political and administrative talents. Michel Béraud, who was three times moderator of national synods in the sixteenth century, demonstrated that the role needed the experience of a networker, someone who had served in a number of different churches and whose efficacy as a controversialist would stand him in good stead.[62] The French churches were not particularly bureaucratic, but because the constitution was federal and pluralist, it required regular consultation and correspondence to work effectively.

There are many examples of this process at work. One of the problems faced by the young French church was that of unauthorized 'hedge' preachers (or 'coureurs') who were accepted by communities in need of a minister. The national synods published the names and descriptions of these colourful characters so that they might be more easily recognized and removed. But, in practice, that meant the churches keeping in touch with one another. So, to take one example, the provincial synod at Ploermel in Brittany on February 1565, found itself confronted by the case of one René Chamviry who had been enthusiastically received as a minister at Vieillevigne.[63] He had told them he had served as pastor at Condom in Gascony but that he had been separated from the church as a result of the first civil war. His story had seemed plausible but, as it turned out, the moderator of the synod had received a letter sent from the province of Berry on 3 September of the preceding year explaining

---

[61] The process is outlined in Bibliothèque Mazarine, MS 2605, fo. 23.

[62] E. and E. Haag, *La France protestante*, 10 vols. (Paris, 1846–58), entry on Béraud.

[63] J.-Y. Carluer, 'Deux synodes provinciaux bretons au XVIe siècle', *BSHPF* 135 (1989), 346.

that, in reality, Chamviry had been deposed and excommunicated by their province. The synod at Ploermel was not impressed by his submission of two suspiciously recent letters, purporting to come from ministers in Berry and attesting to his good character, and he was deposed.

With an implied equality among the churches in France, it was natural that they would seek Geneva's advice and mediation. This led Theodore Beza and the Company of Pastors into deliberating informally on all kinds of difficult or controversial issues affecting the churches. They urged their French 'brethren' to conduct themselves 'in proper unity and fraternity', to proceed 'faithfully and in edification', taking care to avoid 'all factions and dissension, and that to which all this might lead you, namely pride, avarice and ambition, following instead simplicity and charity'.[64] These aspirations were difficult to realize in practice when it came to persuading churches to remunerate their pastors satisfactorily, sustain the rural churches in their neighbourhood, sponsor a student or deliberate on delicate individual issues. There were plenty of the latter. What should the church at Maillé in the Loire do, for example, having discovered its local seigneur, François de la Tour-Landry, had been guilty of gross immorality?[65] The congregation's rights of worship were dependent on the 'culte seigneurial' in the chapel of his château. If they censored him publicly they would probably lose those rights. The problem was compounded by the fact that the minister was Jean le Gasgneux, something of a firebrand. Or again, there was the question of an elder in a church who was accused of attempting to murder a relative who had severely provoked him.[66] Then there was the matter of whether it was morally right or ecclesiastically healthy for Protestants to rent Catholic church property.[67] On the one hand, this might create a situation of split loyalties and was certainly not to be encouraged. On the other hand, these were often the notables in their communities whose support for the church was important. These are just a few of the issues that were referred to Beza and the Company of Pastors. These affairs were either not appropriate for discussion at a provincial or national synod, or they had been discussed there and the issue had not been resolved. The Genevan response often made clear that they knew they had no formal jurisdiction in any of these cases. But they also accepted their responsibility as a sister church, in 'charité commune' to offer advice where appropriate.

Sometimes Geneva politely declined to offer an opinion. As Beza said in reply to a memorandum from La Rochelle in 1594, 'it is unlikely that

---

[64] Bergier *et al.*, *Registres de la Compagnie*, II, p. 175.   [65] *Ibid.*, II, p. 232.   [66] *Ibid.*, VII, p. 378.
[67] *Ibid.*, IV, p. 432.

my letters carry more weight than the provincial synod'.[68] The matters on which they wanted his views in 1594 were, in reality, the substantial questions that had been posed by the civil wars. How was the security of French Protestants to be guaranteed by law? What degree of restriction of public worship would be acceptable in the pacification effort? Were princes sincere and to be trusted? Was it 'lawful (*salva conscientiae pace*) to take up arms'? These were complex matters, which required prudent and confidential treatment. They could be raised in a private forum, one that was probably essential if the Protestants in France were to react to events with a degree of political coherence. The deputies at the French court for the Protestant provinces, the presentation of cases before the privy council, the households of the aristocrats who articulated the Protestant interests, the raising of requisite military and financial resources for the Huguenot war effort all depended on informal networks for their effectiveness. This was how provinces were linked, petitions formulated, answers pressed for, communities mobilized and international connections cemented. The complex social geography of the French Protestant movement with its differing urban, aristocratic and squirearchical roots could only have been brought together to constructive purpose in these informal ways.

Frameworks of friendship provided recurrent ideals and images, which were expressed in the epistolary traffic of the French Huguenot world. They were present, even when the reality was otherwise. Although French Protestantism avoided a major theological fissure in the sixteenth century, it harboured internal quarrels and debates. These were often, however, expressed in terms of one party's failure to observe the benevolent disposition expected between Protestants. In the Mutonis affair of 1561, the provincial synod of lower Languedoc tried to mediate between the resident pastor at Nîmes, Mauget, and his neighbouring colleague Mutonis, pastor at Montagnac, whom a local nobleman wanted to see installed as a second minister at Nîmes.[69] When the synod intervened it detected no doctrinal issue. It recognized that Mutonis might not have sought proper permission to be released from his responsibilities at Montagnac. But the essence of the debate really centred on a letter that Mutonis had written to Mauget, one that they later described to Geneva as 'seditious, scandalous, mutinous and turbulent'. This was emphatically not the example that ministers were expected to set by way of mutual 'benevolence' and 'good conversation'

[68] *Ibid.*, VII, p. 482 and refs.
[69] Briefly described in Kingdon, *Geneva and the Coming of the Wars*, pp. 47–8.

and Geneva adroitly engineered a reproof for the offence and Mutonis's transfer to another church in lower Languedoc.

The Morély affair was much larger and more complex. Jean Morély's famous book, the *Traicté de la Discipline & Police Chrestienne*, published in Lyon in 1562, proposed a shift in the centre of authority within individual churches away from the consistory and towards the community at large. Such a move, had it occurred, would probably have changed significantly the operation of these informal networks. The affair climaxed when a stack of Latin letters that Morély had written to the polemical pastor of the church at Orléans, Hugues Roseau, were confiscated from his study by his and Morély's enemies in the summer of 1566.[70] They were translated by the professor of Hebrew at the new Reformed academy at Orléans and shown to the elders and deacons of the consistory. They were said to contain heresy, although that was not so easily proved as the charge that he had violated the social code of the movement. He had called the respected minister Nicolas des Gallars a liar and a fake, who counterfeited brotherly benevolence. Theodore Beza was referred to as the 'Jupiter of the lake of Geneva' and 'this new Antichrist'. Other ministers were also mocked or attacked. As things turned out, it would be an important turning point for Morély. He wrote apologetically to Nicolas des Gallars and Beza, attributing his letters to a loss of temper. He volunteered not to pursue his ambition to seek changes to ecclesiastical governance. But the damage to his reputation proved too great and Jeanne d'Albret removed him from the post of tutor to the future king of Navarre. His supporters were forced to withdraw and regroup. Beza's final letter to him, dated 25 March 1567, used unusually strong language: 'Because it is you who has violated the virginity of the French churches'. Morély had bruised the soft tissue of the French churches and Beza recognized how vulnerable it would be to abuse its decorum and norms.

If the French Protestants had become the majority faith in the kingdom at any stage in the second half of the sixteenth century, the picture of these informal networks would doubtless have been very different. As it was, however, Catholics resented the private inwardness that these networks represented and suspected them of fomenting sedition. Such views were common currency among Catholics by the time of the League but they were voiced much earlier, too. A member of Lyon's consular elite (possibly Claude de Rubys, the city's *procureur*) expressed his suspicions of the Protestant 'consistoires et sinodes' in an

---

70 R. M. Kingdon, *Geneva and the Consolidation of the French Protestant Movement, 1564–1572* (Geneva, 1967), pp. 83–96.

undated memorandum, perhaps written in the 1570s:[71] 'they confer, treat and resolve all affairs involving the exercise of justice among themselves, raise funds, enlist soldiers, and gather intelligence within and without the kingdom; in short, they have established a republic and exercise a secret hostility, to the ruin of the king and his state, and they have induced their followers to rise up against their natural prince'. If these lateral communicative and corresponding energies of the French Protestant movement were neither unique nor as exclusive as its opponents feared, they nevertheless provided a subtle, pervasive and essential element to the unity and identity of the emerging Huguenot world.

France was a huge kingdom in the sixteenth century, a good deal of it relatively recently acquired by the French crown. Travellers were repeatedly impressed by its cultural and linguistic variety. At its head lay an absolute monarchy that acted as a focus for the unity of its political institutions. Establishing a functioning Protestant community across this expanse would have been a considerable endeavour at any time in early modern Europe. To do so against the determined will of the French monarchy or with only a reluctantly accorded and limited set of concessions to establish churches required exceptional means of sustaining dispersed communities and giving them a sense of common purpose. The 'parti formé' of the Huguenots was more than a way of raising contributions for military purposes and sustaining Protestant aristocrats in French high politics. It was a sense of belonging that was sustained by informal networks of communication, which in turn lifted the horizons of the movement beyond local and regional concerns. These informal networks help to explain how the diffused structures of authority within French Protestantism nevertheless sustained its unity.

---

[71] AM Lyon, GG 77. Cited from T. Watson, 'The Lyon City Council, c. 1525–1575: Politics, Culture, Religion', D.Phil. thesis, University of Oxford (2000), pp. 241–2. I am grateful to Dr Watson for his permission to cite his thesis in advance of its publication.

7. The Edict of Nantes and its institutions

Raymond A. Mentzer

The Edict of Nantes is among the most celebrated documents in French historical memory. The value attached to the legislation, promulgated by Henri IV in April 1598, has been at once real and symbolic. In concrete terms, it provided the legal and institutional framework for bringing an end to some forty years of religious strife. The edict also possessed a strong representational quality, embodying for people within both confessional communities an innovative experiment in religious pluralism and the complex processes of mediation and conciliation. Recent public and scholarly opinion has emphasized the act as an early and important step toward religious coexistence. A few observers have further suggested that it at least implied modern notions of toleration.[1] Whatever the edict's ultimate significance, contemporary reaction was decidedly mixed. Catholics and Protestants benefited from its specific arrangements as well as the overall goals and principles. At the same time, voices in each camp raised objections to many of the provisions and concessions. Not surprisingly, neither party was entirely satisfied.[2] Still, the measure held the promise of peace and protection for French Protestants; it also offered an opportunity for the elaboration of a stable and enduring Huguenot culture.

Although the edict failed to grant Protestants full equality with Catholics, it created an intelligible and logical structure in which followers of the two faiths might live together without violence and bloodshed. It permitted the exercise of the Reformed religion, but under restricted circumstances. Huguenots also received guarantees of their civil and

---

[1] P. Benedict, '*Un Roi, une Loi, deux Fois*: Parameters for the History of Catholic–Reformed Co-existence in France, 1555–1685' in O. P. Grell and B. Scribner (eds.), *Tolerance and Intolerance in the European Reformation* (Cambridge, 1996), pp. 65–93, closely examines the issues of coexistence and toleration.

[2] Recent studies of the edict include B. Cottret, *1598. L'Édit de Nantes. Pour en finir avec les guerres de religion* (Paris, 1997); J. Garrisson, *L'Édit de Nantes* (Paris, 1998); M. Grandjean and B. Roussel (eds.), *Coexister dans l'intolérance. L'Édit de Nantes (1598)* (Geneva, 1998).

political rights, which had been an important feature of the various edicts of pacification, truces and peace arrangements that punctuated the religious wars. In the immediate, the edict gave the Protestant minority religious security, legal identity and juridical status.

The royal legislation confirmed Catholicism as the dominant religion of France.[3] Yet the king's Catholic subjects were far from satisfied and they soon set about contesting its provisions. Catholic worship, above all the celebration of the Mass, was reinstated throughout the kingdom and ecclesiastical property seized during the protracted warfare was returned to the Catholic clergy. The dangerous and detestable 'heresy', however, had not been eradicated. Eventually, the Catholic state and church, supported by a majority of the king's subjects, managed to turn the edict against the very Protestants to whom it extended protection. The crown and clergy found various elements in the legislation useful devices for restricting the Reformed community and even persecuting its members. Accordingly, scholars continue to debate questions surrounding the ultimate beneficiaries of the edict and the extent to which it offered a robust workable solution for the prolonged confessional discord.[4]

The act is a lengthy and complex document, composed of four distinct parts, indeed four separate legislative texts.[5] The edict proper consists of ninety-two 'perpetual and irrevocable' articles focusing on the general pacification effort.[6] Fifty-six secret articles, so labelled because they were not immediately published, complement the general articles. These clauses clarified particular issues and addressed specific individuals and towns to which exemptions applied. Finally, two royal brevets or warrants complete the ensemble. They contained controversial concessions, which the king granted to the Huguenots, realizing that the *parlements* would never agree to the arrangements. The brevets provided an annual royal subsidy for the pastors of the Reformed churches, recognized Huguenot

---

[3] M. Venard, 'L'Église catholique bénéficiaire de l'édit de Nantes' in Grandjean and Roussel, *Coexister dans l'intolérance*, pp. 283–302, deftly explores the manner by which the Catholic church benefited profoundly from the edict.

[4] See, by way of recent examples, the comments of B. Cottret, 'Pourquoi l'Édit de Nantes a-t-il réussi?', in Grandjean and Roussel, *Coexister dans l'intolérance*, pp. 447–61; M. Wolfe, 'Protestant Reactions to the Conversion of Henry IV', in M. Wolfe (ed.), *Changing Identities in Early Modern France* (Durham, NC, 1997), pp. 382–4.

[5] J. Garrisson (ed.), *L'Édit de Nantes* (Biarritz, 1997) provides an annotated edition of the text of the edict. For an English translation, see R. Mousnier, *The Assassination of Henry IV*, trans. by J. Spencer (London, 1973), pp. 316–63.

[6] Though the edict was deemed 'perpétuel et irrévocable', perpetuity was not 'éternité' in the minds of royal jurists and the Catholic faithful. See M. Carbonnier-Burkard, 'Les Préambules des Édits de Pacification (1562–1598)' in Grandjean and Roussel, *Coexister dans l'intolérance*, pp. 91–2.

possession of surety towns (*places de sûreté*), and instituted the crown's financial support of the Huguenot military garrisons that protected these strongholds.

The repercussions were, of course, profound and far-reaching. The document's provisions recognizing the legal existence of the Reformed churches and establishing fortified cities where Protestants could worship freely are probably its best-known feature. The text contained other important clauses, which are frequently overlooked. It also drew considerably, sometimes word for word, from the many earlier edicts of pacification. Since the 1560s, negotiators had repeatedly struggled to find acceptable mechanisms to restore Catholicism, authorize Reformed worship and institute judicial assurances and security arrangements for the Huguenots.[7] In this sense, many of the stipulations in the Edict of Nantes were the culmination of protracted discussion and substantial experience in pragmatic concessions by all parties.

It opened with the king's proclamation of a general amnesty, followed by a statement of intent to restore civil and religious peace. It affirmed the fundamental principle of freedom of conscience, even as it set restraints on Reformed worship. Huguenot nobles with rights of *haute justice* were allowed private services on their estates. The edict also authorized Protestant religious practice in locales where it had been exercised in 1596 and 1597. Finally, worship was permitted at two towns, or more accurately their suburbs, within each *bailliage* or *sénéchaussée*; royal commissioners would determine the appropriate locations.

At the same time, Protestants were forbidden to appropriate Catholic churches. Struggles over sacred space, in this instance places for worship, had been the source of considerable friction. Still, Reformed congregations did have permission to construct temples in towns under their control. Protestants were also assigned their own special cemeteries. Again, disputes over funeral ceremonies and burial sites, sacral ground of another sort, had been and would continue to be particularly severe.[8] The secret articles contained, among other things, permission for the Protestants to have their own bells to summon the faithful, maintain their own

---

[7] F. Garrisson, *Essai sur les Commissions d'Application de l'Édit de Nantes: Règne de Henri IV* (Montpellier, 1964), pp. 12–20. See P. Roberts, 'Huguenot Petitioning during the Wars of Religion', in this volume, chap. 5.

[8] Garrisson (ed.), *L'Édit de Nantes*, pp. 235 49; P. Roberts, 'The Most Crucial Battle of the Wars of Religion? The Conflict over Sites for Reformed Worship in Sixteenth-century France', *ARG* (1998), 247–67; also her 'Contesting Sacred Space: Burial Disputes in Sixteenth-century France' in B. Gordon and P. Marshall (eds.), *The Place of the Dead. Death and Remembrance in Late Medieval and Early Modern Europe* (Cambridge, 2000), pp. 131–48.

schools and, perhaps most important, continue their various religious assemblies.

The Reformed faithful were assured access to public and royal offices as well as admission to educational institutions. Again, these were major concerns among Huguenot professionals, members of the bourgeoisie and aristocrats.[9] The edict even created or, more precisely, confirmed special bipartisan law courts, the so-called *chambres de l'Édit* that were attached to the *parlements* in Protestant regions.[10] Altogether, 40 per cent of the general articles dealt with these judicial arrangements.[11]

There were important provisions designed to reassure Catholics and, in critical ways, reaffirm and restore their pre-eminent religious position and privilege. While the arrangements confined Reformed worship to specific geographic circumstances, Catholics could freely celebrate their religion everywhere in the realm. The Mass and other Catholic religious observances were reintroduced in those places where Huguenots had banned them. Protestants were forbidden to work or keep their shops open on Catholic feast days; restrictions were placed on the printing and sale of Reformed religious books; perhaps most onerously, Huguenots were obliged to pay the traditional tithe to Catholic ecclesiastical officials.

The two royal brevets provided annual financial support for Reformed ministers in compensation for the obligation that Protestants pay the tithe. They also permitted the Huguenots to maintain garrisons in the so-called surety towns that they had controlled as of August 1597. The monarchy agreed to subsidize the Huguenot garrisons in these strongholds.[12] However, the promised payments were always uncertain and the crown made them only irregularly after Henri IV's death in 1610. The brevets were finally withdrawn in 1629, following the Peace of Alès, which ended the Huguenots' unsuccessful struggle with Cardinal Richelieu and Louis XIII.

---

[9] Garrisson, *L'Édit de Nantes*, pp. 292–4; R. A. Mentzer, *Blood and Belief: Family Survival and Confessional Identity among the Provincial Huguenot Nobility* (West Lafayette, IN, 1994), p. 124.

[10] The appellation *chambre de l'Édit* dates not from the Edict of Nantes, but from the Edict of Beaulieu, which in 1576 first envisaged their creation.

[11] An excellent recent study of this aspect of the edict is S. Capot, *Justice et religion en Languedoc au temps de l'Édit de Nantes: la chambre de l'Édit de Castres (1579–1679)* (Paris, 1998).

[12] A helpful introduction to the complexities of the surety places is P. Chareyre, 'Les places de sûreté' in *L'Édit de Nantes* (Paris, 1998), pp. 51–62. According to Garrisson, *L'Édit de Nantes*, pp. 299–300, the substantial number of 'places of refuge' included fifty-nine surety towns, eighteen 'places of marriage' (small towns and villages, often near a place of surety), fifty-seven or so 'particular' fortified places whose garrisons the Huguenots agreed to maintain at their own expense, and a number of Protestant royal free cities, which had the right to provide their own defence.

The edict was conspicuously silent on matters of theological position and did not, in fact, concern itself directly with questions of belief.
Rather, it sought to initiate the pacification process and to create social
and institutional structures conducive to concord among members of the
two faiths.[13] The principal vehicles for promoting peaceful coexistence
between Catholic and Protestant were the royal commissions for implementation of the edict and the special chambers of justice attached to the
parlements in Protestant regions. In both cases, the concept of bipartisan
participation became an important component in gaining acceptance
for the reconciliation process.

The commissions of implementation are the less understood of the two
institutions, due largely to the paucity of documentation. In the interests
of the proper application of the Edict of Nantes, the king, beginning in
I 599, appointed commissions composed of two delegates, one Catholic
and the other Protestant, to verify and execute the edict throughout the
provinces. These officials had the difficult, unenviable task of ensuring
the edict's legal observation and transforming its myriad of complicated
provisions into appropriate everyday conduct. On a practical level, they
sought, within months of the edict's promulgation and registration, to
guarantee Protestant worship in those towns where it was permitted, re-
establish the celebration of the Mass everywhere in the kingdom, restore
ecclesiastical property to the Catholic church and its clergy, and assure
individual and collective security for both Catholics and Protestants. In
all of this, the commissioners displayed in tangible fashion the power of
the monarchical state as the arbiter of civil conflict, guarantor of public
repose, and protector of the rights pertaining to the Catholic majority as
well as the Reformed minority.

The notion of bipartisan commissions – prominent persons from each
faith working together for peace – emerged gradually over the course of
the religious conflict. The crown had attempted to use various officials
and envoys for the implementation of the numerous edicts of pacification,
which preceded that of Nantes. Thus, as Henri IV set about creating the
commissions in I 599, he profited from the previous experience. The
crown's insistence upon confessionally mixed commissions aimed at increased confidence in the balance and impartiality of their decisions. In
addition, the king conferred the title of intendant upon the commission-

---

[13] This innovative focus on political agreement, the interests of the state and the place of the citizen
as opposed to the believer constitute, according to O. Christin, *La paix de religion: l'autonomisation de
la raison politique au XVIe siècle* (Paris, I 997), an autonomizing process, which increasingly developed
support for religious peace in and of itself.

ers, thereby underscoring the importance of their mission, their direct dependence on the monarch and his delegation of royal power. They operated within well-defined geographic limits, which usually corresponded to the territorial jurisdiction of the *parlements*. There were, for example, two commissions for the *parlement* of Toulouse and four within the jurisdiction of the *parlement* of Paris. The Catholic members generally came from the judicial ranks and upper administrative echelons. The Huguenot commissioners were also individuals of stature and influence, especially within the particular provinces that they served. They included judges, governors, political leaders and important nobles.[14]

The commissioners' assignment was thorny, painstaking and highly charged. The process involved far more than the simple execution of the edict; it meant publicizing the legislation and, more important, negotiating its implementation at innumerable towns and villages throughout the realm.[15] The commissioners carefully explained the overall objectives and benefits as well as the specific provisions of the edict to local authorities. As they toured their geographic districts, they met at every stop with clergymen, nobles, royal officials, municipal authorities and other notables. These ceremonial assemblies typically began with a reading of the edict's text and the specific instructions applicable to their region. The commissioners exhorted the assembled leaders to 'assist them with all their power in the execution of the edict'.[16] Lengthy hearings and heated discussions followed. Eventually, in accordance with article 92, the commissioners enjoined the prominent and powerful within each locale to swear a formal collective oath to maintain and observe the terms of the royal legislation and the settlement which the commissioners and townspeople had achieved.[17]

As the commissioners set about their work, it became clear that the antagonism between Catholic and Protestant possessed a twofold dynamic. Catholics were anxious to see the enforcement of article 3. It provided for the restoration of the Mass and the safe return of Catholic priests and members of monastic orders, who promptly reclaimed their tithes, revenues from benefices, and property to include churches, monastery buildings and land, which Huguenots had confiscated or badly damaged

---

[14] Garrisson, *Commissions d'application*, pp. 37–53.
[15] D. Hickey, 'Enforcing the Edict of Nantes: The 1599 Commissions and Local Elites in Dauphiné and Poitou-Aunis' in K. Cameron, M. Greengrass and P. Roberts (eds.), *The Adventure of Religious Pluralism in Early Modern France* (Berne, 2000), pp. 65–83.
[16] Quoted in Garrisson, *Commissions d'application*, pp. 53–4.
[17] *Ibid.*, pp. 53–5; E. Rabut, *Le roi, l'église et le temple. L'exécution de l'Édit de Nantes en Dauphiné* (Grenoble, 1987), pp. 24–5.

during the warfare. Protestants could be less than fully co-operative and sorting out the tangle of rival claims, especially for assets seized, sold and resold, was no simple matter. The courts, particularly the *chambres de l'Édit*, sometimes became the final arbiters in these matters. For Huguenots, the proper application of articles 9, 10 and 11, which assured public Reformed worship, often in overwhelmingly Catholic areas, was vital. Not surprisingly, Catholics frequently opposed these provisions. Among the commissioners' additional duties were securing Protestant access to cemeteries and ensuring the availability of educational opportunities and social welfare services for the impoverished and ailing of both faiths. These mediators even had to negotiate systems for the sale of meat during Lent and the common use of municipal bells in summoning Catholic and Protestant congregations for their respective services.[18]

The vast territory of the *parlement* of Paris required four separate commissions. The principal focus of the deputies despatched for the strongly Catholic Île de France, Picardy and Champagne was the resolution of objections to the introduction of Reformed worship at two places within each *bailliage*. South-west of Paris in the area of Poitou and Aunis, where Protestants were more numerous and more powerful, the major problem was the peaceful re-establishment of Catholic practices in Huguenot towns. The assignment was inevitably sensitive. Protestants at La Rochelle, for instance, eventually agreed to the reintroduction of the Mass, but were more resistant to the restitution of cemeteries to Catholics and public observation of Catholic feast days. Towards the south-east at Lyon and in the Forez, the issue was once again the concession of towns where Protestants could hold sermon services, celebrate the Lord's Supper, baptize their infants, perform marriage ceremonies and bury their dead. Leaders of Catholic towns vigorously opposed the prospect of Reformed services within their walls or even in adjoining suburbs. Commissioners in the Loire valley confronted similar obstacles apropos appropriate places for Reformed religious practice.[19]

In the southern province of Languedoc, Protestants constituted the majority of inhabitants in important towns such as Castres, Montpellier, Montauban, Nîmes and Uzès. In these and many smaller rural settlements, the commissioners' essential goal again was the re-establishment

---

[18] J.-Y. Carluer, *Protestants et Bretons. La mémoire des hommes et des lieux* (Carrière-sous-Poissy, 1993), p. 75; Garrisson, *Commissions d'application*, pp. 195–6; Garrisson, *L'Édit de Nantes*, pp. 346–9.

[19] T. Boffard, 'L'Application de l'Édit de Nantes à Lyon, 1598–1685', *BSHPF* 145 (1999), 285–319; Cottret, *L'Édit de Nantes*, pp. 217–20; P. de Félice, *La Réforme en Blaisois, documents inédits. Registre du consistoire (1665–1677)* (Orléans, 1885), pp. 1–43; Garrisson, *Commissions d'application*, pp. 79–108.

of the religious prerogatives for Catholics. At Montauban, Catholic expectations went beyond the reintroduction of the Mass and the restoration and reconstruction of churches and monasteries. Returning clerics
campaigned, for example, to hold public processions on religious feasts
such as Corpus Christi and demanded a cemetery solely for Catholic
burials. Bishops, abbots and other Catholic officials voiced similar claims
in Protestant towns throughout the region. On the other hand, intensely
Catholic towns resisted Reformed worship and were equally loath to see
Protestants secure positions in the municipal administration.[20]

The commissions established for Dauphiné are perhaps the best
studied of the entire kingdom. In a division suggestive of the overall situation in France, the principal task in the northern and heavily Catholic
portion of the province was the safeguard of the minority Protestants'
right to worship. Further south the commissioners endeavoured to
ensure the return of the Catholic clergy along with the reinstatement of
the Mass and restoration of ecclesiastical property within dense pockets
of Protestantism.

In what was perhaps an indication of the challenge confronting them,
a president of the *parlement* of Grenoble joined the Catholic and Protestant commissioners for Dauphiné. Together, they, or their delegates in
the more remote areas, mediated a delicate process.[21] In predominantly
Catholic towns, they sorted out the appropriate sites, often nearby ham-
lets and suburbs, for Protestant services and construction of temples.
Conversely, they worked to reinstitute the Mass in Protestant locales
and protect the minority Catholic residents. The decisions were sometimes disputed and negotiating acceptable compromises could be trying.
Now and again, the commissioners were themselves divided.[22] In short,
promoting peaceful coexistence proved tedious, demanding and occasionally frustrating.[23]

Huguenot communities, for their part, appear to have regarded the
commissioners as authoritative guarantors of the civil order announced
by the Edict of Nantes. At Dieulefit in Dauphiné, for example, Protestants
were quite explicit in securing 'permission' from the commissioners that
municipal authorities would make a substantial annual payment toward

---

[20] Garrisson, *Commissions d'application*, pp. 197–215, 259–61.
[21] Hickey, 'Enforcing the Edict of Nantes'.
[22] Garrison, *Commissions d'Application*, pp. 149–55, 188–97, 252–9, 265; Rabut, *Le roi, l'église et le temple*, pp. 9–47.
[23] Protestant claims of Catholic mistreatment continued for decades. The Huguenot political assemblies and later the national synods of the Reformed churches of France systematically addressed
cahiers des plaintes to the crown. F. Chevalier, 'Les Difficultés d'application de l'Édit de Nantes
d'après les Cahiers des Plaintes' in Grandjean and Roussel, *Coexister dans l'intolérance*, pp. 303–20.

the pastor's salary. Likewise, in the decade following the edict's publication, Reformed church leaders cited the 'inhibitions' established by
the commissioners when chastising several members of a so-called youth
abbey for participating in a charivari.[24]

Henri IV's mobilization of royal commissions for the swift and systematic application of the edict ultimately represented the beginnings of
an immense effort to root the legislation firmly in people's minds and
actions. The commissioners' work was measured in months. The task
of securing the edict's enduring elaboration and observance in the face
of local and regional hostility fell ultimately to royal justice. In reality,
the commissions of application and special royal courts – the *chambres
de l'Édit* – complemented one another significantly in the pacification
effort.

The Edict of Nantes and supplementary legislation organized *chambres
de l'Édit* for the *parlements* of Bordeaux, Grenoble, Toulouse and, in more
limited fashion, for the high courts at Paris and Rouen. The judicial guarantees contained in the edict were among the most important elements
in the comprehensive effort to end the destructive religious wars. Articles
30 and 31 created special chambers within the *parlements* of Bordeaux,
Grenoble, Paris and Toulouse in the expectation that justice 'without any
suspicion, hate or favour' was 'one of the principal means for maintaining peace and concord'.[25] A royal edict of August 1599 added a *chambre*
for the *parlement* of Rouen.[26] Articles 32 through 64 of the Edict of Nantes
explained the regulations and procedures governing the operation of the
chambres de l'Édit. In brief, these courts had jurisdiction over all judicial
proceedings involving Protestants. Moreover, the tribunals, with an eye to
fairness towards Protestants, were staffed at least partially by Reformed
judges. The *chambres* affiliated with the *parlements* of Bordeaux, Grenoble
and Toulouse were *mi-parties* or bipartisan – that is to say, composed of
equal numbers of Protestant and Catholic judges. The chamber for the
parlement of Toulouse had two presidents and sixteen associate judges
drawn equally from each faith; those for Bordeaux and Grenoble two
presidents and twelve associate magistrates, again with a balance between Protestants and Catholics. The *chambres* for Paris and Rouen, on
the other hand, had but a single Reformed judge; the remainder of the
bench was Catholic.

---

[24] Bibliothèque de la SHPF, MS 654, pp. 30–1.   [25] Mousnier, *Assassination*, p. 326.
[26] The *chambre* at Rouen operated for sixty years. It was dissolved, along with the Parisian *chambre*,
     in January 1669. See F. Burckard, *Guide des archives de la Seine-Maritime*, 2 vols. (Rouen, 1990–3),
     I, p. 195.

The Protestant and Catholic judges who staffed these tribunals had the power to hear any civil or criminal case in which at least one of the litigants was Protestant. Collectively, they adjudicated tens of thousands of cases before their dissolution on the eve of the Revocation. The *chambres* assured Protestants access to unbiased justice or, at least, justice as dispassionate and impartial as possible in the religiously divided world of Reformation France. The court also offered professional and social opportunities for the Huguenot elite, especially those persons who belonged to the office-holding nobility. Finally, in addition to their regular judicial activities, the *chambres* played an important role in lessening tensions and promoting stability during the critical years that immediately followed the promulgation of the Edict of Nantes.

The Huguenots had called for independent justice when violence first erupted in the 1560s. Simply put, the prospect of trial by Catholic judges frightened them. The political leadership of the Huguenot cause had originally sought to create a separate judicial structure. The endeavour, however, proved wholly unworkable. Although they generally dominated the courts in the towns and regions where they exercised political and military authority, controlling or even finding a suitable substitute for the sovereign high courts, the *parlements*, proved infinitely more difficult. The *parlements* were the tribunals of final appeal, possessed jurisdiction over entire provinces and, more than other institutions, represented royal judicial authority. Yet the Protestants could not wrest control of them as they had various lower courts. Only gradually did a solution emerge.

The breakthrough came in the aftermath of the St Bartholomew's Day massacre when the Huguenots forged a critical alliance with the emerging Politique party. The Politiques, for their part, insisted on *chambres mi-parties* rather than entirely Protestant tribunals. These tentative undertakings eventually bore fruit with the Edict of Beaulieu, issued in May 1576.[27] The edict envisaged *chambres*, staffed by equal numbers of Protestant and Catholic judges, attached to the various *parlements*. Several ephemeral judicial sessions occurred in the late 1570s and 1580s.[28]

---

[27] For the text of the Edict of Beaulieu, especially articles 18 through 21 which deal with the *chambre de justice*, see A. Stegmann, *Édits des guerres de religion* (Paris, 1979), pp. 97–120.

[28] For developments within the jurisdiction of the *parlement* of Bordeaux, see: E. Brives-Cazès, *La Chambre de Justice de Guyenne en 1583–84* (Bordeaux, 1874); J. Parsons, 'The Political Vision of Antoine Loisel', *SCJ* 27 (1996), 454–6; for the province of Dauphiné: J. Brun-Durand, *Essai historique sur la chambre de l'Édit de Grenoble* (Valence, 1873); for the *parlement* of Toulouse: J. Cambon de Lavalette, *La chambre de l'Édit de Languedoc* (Paris, 1872), pp. 28–50; Capot, *Justice et religion*, pp. 54–60; R. A. Mentzer, 'L'Édit de Nantes et la Chambre de Justice du Languedoc' in Grandjean and Roussel, *Coexister dans l'intolérance*, pp. 325–7.

Finally, in the mid-1590s, Henri IV resuscitated the Huguenot–Politique project for bipartisan *chambres de justice*. Thus, when the crown promulgated the Edict of Nantes in 1598, it recognized and legitimized arrangements that had been operating in limited and sporadic fashion for some time.

During the course of their stormy existence, the *chambres de l'Édit* were first and foremost courts of law. They adjudicated countless suits from their foundation in the late sixteenth century until the final days in 1679. As with any royal tribunal, the cases ran the gamut from contract disagreements and conflicting business claims, marriage disputes and inheritance squabbles, to major criminal offences such as larceny, arson, forgery and homicide. Among the earliest and more remarkable judicial undertaking of the *chambres* were efforts at what is today labelled conflict resolution. Re-establishing public order in the wake of protracted violence meant a complex process of both recalling and forgetting past hostilities – a practice that one historian has elegantly termed 'adjudicating memory'.[29] Developments surrounding the Paris *chambre* are instructive in this regard.

The Edict of Nantes, in its opening articles, asserted a policy of *oubliance*, suppressing the remembrance of former divisiveness in the express interests of future harmony. Naturally, not all activity could be forgiven and forgotten. A number of cases involved grave offences, such as deliberate destruction or theft of property, assault and murder. The critical issue was amnesty for acts of war and the necessity of distinguishing such deeds from criminal offences that occurred during the conflict but not because of it. The Paris *chambre de l'Édit* heard fifty-seven cases of this nature during the first decade of the seventeenth century. Was, for example, one soldier's slaying of another a legitimate act of self-defence in heated combat or a matter of calculated vengeance stemming from a feud that predated the conflict? The court had the challenging task of settling this and other contradictory readings of past actions.[30]

Other *chambres* were no less diligent in attempting to purge the memory of previous stridency and restore tranquillity. The tribunal for Languedoc, which was attached to the *parlement* of Toulouse but sat at Castres, heard petitions from a number of individuals whose behaviour would normally have been considered criminal. Instead, they claimed benefit

[29] D. C. Margolf, 'Adjudicating Memory: Law and Religious Difference in Early Seventeenth-century France', *SCJ* 27 (1996), 399–418.

[30] See also D. C. Margolf, 'The Paris Chambre de l'Édit: Protestant, Catholic and Royal Justice in Early Modern France', Ph.D. thesis, Yale University (1990).

of royal amnesty. Again, the essential argument was that their deeds were legitimate acts of war and, accordingly, ought to be forgiven in return for obedience to the crown. Thus, the court exonerated some individuals accused of theft, ruin of property, murder and other 'acts of hostility' that under different circumstances would have been deemed crimes.[31] In addition, much like the commissioners for the application of the edict, the magistrates worked to restore Catholic ecclesiastical property and revenues that Protestants had seized during the religious wars. Bishops and abbots demanded the reintroduction of Catholic clergy, worship and other devotional practices in areas where Protestants had prohibited them.[32] Finally, the court sought to reduce confessional friction in the many southern French towns that possessed significant religious minorities. The rival groups clashed, much as elsewhere, over sites for worship and the use of municipal cemeteries.[33] These conflicts, if left unresolved, threatened renewed strife.

The Catholic and Protestant magistrates who participated in the *chambres de l'Édit* had sharply differing ideas regarding the courts' value and place. Developments surrounding the Castres *chambre* are revealing. The Catholic judges, drawn from the militantly conservative *parlement* of Toulouse, approached the venture with considerable mistrust and occasional hostility. They were, on the whole, less than enthusiastic. During the initial years, the jurists despatched from Toulouse appear to have been chosen, above all, for their religious zeal. Several had been prominent members of the virulently anti-Protestant Holy League.[34] Not until the regency of Marie de Medici did the crown take a more active role in the nomination of Catholic judges and promote the despatch of more moderate jurists to Castres.

Upon nomination by their colleagues at Toulouse, moreover, the Catholic judges refused to serve more than one-year terms on the *chambre*

[31] AD Haute-Garonne, chambre de l'Édit, civil, 6 (12 Dec. 1595), 11 (27 Apr. 1599); criminal, 1 (4 Jan., 20 Feb., 4 and 15 Mar., 10 Apr., 13, 14 and 31 May, 10 and 24 Sept., 4 Dec. 1597), 2 (11 Feb., 14 and 17 Apr., 14 and 17 July, 23 July, 4 and 18 Aug., 4 Sept. 1598), 3 (23 and 26 Feb., 12 May 1599).

[32] AD Haute-Garonne, B 173, fo. 306; B 174, fo. 110; chambre de l'Édit, civil, 7 (15 and 26 June 1595), 13 (4 Jan. and 2 Mar. 1600), 14 (13 Sept. 1600). AD Tarn, G 264, fo. 116. BN, Collection Dupuy, 63, fo. 94–94v; J. Faurin, *Journal de Faurin sur les Guerres de Castres*, ed. by C. Pradel (Montpellier, 1878), pp. 217, 223–4, 233–5; J. Gaches, *Mémoires sur les guerres de religion à Castres et dans le Languedoc (1555–1610)*, ed. by C. Pradel (Paris, 1879), pp. 452, 462.

[33] AD Haute-Garonne, chambre de l'Édit, civil, 8 (13 May 1597, 15 Oct. 1597), 11 (15 Apr. 1599), 14 (2 Dec. 1600).

[34] C. Delprat, 'Les Magistrats de parlement de Toulouse durant la Ligue', *Annales du Midi* 108 (1996), 39–62.

at Castres. While the Protestant magistrates sat continuously and permanently, the Catholics insisted upon a fixed rotation, sending a new
group of magistrates each year. They wished to avoid any appearance of
durable commitment. Not until 1604 did the Catholic magistrates from
Toulouse, under considerable royal pressure, allow two of their number to
carry over from one annual session to another and thereby provide some
continuity for the court. Altogether, the Catholic magistrates' behaviour
demonstrated their refusal to accept the *chambre* at Castres as anything
more than a provisional arrangement and, as such, underscored their
lingering opposition to the project.

The Protestant judges were, predictably enough, far better disposed.
They sat permanently at Castres, carefully passed their judicial offices
from one generation to the next, and nurtured a vibrant, sustained cultural experience. Thirteen Huguenot families – primarily from Castres,
Montauban, Montpellier and Nîmes – had between two and four members who served on the *chambre*. They furnished nearly two-thirds of the
sixty-four Protestant magistrates who served the court during its existence. Four generations of des Vignolles, a family of jurists originally from
Montpellier, participated from the earliest experiments during the late
1570s and 1580s until the tribunal's dissolution. Three generations of the
Juge family – father, son and grandson – methodically passed a coveted
office on the *chambre* from one person to the next. The Ranchin observed
a similar meticulous etiquette – in this instance from uncle to nephew to
great-nephew. The d'Escorbiac, an ambitious family from Montauban
with deep roots in the legal professions, and the Lacger, Huguenot jurists
from Castres itself, proved equally adept in acquiring and retaining
judicial positions on the *chambre de l'Édit* for Languedoc.[35]

A similar process took place within the *chambre de l'Édit* of Grenoble,
which had jurisdiction for the provinces of Dauphiné, Provence and
Burgundy. Thirty-three Protestants served as judges in the century between the court's first sessions in the 1580s and its demise in 1679.
Furthermore, in at least ten instances, these magistrates acquired their
positions through close family exchanges. They were the sons, sons-in-
law, nephews and cousins of incumbent magistrates.[36]

This tenacious grip on judicial appointments can be explained as a
trait shared by many economically and socially ambitious families of the

35 Cambon de Lavalette, *La chambre de l'Édit*, pp. 174–81; Capot, *Justice et religion*, pp. 259–73,
    366–92; Mentzer, *Blood and Belief*, pp. 60–72.
36 Brun-Durant, *La chambre de l'Édit de Grenoble*, pp. 61–85.

ancien régime. Yet for the Huguenot magistracy, there was added significance. Since the initial outburst of religious violence in 1562, Protestants had been effectively barred from service in the *parlements*. Only in the final quarter of the sixteenth century, with the creation of the *chambres de l'Édit*, did offices on the sovereign court open to Protestants. The aspiring Huguenot houses immediately set about securing these royal positions for themselves and their heirs. Once acquired, the offices were rarely relinquished. By the early decades of the seventeenth century, it was clear that there would be few openings for advancement beyond royal judicial offices, particularly those in the *chambres de l'Édit*.

For Protestant families such as des Vignolles, Juge, d'Escorbiac and Lacger, aspirations were tied closely to service in the royal judicial system and, in any event, rarely went further than the *chambres*. Those who arrived first held on, usually until extinction of the lineage. Huguenots, in the decades after the Edict of Nantes, discovered that their faith severely curtailed ambitions. Even these tightly circumscribed opportunities on the *chambres de l'Édit* proved a turbulent experience and then completely closed by the last quarter of the seventeenth century when in 1679, as part of its general assault on Protestantism, the monarchy suppressed the *chambres de l'Édit* associated with the *parlements* of Bordeaux, Grenoble and Toulouse. It had already abolished the *chambres* at Paris and Rouen a decade earlier in 1669. In Languedoc, the crown incorporated the Protestant magistrates into the *parlement* at Toulouse. The final blow came with the Revocation of 1685 and the crown's requirement that all royal officials make attestations of Catholicity.[37]

The Protestant magistrates who participated in the *chambres de l'Édit* at Castres were a tightly knit group, bound by ties of blood and marriage, culture and profession. These kinship networks and professional connections operated in fundamental and obvious fashion from the outset. As noted, families frequently passed judicial offices from one generation to the next or sold them to those to whom they were attached by ties of consanguinity and affinity, friendship and occupation. These familial and professional bonds were supplemented in other ways. The judges and their families worshipped together in the same temple, constructed lavish residences along adjoining streets, negotiated marriage alliances among their children, conducted commercial transactions with

---

[37] M. Brenac, 'Toulouse, centre de lutte contre le protestantisme au XVIIe siècle', *Annales du Midi* 77 (1965), 31–6, 43–5.

one another, sent their sons to the same schools, and created a shared cultural experience through poetry readings and artistic patronage.[38]

Among the more ambitious efforts were the various Protestant literary and scientific societies, which flourished by the mid-seventeenth century. Several dozen Huguenot jurists and attorneys associated with the court at Castres created, for instance, an academy in 1648. Their aim was to advance the 'understanding of truth' and the 'practice of virtue'. The members gathered weekly for more than twenty years to discuss political and religious affairs, historical and literary questions, and scientific matters. Some members were poets in their own right; a few even frequented the literary salons of Paris. Together, they sought to render the human spirit 'more learned and wiser'.[39] The Castres academy and others like it throughout the provinces approximated a kind of golden cultural and intellectual age among the Huguenots. While literary and scholarly accomplishments as well as achievements in the architectural and artistic realms[40] were not exactly proof of the election of the Protestant faithful, they remained for many an important demonstration of the virtue and moral worth of Huguenot society.

The rivalry, moreover, between Catholic and Protestant magistrates should not be overdrawn. The academy fostered by the Huguenots at Castres made, for example, important overtures to the Catholic community. A number of Catholics responded constructively to the proposal. Four became permanent members and others occasionally presented their work in the weekly gatherings. The latter included jurists from the *chambre*, various priests, and even a Jesuit father and Franciscan friar. Eventually, the academy's meetings took place in the home of the tribunal's chief Catholic magistrate. The academy of Castres was part of a wider attempt there and elsewhere to bridge the gap between Protestant and Catholic. The membership sought, within the context of the sessions, a forum for toleration and a ground of common culture, where followers of both faiths might conduct an ameliorating dialogue.[41]

---

[38] Capot, *Justice et religion*, pp. 283–307.

[39] AM Castres, II 9 et II 10, Procès-verbaux des séances de l'Académie de Castres; L. Barbaza, *L'Académie de Castres et la Société de Mlle de Scudéry, 1648–1670* (Castres, 1890).

[40] See Andrew Spicer's contribution to this volume, chap. 11.

[41] P. Chabbert, 'L'Académie de Castres' in *Castres et le pays tarnais. Actes du XXVIe Congrès d'études de la Fédération des Sociétés académiques et savantes de Languedoc-Pyrénées-Gascogne* (Albi, 1972), pp. 271–87; O. Granat, 'Une Académie de Province au XVIIe siècle', *Revue des Universités du Midi* (1898), 181–95; D. Roche, *Le siècle des lumières en Province: académies et académiciens provinciaux, 1680–1789*, 2 vols. (Paris and The Hague, 1978), I, p. 20. Several other academies, notably at Paris and Caen, also saw themselves as a common meeting ground for the two religious cultures. See E.-G. Léonard, *Histoire générale du Protestantisme. II. L'établissement* (Paris, 1961), pp. 333–5.

The magistrates' sense of the necessity for pragmatic co-operation is perhaps best exemplified by the rarity of instances in which the judges on the Castres *chambre* – remember an equal number of Catholics and Protestants adjudicated cases – divided evenly along confessional lines. Still, the cases are revealing. To begin, when compared to the massive body of decrees issued by the tribunal, there were very few splits among the magistrates. A sampling of the criminal decrees issued by the Castres *chambre* for the years 1596, 1636 and 1674 suggests that the judges were *mi-partis* in less than 1 per cent of their decisions (3 of 348 *arrêts* for the three years combined). Furthermore, when the judges' decisions did split, the cases touched upon extremely sensitive issues, notably the rights and obligations of Huguenots. These *'contentions'* sometimes focused on appropriate punishment for criminal activity, more frequently on whether the *chambre* had jurisdiction over the matter at issue. The confessional character of many of the matters that polarized the magistrates – Protestants who conducted public business on Catholic feast days, Reformed pastors who gave provocative sermons, inappropriate occasions for singing the psalms, suitable sites for Reformed worship, and the introduction of Catholic instructors into the municipal schools in Huguenot towns – speaks to religious sensibilities and the irritations that continued to separate Protestants and Catholics. As a practical matter, when the court divided, the case was referred to a neighbouring *chambre de l'Édit* or, ultimately, the king's *conseil privé*.[42]

In the end, the *chambres'* success, while limited, must be attributed to the bipartisan character of the three most important tribunals; those attached to the *parlements* of Bordeaux, Grenoble and Toulouse. Bipartisan principles had proven extremely effective in reducing confessional tensions at the end of the sixteenth century. Initially, these bipartisan initiatives, such as the *chambres de l'Édit* and the royal commissions for the proper application of the edict, helped to win approval for the legislation and to resolve enduring issues of contestation between Protestant and Catholic. In the years that followed, however, especially after the Peace of Alès which, in 1629, ended the ill-fated Huguenot revolt led by the duc de Rohan, the monarchy extended the principle of bipartisanship or, more precisely, *mi-partiement* to other institutions – and to the distinct disadvantage of the Protestant populace.

Protestants exercised comprehensive control of the municipal consulates in a number of towns – Castres, Montauban, Nîmes and many

---

[42] Capot, *Justice et religion*, pp. 215–31.

lesser-known places – where they were in the majority. They had also
established municipal schools, staffed exclusively by Protestant instructors in several of these urban localities.[43] After 1629, the king demanded
that these municipal governing councils and schools become bipartisan
with at least half-Catholic consuls and faculty.

   In October 1631, the crown ordered that Catholics and Protestants
share power in communities, particularly in southern France, with substantial Reformed majorities and whose consulates had been wholly
Huguenot. The changes advanced the position of Catholics decisively.
Not only were they admitted to governing circles, but the royal declaration reserved the office of first consul for Catholics. Since the first consul
traditionally represented a town, for example at meetings of the provincial estates, the effect was to concentrate power and authority in Catholic
hands. The other consular offices as well as lesser positions such as treasurer and even watchman were apportioned equally between members
of the two faiths. After 1661 and the onset of Louis XIV's personal rule,
royal officials gradually suppressed this system of bipartisan municipal
governance in favour of exclusive Catholic control.[44]

   In the educational sphere, the municipal colleges at Castres,
Montauban and Nîmes became bipartisan by the mid-1630s. Catholics,
notably the Jesuits, were allocated half of the instructional positions. Although some observers have suggested that the situation led, in small
ways, to salutary contacts between the confessional opponents, the relationship was, on the whole, antagonistic and strident. The two sides
struggled for predominance over the education of the young and, by
extension, control of the future. At Nîmes, the municipal hospital and
the social welfare programmes associated with it became bipartisan at
the same time as the local college.[45] Indeed, education and poor relief
were among the principal arenas in the long struggle between Huguenot
and Catholic for the soul of society. In some places, these bipartisan divisions had occurred much earlier. At Dieulefit, whose population was
two-thirds Protestant, the municipal council and hospital administration
were already *mi-partis* in 1599. The municipal *collège* at Montpellier was
confessionally divided by 1604 and the Jesuits took over completely in

43 See K. Maag, 'The Huguenot Academies: Preparing for an Uncertain Future', in this volume,
    chap. 9.
44 P. Gachon, *Quelques préliminaires de la Révocation de l'Édit de Nantes en Languedoc (1661–1685)*
    (Toulouse, 1899), pp. 25–48; C. Rabaud, *Histoire du Protestantisme dans l'Albigeois et le Lauragais*,
    2 vols. (Paris, 1873 and 1898), I, pp. 275–6.
45 P. Chareyre, 'Le consistoire de Nîmes et l'Édit de Nantes', *Bulletin historique de la Ville de Montpellier*
    23 (1999), 124–5.

1629.[46] Nor were these the only bipartisan institutions that the monarchy transformed in its offensive against the Huguenots.

The commissions for the application of the edict were also revived, again to the disadvantage of Protestants. Louis XIV reconstituted the commissions in 1661 and, like Henri IV, retained the essential principle of two commissioners, one Catholic, the other Protestant. In this renewed effort, however, the intent was not to find common ground for the advance of peace, but to limit the Edict of Nantes and impose greater restriction on the Huguenots. The king appointed religiously conservative Catholic commissioners and weighted the procedures in their favour.[47] In all of this, the crown effectively turned the principle of bipartisanship against Protestants and, in the process, increased the power of the royal government and Catholic church. The anti-Protestant monarchy undermined the French Reformed community by applying bipartisan standards to install typically zealous Catholics within heretofore entirely Huguenot municipal consulates, schools and hospitals.

Although the regime of the Edict of Nantes differed substantially from the vision that Huguenots had entertained early in the wars of religion, the legislation and its associated institutions represented at least the partial realization of goals that the Reformed community had sought. The commissions for the application of the edict strove, during the reign of Henri IV, to assure Huguenots the status granted by the edict. More important, the *chambre de l'Édit* with its divided bench meant the ongoing assurance that Protestant litigants would have access to dispassionate justice. The court also offered opportunities for the professional and social preferment of the Huguenot elite, especially those persons who belonged to the petty, provincial nobility. Finally, in addition to its regular judicial activities, the *chambre* played an important role in the pacification process during the years that immediately followed the promulgation of the Edict of Nantes.

The ordinary circumstances and daily conditions surrounding the Edict of Nantes can be readily grasped and appreciated in the history of

---

[46] D. Julia and M.-M. Compère, *Les Collèges français, 16e–18e siècles. 1. France du Midi* (Paris, 1984), pp. 206–9, 446–50, 490–6; Gachon, *Quelques préliminaires*, pp. 78–9; Garrisson, *Commissions d'application*, pp. 195–6; F. Moreil, 'Le Collège et l'Académie réformée de Nîmes', *BSHPF* 122 (1976), 77–86; R. Sauzet, 'Une Expérience originale de Cohabitation religieuse: le Collège mi-parti de Nîmes au XVIe siècle' in *Les frontières religieuses en Europe du XVIe au XVIIe siècle* (Paris, 1992), pp. 283–90.

[47] Benedict, *'Un Roi, une Loi, deux Fois'*, pp. 81–2; R. Bonney, 'France under the Early Bourbon Monarchy: Confessional Absolutism or Confessional Pluralism' in Cameron, Greengrass and Roberts, *Adventure of Religious Pluralism*, pp. 209–29.

the commissions of application and *chambres de l'Édit*. These institutions met the immediate critical needs of the Huguenot community by promoting greater security, reducing religious tensions and initiating a delicate structure for peaceful coexistence and the flowering of a Huguenot culture. The concerns of the modern observer focus, in particular, on the place of the judicial process in the overall attempt to resolve confessional conflict and the manner whereby bipartisan commissions and tribunals can serve to guarantee civil rights for religious minorities. For the Huguenots of the seventeenth century, the edict opened opportunities while simultaneously marking the limits of aspiration and achievement within the political and cultural spheres. The formulation and implementation of the royal legislation proved a long and difficult experience. The decades that followed the edict's promulgation were frequently trying and embittering. Though the edict remained in force for eighty-seven years, the Peace of Alès in 1629 repealed the military concessions and eliminated the surety towns; 'rigorous' application from 1661 onward further limited its advantages to Protestants; and the monarchy, of course, revoked the whole in 1685. Yet the Edict of Nantes remained a profound accomplishment, one which permitted the Huguenot community to persevere and, in some ways, flourish, despite strict and increasingly harsh restraints.

8. 'Speaking the king's language': the Huguenot magistrates of Castres and Pau

Amanda Eurich

In 1598 the Edict of Nantes confirmed the right of Huguenots to hold judicial and administrative office within the kingdom of France.[1] The edict also permitted the creation of special bipartisan tribunals to hear criminal and civil cases involving Protestants. These *chambres de l'Édit*, as they came to be known, offered Huguenot *officiers* the unique opportunity to mediate the local perceptions and fortunes of Calvinist minorities at the same time that they provided judicial elites with an important avenue of socio-professional advancement.[2] Over the course of the seventeenth century, local challenges and royal decrees repeatedly tested and eroded the privileges and parameters of Huguenot office-holding elites.[3] Torn between the often conflicting demands imposed by royal service and the Reformed community, Huguenot office-holders experienced the challenges of confessionalization in seventeenth-century France more keenly than most of their co-religionists. In their efforts to juggle the interests of the Bourbon monarchy they served against the equally compelling claims of family and faith, Protestant magistrates developed strategies of survival that can be seen as an index of the imperilled status of Calvinist communities in France at large.

This chapter examines the experience of Huguenot office-holding dynasties in two provincial capitals in southern France: Pau and Castres. With a population that may have reached 10,000 by the end of the seventeenth century, Castres was almost seven times as populous as the Pyrenean capital of Pau, which numbered between 1,200 and 1,500

---

[1] B. Cottret, *1598: L'Édit de Nantes* (Paris, 1997), pp. 361–84. See articles 27, 31, 34 and 41–8 of the edict.

[2] D. Margolf, 'The Edict of Nantes' Amnesty: Appeals to the Chambre de l'Édit, 1600–1680', *Proceedings of the Western Society for French History* 16 (1988), 49–55; R. A. Mentzer, *Blood and Belief: Family Survival and Confessional Identity among the Provincial Huguenot Nobility* (West Lafayette, IN, 1994), pp. 62–4.

[3] A. Th. van Deursen, *Professions et métiers: un aspect de l'histoire de la Révocation de l'Édit de Nantes* (Groningen, 1960), pp. 165–92.

inhabitants over the course of the seventeenth century.[4] Both towns, however, could claim to be the political centre of gravity within their respective regions and were home to the complex matrix of royal councillors, administrators and lawyers who comprised the rapidly expanding bureaucracies of the Bourbon state. By the early seventeenth century, Castres and Pau were also the seats of provincial law courts, dominated by Huguenot dynasties that had achieved prominence during the religious wars within the clientele networks of Henri de Navarre. The preeminence of these Huguenot loyalists profoundly influenced the contours of local society and politics, but the different fates of the two communities after the 1620s reveal diversity of Huguenot experience in seventeenth-century France.

The emergence of dynastic office-holding elites within the Huguenot community confounded the provisions of the Edict of Nantes and the deliberations of the Protestant political assemblies, which had placed the selection of magistrates under the purview of regional synods, the provincial governing bodies of the Reformed churches of France.[5] Delegates to the political assembly at Chatelleraut in June 1598 asserted that magistrates should resign their office in favour of the candidates chosen by the provincial synod. The implementation of the *paulette* in 1604, however, challenged the authority that royal as well as synodal authorities claimed over high judicial appointments and contributed to the creation of a virtually unshakeable rank of hereditary royal office-holders, many of whom penetrated the second estate as a consequence of the noble status attached to high judicial office.[6] Both Catholic and Protestant magistrates recognized the considerable economic and political advantages of the *paulette*, which allowed investors to preserve the office for their children or close relatives for a nominal tax levied annually at $\frac{1}{60}$ of the value of the office and rewarded loyal office-holding dynasties with irrevocable noble standing after three generations of royal service. The strictures levied by the Bourbon state, which barred Protestants from a growing catalogue of royal offices and honourable professions, however, imparted an especial sense of importance to the value Huguenot office-holding families attached to positions in the bipartisan *chambres de l'Édit*

---

4 P. Benedict, *The Huguenot Population of France: The Demographic Fate and Customs of a Religious Minority* (Transactions of the American Philosophical Society, 81, 1991) pp. 52–3; P. Tucoo-Chala, *Histoire de Pau* (Toulouse, 1989), pp. 48–9.

5 L. Anquez, *Histoire des assemblées politiques des réformés de France, 1573–1633* (Paris, 1859), pp. 197–8.

6 See R. Mousnier, *La Vénalité des offices sous Henri IV et Louis XIII* (Paris, 1971), esp. pp. 222–48; S. Kettering, *Patrons, Brokers, and Clients in Seventeenth-century France* (Oxford, 1986), pp. 177–9.

and in subsidiary courts, such as the *cours des aides*, where neither customary nor legal prohibitions kept them from holding office. Huguenot jurists were willing to invest dearly – perhaps as much as one-third more than their Catholic counterparts – to secure these offices and advance their family ambitions.[7]

Within the bipartisan system of *chambres de l'Édit*, the degree to which Huguenots could monopolize offices and control the politics of the *chambres* varied enormously. At one extreme was the *chambre de l'Édit* in Paris, where only one Huguenot judge served alongside his Catholic colleagues. In contrast, the court created at Castres, a subsidiary of the *parlement* of Toulouse, much more clearly reflected the confessional parity intended by the Edict of Nantes. Eleven Protestant members (ten *conseillers* and a presiding judge) shared power with a like number of Catholic colleagues, while subaltern positions, such as *procureurs généreaux* and substitutes, generally fell to Catholics.[8] It was perhaps this parity, the relative stability of the *chambre* (only briefly suspended during the rebellions of the 1620s), and the provincial isolation of Castres itself which allowed the Huguenot magistrates to dominate local society until the dissolution of the *chambre* in 1679.

Many first-generation magistrates within the *chambre de l'Édit* in Castres, such as Fulcrand des Vignolles, Guiscard d'Escorbiac and Jean de Lamer, had risen to political prominence during the religious wars and could directly attribute their offices to the rewards of the patron–client system.[9] The credit they enjoyed as clients of Henri de Navarre or Henri de Montmorency-Damville, governor of Languedoc, led quite naturally to political and diplomatic appointments on behalf of the Reformed churches in France. Even after the conclusion of the religious wars, a number of Huguenot magistrates within the *chambre* remained active within the network of the Huguenot provincial and national political assemblies,[10] willingly embracing such religio-political brokerage as a natural corollary of office-holding. They happily ceded, however, the interminable business of spiritual correction to cadet branches of the family or lesser legal officials, who comprised the corps of the consistory. In the mid-seventeenth century, councillors evinced only perfunctory interest in the honorary position they were granted on the *corps d'Église*,

[7] S. Capot, *Justice et religion en Languedoc au temps de l'Édit de Nantes: la Chambre de l'Édit de Castres, 1579–1679* (Paris, 1998), pp. 292–4.
[8] Margolf, 'Edict of Nantes' Amnesty', 49–55; Capot, *Justice et religion*, pp. 121–34.
[9] Capot, *Justice et religion*, pp. 266–7, 272–7. [10] *Ibid.*, pp. 374, 392.

whose members handled thorny fiscal and administrative issues, such as pastors' salaries, and battled with civic authorities over the contours of confessional coexistence.[11]

The re-emergence of Protestant militancy under the direction of the duc de Rohan in 1621 challenged the brokerage abilities of Huguenot magistrates in Castres.[12] By virtue of family connections, professional ties and aristocratic service, office-holders were often drawn into extensive patronage networks which straddled divisions within Huguenot party leadership. The Lacger, for example, were clients of the powerful La Trémoille family, high-ranking Huguenot aristocrats, who energetically opposed Rohan as a dangerous adventurer. When the first rumours of war reached Castres, Jacques de Lacger, along with his brother Pierre, a municipal judge, and many of his colleagues in the *chambre*, enjoined the town consulate to embrace the politics of prudence. They struggled throughout the war to defend their religious orthodoxy against a number of local nobles, artisans, and even some lesser members of the *chambre*, who comprised the nucleus of the pro-war party. This proved difficult, especially when they joined forces with Catholic sacred and civic officials, whom they urged to remain in Castres to bolster the forces of moderation. When this cross-confessional initiative failed to stem the tide of rebellion in late 1621, Lacger and his supporters provided their Catholic colleagues with an armed escort out of the city. Soon thereafter the *chambre* was dissolved, and a number of Huguenot jurists sought refuge and anonymity on their rural estates.[13]

During the revolt, provincial Protestant magistrates became crucial links between the centre and rebellious peripheries, providing a steady flow of information to royal agents that made it easy to cast them as traitors to the cause. As a consequence, they often became the targets of intraconfessional violence and feuding, subject to reprisals by local radicals and Rohan's partisans. Huguenot families with multiple ties to aristocratic and bureaucratic court circles, such as Lacger and Suc, were especially vulnerable and sustained repeated attacks on their rural properties and townhouses.[14] Vilified as turncoats and opportunists by local partisans of the duc de Rohan, the Huguenot jurists of Castres emerged from the crucible of rebellion even more firmly convinced that the preservation of their family fortunes as well as civic order lay solidly

[11] Mentzer, *Blood and Belief*, pp. 162–7.
[12] R. Artigaut, *Les Protestants de Castres et l'Édit de Nantes* (Castres, 1984), pp. 15–20; Mentzer, *Blood and Belief*, pp. 165–6.
[13] Mentzer, *Blood and Belief*, pp. 20–1, 69–71.   [14] *Ibid.*, p. 71.

with the crown. By the mid-1620s, even lower-level *chambre* officials, some of whom had initially been warm supporters of Rohan, distanced themselves from the more militant wing of the party. In the aftermath of the 1620s rebellion, the crown readily exploited this nascent royalism, relying heavily on Huguenot officials to mediate the conditions of surrender and to implement bipartisan programmes of governance. Pierre de Lacger's political activism within the provincial assemblies, synods and local colloquies of the Midi, for example, only underscored his potential utility to the crown, especially after he repeatedly lobbied town councils in Castres to remain loyal to the crown. Two years after being awarded a royal pension of 600 *livres* for service rendered, he was formally drafted into the king's service as a commissioner to provincial synods, in which capacity he reported on the activities of his co-religionaries to the crown.[15] Samuel d'Escorbiac played a similar role in the Huguenot stronghold of Montauban, where he urged municipal leaders to maintain their obedience to royal authority in 1621, only to be driven out of town by party radicals. In return for his good offices, Louis XIII gave d'Escorbiac asylum in a nearby château, later promoted his candidacy as judge within the *chambre* at Castres, and in 1632 charged him with the thorny task of overseeing the creation of the first bipartisan consulate in Montauban in over sixty years. Many, like Abel de Suc who secured a pension of 15,000 *livres* from Phélypeaux d'Herbaut, secretary of state for Protestant affairs, to compensate for his loss of property and office, expressed their gratitude by a lifetime of loyal service to the crown within the *chambre*.[16]

Over the course of the seventeenth century, deft manipulation of the *paulette* encouraged the emergence of veritable judicial dynasties in Castres, where eight of the eleven offices controlled by Huguenots remained in the hands of the same families for sixty-six years. Huguenot officers meticulously channelled their financial resources and painstakingly cultivated their political networks and clienteles in the capital and the provinces to assure the hereditary transmission of their office to their eldest male child.[17] Groomed from birth to assume the mantle of parlementary office, these heirs apparent trained in law (in most cases in regional universities) and were encouraged by anxious parents to enrol for the bar while in their teens.[18] Protestant royal officials even encouraged younger sons to study law in the hopes they might find lucrative professional opportunities within the broader legal network surrounding sovereign courts. For much of the seventeenth century, the younger sons

[15] *Ibid.*, pp. 70–2.   [16] Capot, *Justice et religion*, p. 293, n. 38.
[17] *Ibid.*, pp. 261–73.   [18] *Ibid.*, pp. 265–7.

Table 8.1. *Occupational choice of children,* chambre de l'Édit, *Castres*

Castres	1590–1609		1610–64		After 1665	
High official	3	23%	15	38%	7	17%
Military/Noble	10	77%	14	36%	32	76%
Legal profession	–	–	10	26%	3	7%
Total	13	100%	39	100%	42	100%

Source: S. Capot, *Justice et religion en Languedoc au temps de l'Édit de Nantes: la chambre de l'Édit de Castres, 1579–1679* (Paris, 1998), pp. 366–92.

of Reformed magistrates served as court attorneys, functioning, albeit as lesser luminaries, in the same professional and social circles as their older siblings and fathers, and sometimes following them in office (see table 8.1, above).

In their desire to protect their investment in office, Protestant magistrates were no different from their Catholic counterparts. Remarkably, the evidence suggests that Protestants faced no greater difficulties transmitting their legacy to their heirs, even when candidates violated legal provisions that stipulated that councillors should be at least twenty-five years of age before assuming office. Three families – Montcalm, des Vignolles and Rozels – successfully advanced under-age candidates to office twice over the course of the seventeenth century.[19] When the failure to produce the requisite male heir threatened patrimonial ambitions, relatives cobbled together resources (much like they did for dowries) to assure that the office passed to a collateral branch of the family.[20]

The tenacious defence of patrimonial rights to office, repeated intermarriages among distinguished parlementary families, and shared traditions of service perpetuated the political influence of venerable parlementary clans, such as the Montcalm, de Lacger and d'Escorbiac, who readily closed ranks against relative newcomers whose lack of experience or lacklustre pedigree threatened the distinction of the *chambre* and their own deeply entrenched patronage networks. In 1655, for example, Isaac Brugière, considered a relative *parvenu* from Périgord, resigned his office in favour of his brother, a captain in the regiment of Guyenne. Under the leadership of Thomas d'Escorbiac, who had targeted the office for one of his own relatives, Huguenot *officiers* in Castres staunchly refused to register Pierre de Brugière's letters of appointment, claiming he had

[19] *Ibid.,* p. 266.   [20] Mentzer, *Blood and Belief,* pp. 131–2.

not served the requisite number of years as a practising lawyer in spite of papers which proved Pierre had qualified as a lawyer to the *parlement* of Bordeaux. Threats levied by the royal council in 1658 and the intervention of agents from the national synod of Reformed churches in 1659 failed to budge d'Escorbiac and his party, who refused to recognize Brugière's candidacy, even after Pierre enlisted the help of a kinsman in the *cours des aides* in Montpellier, where his papers were finally registered.[21]

Internal conflicts, such as the Brugière affair, obscure the normal esprit de corps which united the Huguenot magistrates of Castres. Dense familial networks reinforced by patterns of professional endogamy created ties of fictive kinship and mutual dependency among office-holding elites. With few exceptions, the *parlementaires* of Castres married within the faith to women whose social profile closely resembled their own.[22] Over the course of the seventeenth century, roughly a quarter of Castrais magistrates chose the daughters of fellow councillors as their brides. The proximity of a number of prosperous Huguenot urban communities throughout Languedoc also permitted them to forge strategic alliances with regional Protestant elites. By the second half of the seventeenth century, parlementary families had established sufficient fortunes and political *crédit* to strike marriage bargains on a regular basis with the petty seigneurs in the surrounding region.

From the mid-1620s onward, shifting patterns of migration, the conversion of a number of prominent Protestant leaders to Catholicism, and the growing Catholic presence in municipal and provincial office threatened the veritable hegemony that Calvinists had enjoyed throughout much of the Huguenot crescent, which stretched from Poitou south through Gascony and eastward into Languedoc. Inspired by their growing political and economic dominance and increasingly restrictive royal policies toward Protestants, Catholic elites repeatedly lobbied the crown to prohibit Huguenots from holding key royal offices in the province.[23] In Castres, where the presence of a politically vital Huguenot magistracy was an essential feature of the city's political culture, sustained efforts by the *parlement* of Toulouse to introduce subtle gradations in the honorific perquisites and duties of office inexorably reduced Calvinist jurists to second-class status. In 1638, a bitter, thirty-year struggle between the two *présidents à mortier*, one Catholic and one Protestant, to claim control within the *chambre* was formally settled by a decree of

[21] Capot, *Justice et religion*, pp. 309–10.   [22] *Ibid.*, pp. 283–9, 365–92.
[23] P. Benedict, 'Faith, Fortune and Social Structure in Seventeenth-century Montpellier', *Past & Present* 152 (1996), 70–1.

the *parlement* of Toulouse which gave Catholics alone the right to pre-
side over the deliberations and assemblies of the magistrates. Protestants
perceived this affront as one of many procedural *coups* that contravened
the intentions of the Edict of Nantes. Royal agents, however, boasted to
Chancellor Séguier that the willingness of Protestant moderates, such as
Abel de Suc, to accommodate royal policy facilitated the slow and inexorable marginalization of his Huguenot colleagues within the *chambre*.
Under the leadership of Gaspard des Vignolles, *président à mortier* from
1638 to 1674, the Huguenot magistrates of the *chambre* attempted to challenge the new system of precedence and distribution but failed in the face
of the broader royal and provincial assault on Huguenot privileges.[24]

By the 1660s, the cumulative impact of this interminable legal wran-
gling cast a pall on the lure of office and encouraged Calvinist office-
holding elites to steer their male progeny toward other career alternatives. Table 8.1 demonstrates the clear predilection of the children of the
Huguenot officers for *robe* careers before the changing legal and political climate of the 1650s and 1660s compelled the drastic reorientation
of familial strategies. From 1610 to 1665, almost two-thirds of young
Huguenots from among the ranks of *robe* followed their fathers into royal
officialdom or pursued legal careers. After 1665, the percentages nearly
reversed. Forced to abandon familial traditions of judicial office, many
sons of the Huguenot *noblesse de robe* refashioned themselves as military
officers in the later seventeenth century, thereby perpetuating the familial legacy of royal service and the aristocratic dignity they accrued from
it. Others embraced the quiet life of a country squire. Ironically, both
strategies better equipped Huguenots to face the crucible of religious
persecution and emigration after the Revocation of the Edict of Nantes.
Many aspiring officers accepted military commissions in the service of
foreign Protestant princes, where they were in a position to help Calvinist
relatives find a suitable *pays de refuge*. Others entered French royal regi-
ments, where public attestations of Catholicity were not required until
1685, and they learned to model the kind of nominal conformity to the
rites of the Catholic church that allowed many Huguenot families to
convert gracefully to the dictates of 1685.[25]

The efflorescence of the academy of Castres, a literary society established in 1648 at the behest of several jurists in the *chambre de l'Édit*, is
a testament to the cultural capital which Huguenot officials continued to
wield in provincial society until the dissolution of the *chambre* in 1679. The

---

[24] Capot, *Justice et religion*, pp. 121–4, 240–4.   [25] See Mentzer, *Blood and Belief*, pp. 72–80.

bipartisan composition of the academy at Castres emphasized the common classical training, professional interests and royalist ethos shared by elites of both confessions.[26] Some of the most devoted participants had spent a portion of their formative years in Paris, where they sought as aspiring provincials to establish their reputations in salon society, and the tenor of the academy's meetings drew inspiration from the gallant poetic exercises and debates in which many of them had engaged in the salons of Mademoiselle de Scudéry and other *précieuses*. The academy thus reinforced the cultural hegemony of office-holding elites – Protestant and Catholic – and tied them both even more firmly to the discursive practices of polite society and court culture.[27]

The dissolution of the *chambre de l'Édit* in Castres in 1679 and its incorporation into the *parlement* of Toulouse almost completely destroyed the hard-core Huguenot dynasties, whose painstaking strategies had permitted them to dominate provincial politics and cultural life for almost a century. The financial and psychological toll of relocating to Toulouse, the diminution of political clienteles and social credit, the economic devaluation of the offices themselves all left venerable Huguenot *robe* dynasties scrambling for position in ultra-Catholic Toulouse. Some attempted to preserve their candidacies on the high court by converting to Catholicism and even received handsome royal pensions for their exemplary actions. Thomas d'Escorbiac, who held out until 1685, compensated for his recalcitrant behaviour by travelling to Versailles to abjure in the presence of the Sun King himself, an action which earned him a royal pension of 3,000 *livres* and the right to pass his office on to his *nouveau converti* son a few years later.[28] Others retained both their offices and confessional identities, only to be forced to relinquish their investment at cut-rate prices to Catholic buyers after 1685. The fortunes of the formidable de Lacger clan reveal the tremendous toll that recusancy and cypto-Protestantism exacted on the market for offices. When the sons of Jacques de Lacger tried to sell their father's office after his death in 1688, they only managed to get 39,000 *livres* for an office that had been valued at 80,000 *livres* only a few years earlier.[29] Across France, the collapse in the market for Protestant councillorships wrecked the fortunes of Huguenot *robe* dynasties and rendered the task of reconstituting family finances even more difficult.

[26] *Ibid.*, pp. 133–41.
[27] For further discussion of the academy at Castres, see R. A. Mentzer, 'The Edict of Nantes and its Institutions', in this volume, chap. 7.
[28] Mentzer, *Blood and Belief*, p. 170.   [29] Capot, *Justice et religion*, p. 294.

The experience of Protestant parlementary elites in the viscounty of Béarn followed a radically different trajectory from their *confrères* in Languedoc. In the late sixteenth century, Jeanne d'Albret, with the assistance of Pierre Viret, imposed a full-scale Reformation on her subjects in the tiny principality of Béarn.[30] The alacrity with which many artisans, merchants and *officiers* attached to Jeanne's court in Pau, embraced Calvinism and facilitated the process of reform earned them royal favour and preferments. Many of the most powerful office-holding dynasties in seventeenth-century Béarn, such as the Gassion and Loyard, rose to power through the ranks of Jeanne d'Albret's clientele networks, and those of her son and heir, Henri de Navarre. By the 1570s, the implementation of the Ecclesiastical Ordinances assured the political ascendancy of Huguenot elites in Béarn, who claimed the exclusive right to municipal and royal offices throughout the realm.[31] For the next fifty years, the Huguenot magistrates of the *conseil souverain*, the court of last appeal established in 1519, and the *chambre des comptes*, vigorously defended Béarnais liberties, which they viewed as the essential guarantee of Protestant hegemony in the viscounty.[32]

From 1569 to 1620, Pau itself became one of the most vibrant nerve centres of Protestantism within the tiny principality. Even the reintroduction of Catholicism in Béarn by virtue of the 1599 Edict of Fontainebleau, a mirror image of the Edict of Nantes, did little to dismantle the virtual monopoly that Protestants enjoyed over royal offices.[33] Although the newly installed bishops of Oloron and Lescar were granted the right to vet new candidates for the *conseil souverain* and serve as *ex officio* members, the composition of the council remained staunchly Calvinist and deeply loyal to the memory of *la bonne Regine Jehanne*.

The early seventeenth century also witnessed the transformation of the fortunes of many Huguenot office-holding families, whose shrewd manipulation of the volatile marriage and real-estate markets allowed them to consolidate their socio-economic position in Béarnais society (see tables 8.2 and 8.3). During these decades, many royal servitors shed their *routurier* origins and confirmed their entry into ranks of the local nobility through the acquisition of seigneurial estates and titles. Marriage

---

[30] M. Greengrass, 'The Calvinist Experiment in Béarn' in A. Pettegree, A. Duke and G. Lewis (eds.), *Calvinism in Europe, 1540–1620* (Cambridge, 1994), pp. 119–42; T. Issartel, *Les chemins de la tolérance en Béarn: les catholiques, les protestants et l'État* (Biarritz, 1999), pp. 32–64.

[31] For the full text of these ordinances, see BN, MS Brienne, 271.

[32] Greengrass, 'Calvinist Experiment in Béarn', pp. 138–41.

[33] C. Desplat, 'Édit de Fontainebleau du 15 avril 1599 en faveur des catholiques du Béarn' in *Réformes et Révocation en Béarn* (Pau, 1986), pp. 223–46.

Table 8.2. *Huguenot and Catholic dowries compared (in livres)*

Huguenot	1570–99	1600–19	1620–40	1660–83
Noble	4,812 (4)	2,000 (2)	6,119 (7)	6,450 (6)
Agensament			2,120 (5)	3,500
High official	1,937 (12)	5,343 (24)	6,031 (8)	–
Agensament	1,750 (2)	1,929 (7)	1,412 (4)	
Minor officer	975 (6)	1,771 (14)	2,759 (14)	3,627 (14)
Agensament	750 (2)	960 (1)	867 (3)	1,840 (6)
Profession/Bourg	400	1,200 (2)	4,266 (3)	2,320 (5)
Agensament			100 (1)	2,666 (5)
Catholic				
Noble	–	–	17,500 (3)	28,555 (4)
Agensament				3,133 (3)
High official	–	–	9,714 (14)	22,928 (7)
Agensament			6,888 (1)	
Minor officer	–	–	2,720 (4)	5,560 (5)
Agensament			1,475 (3)	1,125 (2)
Profession/Bourg	–	–	–	–
Agensament				

Source: AD Pyrénées-Atlantiques, E2000-53.

Table 8.3. *Land transfers, Pau*

	1600–20		1624–59		1660–85	
Seller	Number	*Livres*	Number	*Livres*	Number	*Livres*
Noble	33	74,862	31	60,106	19	44,796
Parlementaire	60	48,869	67	66,957	16	38,601
Minor officer	25	28,094	38	33,849	10	10,170
Total	118	151,825	136	160,912	45	93,567
Buyer	Number	*Livres*	Number	*Livres*	Number	*Livres*
Noble	21	67,670	17	66,140	9	64,469
Parlementaire	48	35,287	29	38,414	4	8,391
Minor officer	48	20,156	23	21,530	1	1,000
Total	117	123,113	69	126,084	14	73,860

Source: AD Pyrénées-Atlantiques, E2020-53.

contracts corroborate the emergence of a self-confident, new political
elite, whose successful quest for landed wealth and title permitted them to
negotiate strategic alliances with provincial noble houses as well as office-
holding dynasties. As the prestige of their marital unions increased and
their own fortunes flourished, the average dowries offered by Huguenot
robe officials in Béarn almost tripled, outstripping inflationary trends.
During this same period, dowries offered by minor office-holding families doubled.

The dramatic events which culminated in the *reattachment* (to use contemporary parlance) of Béarn to the kingdom of France exposed profound
political cleavages among the largely Calvinist members of the *conseil
souverain* and provincial estates. The promulgation of the Edict of Restitution in 1617, whereby Louis XIII ordered the return of church lands
and revenues confiscated by Jeanne d'Albret, unleashed vigorous debates
within the Estates and *conseil souverain* over the precise nature of Béarnais
sovereignty as enshrined in the *fors* or customs. Militants within the
Estates of Béarn, such as the baron Gabaston, military governor of the
fortified stronghold at Navarrenx, couched their resistance to the edict
in terms of fundamental law and popular sovereignty.[34] The growing
influence of a party of moderates around Jacques de Gassion revealed
the centripetal force of Bourbon absolutism and nascent royalist ethos
among judicial elites of both confessions.[35] Protestant councillors, such as
Gassion, often found themselves at odds with their more radical *confrères*,
who were not above imposing disciplinary sanctions to censure political moderates. On a diplomatic mission to court in 1617, for example, de Gassion and his fellow councillor, Dupont, were refused the
Lord's Supper by the Paris community of saints. Rumours that the
two councillors had supported the ecclesiastical party led by Pierre de
Marca, the future archbishop of Paris, and championed the restoration of church lands and revenues in Béarn further fuelled the consistory's determination to withhold Communion from the two Béarnais
agents until they pledged to do everything in their power to frus-
trate the implementation of the edict of 1617. While Dupont quickly
acquiesced to their demands, de Gassion protested that such blatant
political manoeuvring was an affront to his personal dignity and his
public commission as a royal officer. Upon his return to Pau, de
Gassion immediately joined the Catholics in the *conseil souverain* in
demanding that the Reformed church in Béarn break off relations

34 See Issartel, *Les chemins de la tolérance*, pp. 96–102.   35 *Ibid.*, pp. 178–86.

with the French Assembly of Reformed churches.[36] De Gassion's actions sealed the union of moderates of both confessions and underscored the growing political and cultural chasm among Huguenot elites.

The public capitulation of the Calvinist leadership in Béarn to Louis XIII and his troops in October 1620 failed to stem the vigorous and ongoing commitment to militant resistance among some members of the Huguenot nobility. After Louis XIII departed for Paris with the majority of his military retinue in late October, local warlords and their supporters waged a successful guerrilla war for several months, capitalizing on feudal and communal fears over the abolition of the local militias and military contributions system (*parsan*) prescribed by the Edict of Union. Venerable Huguenot warlords such as the redoubtable Jacques de Brassalay refused to cede fortified strongholds to royal garrisons. Minor nobles, who had been largely ignored in the pacification process, readily took up arms to defend their honour and hereditary privileges. Captain Bensin, the nephew of the baron Gabaston (who himself had been richly compensated with a 100,000 *livres* pension), penetrated the garrison at Navarrenx, confiscated stockpiled arms, and occupied the château at Montgiscard in a classic *prise des armes*. The refusal of newly compensated loyalists, such as the former governor of Béarn, Caumont de la Force, to rally troops against former clients, friends and family members exposed potent ties of patronage and blood which jeopardized the peaceful transfer of power and threatened to plunge Béarn anew into civil war. The timely intervention of a bipartisan parlementary commission, which negotiated Bensin's surrender, defused military tensions and revealed the political authority of the moderate party. Two months later, de la Force fled Béarn in the face of advancing royal forces, led by the duc d'Epernon. Deprived of a protector, the leadership of the Reformed church in Béarn repudiated the actions of the political assembly in La Rochelle, ordered their representatives to return home, and sent a deputation to the king to protest their loyalty.[37]

The promulgation of the Edict of Union in 1620, followed by the dissolution of the *conseil souverain*, and the creation of the *parlement* of Navarre in its place, almost completely reversed the monopoly that Huguenot elites had exercised over financial and judicial institutions in Béarn. Louis XIII's decision to unite the *conseil souverain* of Béarn and the chancellery of Saint-Palais in Navarre, composed almost entirely of Catholic

---

[36] BN, MS Dupuy 153, fo. 228.
[37] Issartel, *Les chemins de la tolérance*, pp. 170–83.

officers, in a single parlementary body, and his nomination and promotion of Catholic loyalists to positions within the new *parlement* of Navarre
critically undermined the confessional unanimity so pivotal to Huguenot
hegemony and left venerable Protestant families scrambling to protect
their offices and insinuate themselves into the new institutional framework. Doing so proved to be even more difficult because of Louis's
steadfast refusal to establish a bipartisan chamber within the *parlement*
of Navarre.[38]

In 1629, Louis sealed the dynastic aspirations of Huguenot *officiers*
when he acceded to Pierre de Marca's request to give precedence to
Catholic *présidents* within the *parlement*, citing the honour royal officials
owed to the Catholic church.[39] This action virtually assured the whole-
sale repatriation of the corps of high-ranking magistrates within the *parlement* to the Roman Catholic church over the next decade. Within weeks,
Jacques de Gassion staged a highly public conversion to Catholicism, thus
preserving his office for his oldest son.[40] Over the next several years, the
flurry of conversions to Catholicism among Béarn's office-holding elites
after 1629 suggests how critical public conformity to the religious policies
of the Bourbon state could be to the preservation of a family's political
fortunes. As access to the highest parlementary offices increasingly was
limited by royal decrees, *conseillers* as well as *présidents* abjured the Calvinist
faith in order to consolidate their credit as loyal servitors of the crown and
to preserve their investment for their heirs. Over the next decade, officers in subsidiary courts and financial institutions, such as the *chambre des
comptes*, followed suit, transforming the confessional composition of the
highest levels of the provincial magistracy in Béarn. Staunch Huguenot
loyalists, who refused to embrace the politics of expediency, condemned
their heirs to subordinate positions within *chambre des comptes* or *parlement*,
where they rarely rose above the circle of lawyers, notaries and clerks,
who serviced the needs of the high court.

By mid-century royal policies had crystallized a profound confessional
divide between the highest levels of the parlementary magistracy and
the minor judicial and administrative officers, lawyers and clerks, who
assumed political and moral leadership of the Reformed community in
Pau.[41] In a memoir penned to Colbert in 1663, the *intendant* Pelot could
relate the heartening news that only two high-ranking officers in the

---

[38] M. Forissier, *Histoire de la Réforme en Béarn*, 2 vols. (Tarbes, 1953), I, pp. 136–55.

[39] Issartel, *Les chemins de la tolérance*, p. 309.

[40] P. Salefranque, *Histoire de l'hérésie*, ed. by V. Dubarat, 2 vols. (Pau, 1928), II, pp. 267–9.

[41] F. Guistiani, 'De la Coexistance à l'éxil', thèse, École Nationale de Chartes (1996), esp.
pp. 187–95.

chambre des comptes, the first president Dupont and the ageing master of the accounts, Guillaume Loyard, were adherents of the so-called Reformed faith in Béarn.[42] Two decades later, Pelot's successor, Nicholas Foucault, filed a somewhat more ambivalent report in which he described how the exclusion of members of the RPR from 'all offices and charges' had encouraged those who did not raise their children to take up arms or commerce to study law. As a consequence, Foucault noted ruefully, 'of the 200 or so lawyers who composed the bar of this *parlement*, at least 150 of them are RPR'.[43]

The fortunes of the Loyard family illustrate the singular challenges facing Huguenot elites in the seventeenth century. Like a number of prominent office-holding families, the Loyards owed their political and economic ascendancy in no small part to shrewd marriage alliances and their close association with the house of Navarre. In the mid-sixteenth century, Daniel Loyard, a modestly successful Palois merchant, married Françoise de Sarraberre, the daughter of Pees de Sarraberre, an auditor in the *chambres des comptes*, who resigned his office in favour of his son-in-law.[44] From 1563 to 1582, Loyard served as auditor in the *chambre des comptes*, passing the post to his eldest son Pierre and securing two positions in the *chambre des comptes* for two younger sons, Augustin and another Pierre. A fourth son, Jean, who entered the medical profession, consolidated the family's role in municipal government, serving as *jurat* in Pau at various points during the seventeenth century.[45] To bolster his fortunes and social standing, Loyard aggressively pursued rural properties commensurate with his political status, purchasing the seigneury of Usos, which allowed successive generations to distance themselves from their commercial origins and style themselves as gentlemen.[46]

By the early seventeenth century, the Loyards had established an extensive kinship network that reached outward and downward into the Huguenot/Reformed community. Daniel Loyard parlayed his rising fortunes into advantageous matches for his two younger sons, Augustin and Jean, whose wives brought dowries three to five times higher than the dowries Daniel had paid to the solid, but undistinguished, merchant families to whom he had married his two daughters.[47] In 1602, Augustin

[42] G. B. Depping, *Correspondance administrative sous le règne de Louis XIV*, 2 vols. (Paris, 1851–2), II, p. 116.

[43] N.-J. Foucault, *Mémoires*, ed. by F. Baudry (Paris, 1862), p. 107. See also M. Grosclaude, 'L'intendant Nicholas Foucauld en Béarn en 1684–1685' in *Réformes et Révocation en Béarn*, pp. 61–8.

[44] AD Pyrénées-Atlantiques, B767 (1569), B257 (1568–9), B267 (1581), B2636 (1583).

[45] AD Pyrénées-Atlantiques, E2037, fo. 48.   [46] AD Pyrénées-Atlantiques, E2020; E2134, fo. 1.

[47] AD Pyrénées-Atlantiques, E2000, fos. 81, 98.

willingly set aside confessional differences to marry the daughter of a
petty seigneur from Gan, Jeanne de Labarthe, to whom he promised
'toute liberté de religion' in return for her dowry of 10,000 *francs*;[48] and
by 1605, he had secured a lucrative post within the *conseil souverain*, thus
penetrating the highest ranks of the judicial magistracy. For the next three
decades, the notarial registers bear witness to his painstaking efforts to
enhance his modest estate and establish a strong financial and territorial
hold over the rural community of Rontignon, where he purchased noble
properties.[49] Swapping a few *jornades* of land here and there with fellow
officiers, ruthlessly foreclosing on properties mortgaged by cash-strapped
labourers or occasionally purchasing property outright, Augustin assembled an important collection of rural properties in Rontignon and Gélos,
where he doggedly pursued every minor feudal privilege due him. His
younger brother, Jean, also traded vigorously in real estate and *rentes*,
but the noble status conferred by seigneurial holdings and high office
effectively remained beyond his grasp.[50]

Within a decade of the Edict of Union, the office-holding branches
of the Loyard family split ranks on religious issues. Like many of his
fellow councillors, Augustin readily embraced his wife's Catholicism,
supported his daughter's decision in 1632 to enter the newly established
Ursuline convent in Pau, and aggressively sought marital alliances for his
remaining children from among local nobility.[51] As a consequence of his
efforts, his son, Théophile, and his grandson, Pierre, succeeded him in
parlementary office.[52] By contrast, Guillaume Loyard, who succeeded
his father Pierre as doyen of the *chambre des comptes* in 1625, resisted the
pressure to convert and remained a stalwart member of the Reformed
community. The decision had very little immediate impact on the evolution of his fortunes. He continued to extend his patrimonial holdings in
the community of Usos. His children from a youthful marriage to Marie
de Poeyferre all made distinguished matches with prominent Huguenot
noble and official-holding dynasties.[53] And in 1680, he negotiated a

[48] AD Pyrénées-Atlantiques, E2134, fo. 1.
[49] AD Pyrénées-Atlantiques, E2019, fo. 290 (Gélos); E2024, fos. 422, 690, 764v (Gélos and Rontignon); E2027, fo. 247 (Rontignon); E2031, fo. 219v, 226 (Jurançon); E2035, fo. 196 (Rontignon); E2038, fo. 20, 75, 136 (Rontignon); E2036, fo. 81v, 113 (Gélos); E2040, fo. 163 (Rontignon).
[50] AD Pyrénées-Atlantiques, E2024, fos. 73–4, 419–20, 493–4, 624v; E2031, fos. 241, 280v; E2031, fo. 191; E2039, fos. 2v, 9, 59.
[51] AD Pyrénées-Atlantiques, E2035, fo. 46, E2038, fo. 214, 233.
[52] AD Pyrénées-Atlantiques, E2053; AC Pau, GG5.
[53] AD Pyrénées-Atlantiques, E2025, fo. 28v; E2022, fo. 22.

strategic second marriage with Demoiselle Marie-Thérèse de Bordes, whose father promised his office in *parlement* valued at 36,000 *livres* as her dotal settlement.[54]

By the late-seventeenth century, however, most of Guillaume Loyard's children had converted to Catholicism. Some responded to the tremendous pull of Tridentine spirituality and took religious orders.[55] Others probably embraced Catholicism out of political interest, or perhaps religious indifference, such as Guillaume's two oldest surviving sons, Pierre and Antoine, who could only inherit their patrimonial offices in the *parlement* of Navarre and *chambre des comptes* if they demonstrated nominal allegiance to the Catholic church.[56] Jean Loyard, whose own religious affiliation remains unclear in his testament, saw all of his surviving male children enter the Catholic fold. Only his daughters retained their Calvinist identities, although Jeanne married Abraham Bélaguer, a Catholic *procureur général* (albeit from a family of mixed confessions as well), and baptized her children in the church of Saint Martin.[57]

The chequered pattern of conversion within the Loyard clan reveals how royal office-holding and rallying to royal policies at critical junctures could reverse the advantages of primogeniture, narrow the gulf between cadet branches of office-holding dynasties, and preserve patrimonial fortunes. Neither religious differences nor the striking reversal of rank and privileges, however, adversely affected their profound commitment to the ties of blood and family solidarity. The insular, almost incestuous nature of the marital alliances forged by office-holding elites in Pau exacerbated the dense and confusing thicket of family relationships and brought members of the Reformed church into close social contact with Catholic kindred and friends, especially at liminal moments in the life cycle – baptism, marriage and death – when displays of lineage loyalty became a visible symbol of a family's pre-eminence. Shared professional interests, family attachments and personal affection undoubtedly prompted Abraham Bélaguer and his wife Jeanne Loyard to select Protestant relatives as godparents for at least three of their seven

[54] AD Pyrénées-Atlantiques, E2053. For Guillaume's extensive real-estate dealings, see E2036, fos. 19, 27, 122 (Gélos, Usos); E2038, fos. 7, 212 (Masères, Usos); E2039, fos. 28, 32 (Nay, Usos); E2040, fos. 21, 25–6, 129, 137 (Usos); E2046, fo. 220 (Usos); E2049, fo. 278 (Usos); E2051, fo. 2 (Pau); E2052, fo. 117 (Gélos).
[55] See, for example, the references to Jean de Loyard's third son and namesake, who forsook family fortunes to enter a monastery in Paris: AD Pyrénées-Atlantiques, E2024, fo. 914 (1614). Guillaume de Loyard's youngest son, Cyprien, became archbishop of Perpignan: E2085, fo. 90v.
[56] See AD Pyrénées-Atlantiques, E2063, fo. 344; E2075, fo. 90v.
[57] AD Pyrénées-Atlantiques, E2020, fo. 567; E2053, fo. 663, E2056, fo. 28; AC Pau, GG6.

children.[58] Similar examples of cross-confessional family connections, especially the privileged kin relationships between uncles and aunts and their nieces and nephews, abound in notarial and parish records.

As the case of the Loyard family also illustrates, the political consequences of recusancy weighed much more heavily on men, who risked their offices and dynastic ambitions, than on women whose confessional allegiance posed little immediate threat to their family's public status.[59] In Pau, as in Castres, the wives of Huguenot *officiers* did not necessarily follow their husband's lead and renounce their Calvinist faith when political expediency demanded it. This decision, as Raymond Mentzer has suggested, may have been a 'deliberate and mutual' strategy on the part of some Huguenot couples, who constructed a dual family identity in which women conserved religious traditions within the private, domestic world while their husbands preserved the public face of conformity.[60] The veil of silence, which usually shrouded such decisions, makes it virtually impossible to speculate on how frequently couples embraced this stratagem. The practice was common enough, however, to provoke the *parlement* of Navarre to invoke sanctions against Catholic councillors who permitted their wives to escort children of both sexes to Calvinist services on the spurious pretext that their spouses were of the contrary faith. By the 1670s, parlementary threats to deprive magistrates of their office unless their children made a public profession of Catholic faith rendered such spousal subterfuge extremely precarious.[61]

Considerable pressure, public and private, was often brought to bear on wives of *nouveaux convertis* who refused to adopt their husband's religion. Split households often became the focus of intense confessional battles in which Catholics clerics, friends and neighbours relentlessly lobbied the recusant spouse while Protestant ministers struggled to counterbalance the centripetal dynamic of conversion within the family cell. In 1638, for example, a Palois minister, Pierre d'Abbadie, recounted the covert efforts to convert the wife of a prominent Catholic jurist, Sieur Pardies.[62] For months, relatives and friends had pressured the honourable demoiselle to embrace her husband's faith. Given the porous boundaries of confessional communities, religious conversations and debates were

[58] AC Pau, GG6; see also, Dufau du Maluquer, *Armorial du Béarn*, 3 vols. (Paris, 1889; repr. Marseilles, 1976), II, pp. 322–3.
[59] B. Diefendorf, 'House Divided: Religious Schism in Sixteenth-century Parisian Families' in S. Zimmerman and R. Weissman (eds.), *Urban Life in the Renaissance* (Newark, 1988), pp. 80–99; Mentzer, *Blood and Belief*, pp. 171–4.
[60] Mentzer, *Blood and Belief*, p. 172.   [61] AD Pyrénées-Atlantiques, B4538, fo. 69v.
[62] Pierre d'Abbadie, *La Victoire de la Verité opposée au Triomphe* (Orthez, 1638).

commonplace, and Calvinist ministers themselves even fanned the fires of religious controversy by staging public debates with renowned Jesuit apologists *en mission*.[63] None the less, the delivery of a clandestine note, written by an unknown hand, alerting Abbadie that Demoiselle Pardies was in conference with two Catholic women and a Jesuit, compelled the minister to set aside his sermon notes to engage in a more urgent defence of the faith. For the next six hours, Abbadie records, he sparred with his adversary, Etienne Audibert, until Demoiselle Pardies's assurance that she was 'fortement satisfaite' by his proofs sent Abbadie back to his study. Her subsequent conversion three years later, which Audibert quickly proclaimed in print as proof of the inexorable logic of conversion, prompted Abbadie to engage in a vigorous volley of counter-replies, fearing the ripple effect within the Reformed community.

Nothing comparable to the academy in Castres fostered intellectual co-operation between Catholic and Calvinist magistrates in Pau. The dissolution of the Protestant University of Béarn in 1620, the rapid establishment of two Catholic *collèges*, one by Barnabites in Lescar, the other by Jesuits in Pau, and suppression of scholarship for the sons of Calvinist magistrates forced most office-holding families to educate their male children within institutions that mirrored the re-Catholicization of civic culture in Pau. At the same time, the resurgence of confraternities and penitential societies in the 1630s and 1640s marginalized the Huguenot *noblesse de robe* from participation in key civic institutions.[64] Recruiting primarily among parlementary and judicial elites, confraternities became one of the principal catalysts behind the formation of a cadre of politically powerful 'nouveaux catholiques'. By mid-century royal officers were required to participate in the Candlemas and Corpus Christi processions, which had become potent symbols of public conformity to the religious policies of the Bourbon state.[65]

Marriage contracts and real-estate sales strikingly document the reversal of fortunes that accompanied the slow erosion of political influence, economic power and demographic strength of Huguenot elites in the Pyrenean principality. In contrast to Huguenot communities in the Midi, where Protestant grooms and brides continued to promise settlements at rates significantly higher than their Catholic counterparts, Huguenot

---

[63] A. Eurich, 'La Politique de Différentiation: Controverse et Conversion en Béarn au 17e siècle' in P. Mironneau and I. Pébay-Clottes (eds.), *Actes du Colloque paix des armes, paix des âmes* (Paris, 2000), pp. 332–42.
[64] 'Confrérie du Saint Sacrement', *Bulletin des Sciences, Lettres et Arts de Pau et Béarn* (1909), 192–3.
[65] AD Pyrénées-Atlantiques, B3920.

nobles in Béarn exchanged dowries and widows' jointures which lagged seriously behind their Catholic counterparts and eventually stagnated by the 1660s[66] (see table 8.2, above). While the average dowries offered by members of both confessions increased between the 1620s and 1660s, Huguenot officials could neither match the generous dowries offered by Catholic *officiers* nor attract grooms of similar social status for their daughters. By the 1660s, dotal amounts among Huguenot officers had stagnated, except among minor officials. A similar pattern can be traced in the land sale contracts, where Catholic *parlementaires*' vigorous trading in the real-estate market clearly marked their economic ascendancy and allowed them to increase their fortunes dramatically between 1620 and 1659 against the minor gains of their Huguenot colleagues in lesser offices (see table 8.3, above).

Huguenot officers and their wives responded to their loss of political influence and social standing within the larger community by insisting even more strenuously on the privileges conferred by rank and social status within the Reformed community. The struggles over precedence, which disrupted social relations in Calvinist communities, took on a particularly gendered cast in Pau, where the wives of officers repeatedly elbowed their way to the front of the temple, broke the gendered conventions of space and appropriated benches reserved for male officials, and on busy Communion Sundays sent maids or lackeys in advance to guard their seats.[67] In April 1674, the consistory banned servant retinues, charging that most were 'of the contrary religion' and therefore prone to irreverent and scandalous behaviour, a powerful reminder of the increasingly Catholic universe in which many Huguenot gentlewomen lived.[68] The suppression of royal subventions for ministers' salaries and other fiscal needs after Louis XIII's death in 1643[69] also profoundly tested the commitment of Calvinist consistories to common, cemetery funerals.[70] To raise funds, the consistory in Pau began to grant any wealthy parishioner, with resources to pay the 300 *livres* burial fee, the right to burial inside the temple. Officers and families were among the first to seize this renewed opportunity to establish visual markers of family influence within the temple.[71]

---

[66] Benedict, 'Faith, Fortune and Social Structure', 75–95.
[67] AD Pyrénées-Atlantiques, 60 J 56(1), fos. 16, 98, 117, 157.
[68] AD Pyrénées-Atlantiques, 60 J 56(1), fo. 117.
[69] See AD Pyrénées-Atlantiques, B317 (1610–11), B338 (1623), B363 (1644).
[70] C. Desplat, 'Sépulture et frontière confessionelle: protestants et catholiques de Béarn (XVI et XVIIe siècle)', *Revue de Pau et du Béarn* 23 (1996), 67–75.
[71] AD Pyrénées-Atlantiques, 60 J (56)1, fo. 118.

Through their testamentary and charitable bequests, sometimes amounting to hundreds of *livres*, Huguenot elites, many of them from lesser officials or recusant wives of magistrates, became crucial to the survival of the community and pastoral sustenance.[72] The persistent refusal of heirs, both Catholic and Protestant, to honour the bequests of their benefactors, however, made these legacies difficult to collect and pressed the consistory in Pau to adopt a number of strategies to secure this much-needed income, including commissioning collateral relatives to serve as agents on behalf of the church. In 1668, for example, Pierre de Bélaguer, a clerk in the *parlement* of Navarre, was enjoined to use his professional and familial connections to collect delinquent legacies.[73] Ten years later legacies worth over 2,000 *livres* from the Casaux, Dupont, Gassion, Loyard and St Orenx families were still outstanding, testifying to the waning influence of the Reformed community and the spiritual and material defection of the families who had once sustained it.[74]

The religious wars of the sixteenth century witnessed the critical ascendancy of powerful Huguenot office-holding dynasties throughout France. By the early seventeenth century, the provisions of the Edict of Nantes and the *paulette* guaranteed Huguenot elites access to and dynastic control of high judicial office. Over the course of the seventeenth century, Huguenot office-holding families consolidated their prominence in provincial society by employing the same time-honoured strategies of social promotion and survival as their Catholic counterparts. The renewal of religious conflict in the 1620s, however, marked a significant shift in their social and political fortunes and their relationship with the larger Reformed community. Throughout the Huguenot crescent, Calvinist magistrates counselled their co-religionaries to remain loyal to the crown, constructed moderate political coalitions with local Catholic leaders, and struggled to defend the legitimacy of their nascent royalism against the rising tide of militancy. In the aftermath of the 1620s rebellions, their political and moral authority within the Reformed community was jeopardized even further when they emerged among the chief beneficiaries of the spoils system by which the crown had rallied the opposition leadership behind its policies throughout the entire course of the religious wars. To interpret the ease with which some members of the magistracy accepted financial emoluments, titles and offices from

---

[72] AD Pyrénées-Atlantiques, B2043, fos. 94, 163, 249–50, 271.
[73] AD Pyrénées-Atlantiques, 60 J 56(1), fos. 9–14.
[74] AD Pyrénées-Atlantiques, 60 J 56(1), fos. 178–9.

the crown as mere self-interest ignores the deeply entrenched paternalism of Huguenot governing elites, who continued to envision themselves as brokers on behalf of the Reformed community. None the less, royal patronage transformed them into the chief architects of bipartisan programmes which increasingly restricted the presence and influence of their co-religionists in civic life and society.

In Béarn the complete destruction of the institutional grid that had perpetuated Huguenot hegemony in the principality forced ambitious families into at least public religious conformity with the state by the 1630s. In the dense Huguenot communities of the Midi, the Calvinist magistrates in towns such as Castres, Nîmes and Montpellier continued to dominate civic and cultural life, thanks to the continuing vitality of a broad array of political and cultural institutions which preserved their influence. Through their personal and professional connections with Catholic elites with whom they shared common dynastic ambitions, royalist loyalties and cultural interests, they modelled standards of peaceful coexistence which allowed them to mediate the restoration of Catholic hegemony and royal power. From the mid-seventeenth century onward, however, the politics and practice of confessionalization limited the reach of Huguenot office-holding families, even in the Midi, and forced them to reconfigure their political aspirations and public identities. By encouraging members of the next generation to convert or to seek their fortunes beyond the judicial bureaucracies of the Bourbon state, they sanctioned strategies of survival that sealed the withdrawal of Huguenots from political life even before the crown fully proscribed it.

On 5 September 1625, Arnaud Bordenave addressed the *parlement* of Navarre in French rather than his native Béarnais and proclaimed his desire 'henceforth to speak the language of the king in a dignified fashion'.[75] As brokers of royal power in the provinces, Huguenot office-holders struggled to speak the language of the king in word and deed while remaining loyal to their family and religious identities. Over the course of the seventeenth century, their integration into the larger administrative and cultural apparatus of the Bourbon state signalled the marginalization and transformation of the Huguenot magistracies of southern France and the inexorable disappearance of the Reformed communities they served.

---

[75] Issartel, *Les chemins de la tolérance*, p. 269.

9. The Huguenot academies: preparing for an uncertain future

Karin Maag

As the Reformation gained ground in France during the sixteenth century, French Protestants established academies to provide higher education and training for the Huguenot intellectual elite and their future pastors. The late sixteenth and early seventeenth century saw the creation of eight academies, from Saumur and Sedan in the north, to a concentration of academies in the south, at Orthez, Montauban, Montpellier, Nîmes, Orange and Die.[1] The life-span and history of these institutions mirrors that of Protestantism at the time: a first wave of academies was created during the 1560s and 1570s, at a moment of expansion for Calvinism in France. The second set of academies appeared around the time of the Edict of Nantes in 1598 as the Huguenots began to establish themselves more confidently for the longer term, albeit constrained by the relatively narrow restrictions of the edict. All of these centres of Protestant higher education were then shut down one by one, mainly in the latter half of the seventeenth century as the allied powers of a rejuvenated Catholicism and the crown moved against these public manifestations of the Huguenots' continued existence.

What led the French Reformed leadership on a local, regional and national level to expend significant time and financial resources on the provision of higher education? What did their investment say about the value of centres of higher study for the Calvinist communities? Why and how were the Huguenot academies targeted so strongly by the Catholic authorities in the later seventeenth century? This essay seeks to address these questions by examining surviving sources which detail the phases of the academies' existence and by setting the analysis in the context of Reformed higher education in the early modern period.

---

[1] In chronological order, the foundation dates were Nîmes in 1562, Orthez in 1566, Orange in 1573, Montpellier in 1596, Saumur and Montauban in 1598, Sedan in 1602 and Die in 1604.

The ninth national synod of the French Reformed churches, meeting at Sainte-Foy in 1578, urged delegates, in its second article, 'to consider all the possible options to establish schools, in which youths will be brought up and trained to serve the church of God in the future, by entering the holy ministry'.[2] In spite of the pressures of endemic civil war, the Huguenots saw the provision of education as a priority.[3] To understand both the reasons for the Huguenots' commitment to education and the shape this education took, one must first consider the situation which the French Reformed churches faced in this domain in sixteenth-century Europe.

Until the first decades of the sixteenth century, higher education was primarily offered in universities, institutions whose privileges and rights to confer degrees were confirmed through papal and imperial or royal charters. These centres of higher learning were accessible to all young men who could afford the time and money for these studies.[4] Yet as the Reformation gained momentum in France, committed Calvinists were increasingly unwilling to send their sons to these less welcoming Catholic universities. By 1564, for instance, Pope Pius IV had stated that only Catholics could receive degrees in the universities.[5] Furthermore, as the Reformed churches in France expanded in number and established themselves for the long term, the Huguenots began to realize that they needed to train sufficient numbers of pastors for the increasing congregations. At the fifth national synod in Paris in 1565, the delegates urged wealthier churches to support young men in their university studies, so that they could later serve as pastors.[6] One possibility for Huguenots was to send their sons outside France to study. For instance, the creation of the Genevan academy in 1559 provided a welcoming and respected place of training for the future French Calvinist leadership.[7]

However, sending young Frenchmen to study beyond France's borders raised a number of difficulties. First of all, these universities and

---

[2] Aymon, I, p. 126. See also the first paragraphs of Solange Deyon's overview, 'Les Académies protestantes en France', *BSHPF* 135 (1989), 77–85.

[3] To preserve the focus of this contribution, I will not discuss in detail the provision of education at the level of the vernacular schools or the *collèges* (Latin schools), except where they are directly connected with the academies.

[4] L. W. B. Brockliss, *French Higher Education in the Seventeenth and Eighteenth Centuries: A Cultural History* (Oxford, 1987), pp. 13–16.

[5] M. R. di Simone, 'Admission' in H. de Ridder-Symoens (ed.), *A History of the University in Europe*, 4 vols. (Cambridge, 1996), II, pp. 293–4.

[6] Aymon, I, p. 70.

[7] K. Maag, *Seminary or University? The Genevan Academy and Reformed Higher Education, 1560–1620* (Ashgate, 1995), pp. 103–28. See also D. Bourchenin, *Étude sur les académies protestantes en France au XVIe et XVIIe siècles* (Geneva, 1969), pp. 93–6.

academies could not necessarily train sufficient numbers of French pastors to meet the needs of the growing number of congregations.[8] Secondly, and perhaps more importantly, the Huguenot church was increasingly keen to oversee ministers' training directly, to ensure that the doctrinal and educational standards the authorities sought were actually met. In part, this increasing interest in direct oversight was a result of the growing institutionalization of the Huguenot church: as it became more established, its vested interest in having clergy whose orthodoxy and academic achievements were beyond question correspondingly grew. The combination of these pressures increasingly led the Huguenots to consider creating their own centres of higher education.

However, establishing the Huguenot academies was a gradual process. The first phase of expansion in the 1560s came to an end with the disruption of the civil wars.[9] Apart from the damaging effects of warfare, at the heart of the Huguenot academies' slow establishment and longer-term difficulties were financial issues. Even if at a local level certain French cities such as Montauban had a majority of Protestants on the city council, the overall political situation was still one in which Catholicism remained dominant. Hence the Huguenots could not expect to be able to redirect significant public funds into education. As for any extra funds coming from the Huguenot communities, these normally went to the urgent tasks of defence and paying the salaries of the clergy. By examining firstly the establishment and structure of the academies, and then analyzing in greater depth the weaknesses these institutions faced, this essay considers the feasibility of the plans of the French Calvinists for locally available higher education.[10]

It should be noted that series of Calvinist public lectures had been given in a few cities on an occasional basis in the 1560s, in Caen and Orléans, for example. For instance, the public lectures organized by the Reformed in Hebrew, Greek and theology in Orléans began in 1561 as the Huguenots occupied the city, and stopped in 1568, after the end of the second religious war, as the city returned to Catholicism. It is unclear what formal status these lectures had. Nathaniel Weiss, basing himself on Paul de Felice, writes of a 'faculté de théologie', attached to the university in Orléans, which specialized in law. However, evidence is lacking

---

[8] Bibliothèque Publique et Universitaire, Geneva, MS Fr 197a, fo. 92. The church of Nîmes wrote to Geneva on 12 May 1561, asking for a pastor, and pointing out that at the recent provincial synod in Saintes, there were only ten ministers for fifty-four churches.

[9] See Richard Stauffer's analysis of the academies' difficulties in the early period in 'Le Calvinisme et les Universités', *BSHPF* 126 (1980), 42.

[10] See *ibid.*, 41–6.

to confirm that a faculty of theology was formally established. Claude de la Grange, who attended these lectures, noted that about a hundred students had received bursaries from the Calvinist cardinal, Odet de Châtillon, to follow these courses.[11] As no formally constituted academy was established in these cities, they will not be discussed at length, but do serve as a reminder that Huguenot higher education could also be provided outside officially established institutions.[12] Eight academies served the needs of the French Huguenots, even though three of these (Orthez, Orange and Sedan) were in independent territories outside the borders of France in the sixteenth century. Three others within France were essentially municipal foundations, which only gradually received support from the French national synods (Montpellier, Nîmes and Die). The final two, Montauban and Saumur, were officially established and supported by the national synods from their foundation onwards. Indeed, these two seemed to have the best chance to survive and flourish, as they could hope to receive the lion's share of available funding from the Huguenot church. Yet even these two institutions faced difficulties almost from the very beginning.

The foundation date of the academy of Montauban is unclear: while the national synod of Montpellier in 1598 granted Montauban 1,110 écus for the creation of its academy, the synodal proceedings speak of the academy in the future tense: it was a project, not a completed undertaking.[13] As the majority of Montauban's population was Calvinist, it seemed to the magistrates and to the national Huguenot church to be an ideal location for a collège (Latin school) and linked academy. The collège focused on providing education in Latin at a grammar-school or high-school level. Municipal collèges had flourished in France since the early years of the sixteenth century, and had in fact been one of the first provincial settings for the dissemination of Protestant ideas through the influence of the teachers, known as regents. By the second half of the sixteenth century, urban centres under Huguenot control took over pre-existing collèges or created new ones, thus building a network of Calvinist Latin schools for the sons of Huguenot families.[14]

---

[11] See N. Weiss, 'Une des premieres Écoles de Théologie protestantes en France (Orléans 1561–1568)', *BSHPF* 60 (1911), 218–24.

[12] See the brief remarks by Henri Meylan, 'Collèges et académies protestantes en France au XVIe siècle' in his (ed.), *D'Erasme à Théodore de Bèze: problèmes de l'Église et de l'École chez les Réformés* (Geneva, 1976), p. 306, and G. Lewis, 'The Geneva Academy' in A. Pettegree, A. Duke and G. Lewis (eds.), *Calvinism in Europe, 1540–1620* (Cambridge, 1994), p. 51.

[13] Aymon, I, p. 225.

[14] For information on the municipal *collèges*, see G. Huppert, *Public Schools in Renaissance France* (Urbana, IL, 1984). For the impact of Protestantism introduced by the regents and then

The statutes of the *collège* and academy of Montauban were promulgated in 1600.[15] These statutes established Montauban, on paper at least, as a leading centre of contemporary higher education. The regulations called for two professors in theology, as well as chairs of Hebrew and Greek. There were also provisions for professorships in law, medicine and mathematics, though there is no evidence that these chairs were ever formally occupied. Finally, the statutes established two chairs in philosophy, the foundational field for all students pursuing higher studies. The *collège* was to have seven classes, headed by a principal, who would in turn report to the rector of the academy. The latter had overall charge over educational matters, and the statutes indicate that he was to be appointed from among the pastors and professors of the city.[16]

The creation and structure of Montauban's academy reflected the standard approach taken by these Calvinist centres of learning, following the pattern of others such as Strasbourg's Latin school and the Genevan academy.[17] Geneva in particular provided the model of an institution divided into two parts, a Latin school and a university-level section, enabling students to continue their training without interruption at the same location. The academy of Saumur, in northern France, adopted a similar path. As well as receiving synodal support from 1598 onwards on a par with Montauban, the Saumur academy came into being largely through the efforts of Philippe Duplessis-Mornay, royal governor of Saumur since 1588. Duplessis-Mornay was actively involved in the academy's affairs, from his appeal to Henri IV for official permission to establish it, to his search for suitable professors. In 1593, Duplessis-Mornay requested a copy of the statutes of Leiden University (founded in 1575) as a model, undoubtedly in part to compare his project with the curriculum of the increasingly flourishing Dutch university. Duplessis-Mornay was also hoping to have direct input from Leiden, as he sought (unsuccessfully) to attract Franciscus Junius from there to Saumur.[18] The academy of Saumur was established only gradually, for although the

established in Calvinist *collèges*, see J. Fouilleron and A. Blanchard, 'En Conclusion: réforme et education: positions et propositions' in Jean Boisset (ed.), *La Réforme et l'éducation* (Toulouse, 1974), pp. 181–90. Accounts of particular *collèges* include: F. Delteil, 'Le Collège protestant de Millau' and M. Reulos, 'L'Organisation, le fonctionnement et les programmes du collège protestant de Saint-Lo (1563)' both in Boisset, *La Réforme et l'éducation*, pp. 19–34 and pp. 143–51.

[15] The text of the statutes is available in Abbé Marcellin and M. G. Ruck, 'Lois et règlements de l'Académie de Montauban', *BSHPF* 9 (1860), 394–408.

[16] Marcellin and Ruck, 'Lois et règlements', 398–9, 402–4.

[17] H. Meylan, 'Le Recrutement et la formation des pasteurs dans les Églises Réformées du XVI siècle' in Meylan, *D'Erasme à Théodore de Bèze*, pp. 235–58.

[18] R. Patry, *Philippe Du Plessis-Mornay: un huguenot homme d'état (1549–1623)* (Paris, 1933), p. 436.

first professors were appointed in 1599–1600, the official dedication ceremony did not take place until 1606.[19] The academy made no attempt
to offer courses in law or medicine: instead it focused on the humanities, the ancient languages and theology, appointing two professors in
each area. The *collège* of Saumur also had a more limited scope than its
Montauban counterpart, as it offered only five classes to Montauban's
seven.[20]

The significant influence of Duplessis-Mornay as a local organizing force for Saumur's academy points to a decisive factor in the creation of three other Calvinist academies serving the Huguenot church,
namely the central role of local powers in establishing centres of higher
education in their areas. Thus the academy of Orthez in Béarn was set
up thanks to the support of the princely house of Navarre, which ruled the
territory. Established in 1566, the academy of Orthez had professors in
theology, Hebrew, Greek, philosophy and mathematics, and once again
was linked to a *collège* with five classes for the Latin school pupils. There
is no evidence of professors of law or medicine in Orthez.[21] Funding for
the academy did not come from the national synods, although Orthez
appeared in 1607 and again in 1612 in the synod records as a legitimate
place for young Huguenots to study.[22] Instead, the academy's income
came primarily from secularized Catholic benefices held in Béarn. The
arrangement ensured a measure of financial stability for the academy,
although professors began to complain about their low salaries and poor
working conditions even before the kingdom was occupied by France
in 1620.[23] Béarn's academy did, however, succeed in attracting leading
Calvinists: both the Reformer Pierre Viret and the scholar and theologian Lambert Daneau were active in Béarn and its academy towards
the end of their very productive lives. These men had made significant
contributions to the Reformation across Europe: their presence in Béarn
highlights once again the importance of these centres of learning on the
broader European scene.[24]

Like its counterpart in Navarre, the academy in Orange played a major
role in Calvinism beyond its territorial borders. A university was founded
in Orange in 1365, but by 1573 the institution had been transformed

---

[19] *Ibid.*, pp. 437–8.   [20] Bourchenin, *Étude*, p. 144.
[21] J. Lourde-Rocheblave, 'Académie protestante d'Orthez', *BSHPF* 3 (1855), 286–7; Bourchenin,
Étude, pp. 107–10; M. Greengrass, 'The Calvinist Experiment in Béarn' in Pettegree, Duke and
Lewis, *Calvinism in Europe*, p. 137.
[22] Aymon, I, pp. 312, 430.
[23] Lourde-Rocheblave, 'Académie protestante d'Orthez', 283–4.
[24] Meylan, 'Collèges et académies', p. 307; Greengrass, 'The Calvinist Experiment', p. 137.

into an academy and was in the hands of Protestants, as the territory was part of the lands held by the Nassau family. Officially, the academy of Orange survived until 1789, but little information remains about its workings, curriculum or finances.[25] The *collège* of Orange did, however, serve as an alternative educational resource for young Protestants in the later seventeenth century, especially for those from Nîmes after 1634, when their own *collège* was officially divided between Jesuit and Reformed regents. Young Nîmes Protestants who did not wish to attend classes taught by the Jesuits in their local *collège* travelled to Orange to enrol in equivalent classes within an institution wholly run and staffed by Calvinists.[26]

Another option for higher study among young Huguenots by the early seventeenth century was the renowned academy of Sedan, founded officially in 1602 through the work and support of the ducal de Bouillon family, which ruled the principality of Sedan. The *collège* of Sedan had been established in 1579. Sedan's academy offered the widest range of subjects of any of these centres of learning, as there were professors of philosophy, mathematics, Hebrew, Greek, theology and law, but not medicine. The academy was funded, like Orthez, through the use of the secularized benefices of the principality. Although the territory of Sedan lay outside France, the French national synods quickly came to consider Sedan's academy as one of their own. Not only did they list Sedan alongside the other academies on French soil, but the national synod of Gergeau in 1601 began a policy of helping to fund the Sedan academy, to contribute to its flourishing state. By 1603, the national synod of Gap increased the church's contribution from 500 to 800 *écus* per year.[27]

One further group of academies were mainly municipal foundations and, as such, faced a more uncertain destiny, as they lacked both a steady source of funds and the higher profile of their sister institutions. The first of these, the academy of Montpellier, developed from a series of intermittent public lectures given by Protestant scholars in the city beginning in the late 1540s. The university of Montpellier, a separate institution, already taught law and medicine. Prior to the civil wars, Montpellier had also had a faculty of arts, known as the *école mage*, which had closed during the conflict. By 1596, the consuls of Montpellier petitioned Henri IV to grant letters patent to restore the faculty of arts, and he complied

[25] Bourchenin, *Étude*, pp. 111–12.
[26] See P. Chareyre, 'Les derniers feux de l'Académie de Nîmes' in Roger Grossi (ed.), *Le Collège Royal et l'Académie protestante de Nîmes aux XVIe et XVIIe siècles* (Nîmes, 1998), pp. 259–60.
[27] Bourchenin, *Étude*, pp. 122–3; Aymon, I, pp. 251–2, 276.

with their request. The *collège des arts* was to be half Catholic, half Protestant, and salaries were to come from the *gabelle*, or salt tax. Among the first professors, intended to attract students and revive learning, was the Calvinist Greek scholar, Isaac Casaubon.[28] The Huguenots added posts in theology and Hebrew to these chairs sanctioned by the king, so that the institution did receive some synodal support: the national synod of Montpellier in 1598 granted it a share of the money provided by Henri IV, but only assigned less than half the amount given to Montauban and Saumur, namely 500 *écus* rather than 1,100 *écus*.[29] Clearly, the academy of Montpellier did not rank as high in the synod delegates' estimation as did the other two, perhaps because of Montpellier's more limited scope.[30]

Another small academy was that of Nîmes, geographically close to Montpellier. The city of Nîmes established a *collège* and a faculty of arts in 1539, thanks to privileges granted by François I. These schools had been open to all, both Catholics and Protestants.[31] Over the years, however, Nîmes's population increasingly supported the Reformation, and by 1562, the consistory of Nîmes established a school of theology, complete with professors in theology, Hebrew and Greek. By 1582, the statutes of the Nîmes academy added chairs in Latin eloquence and in law. Nîmes's academy received slightly more support than Montpellier's from the national synod of 1598, namely 560 *écus*. That disparity continued even in subsequent years, as by 1603 Nîmes received 611 *écus*, while Montpellier still only received 500.[32]

The last academy under discussion is that of Die, in south-eastern France. The area of the Dauphiné in which Die lay was heavily Protestant. Die's academy, like Montpellier, only had a minimal range of subjects: there was one chair of theology, one of Hebrew and two of philosophy, and at times these were held jointly.[33] The academy of Die was slow to receive financial support from the national synods and consistently received smaller amounts than the other academies. In 1612, the delegates from the Dauphiné appealed for help from the national synod of Privas, and were granted a single payment of 1,000 *livres*, taken

[28] Bourchenin, *Étude*, pp. 125–7. See also M. Pattison, *Isaac Casaubon 1559–1614* (Oxford, 1892), pp. 79–82.

[29] Aymon, I, p. 225. [30] Bourchenin, *Étude*, p. 128.

[31] On the early period of higher education in Nîmes, see M. J. Gaufrès, *Claude Baduel et la réforme des études au XVIe siècle* (Geneva, 1969).

[32] Bourchenin, *Étude*, pp. 106–7; F. Moreil, 'Le Collège et l'Académie réformée de Nîmes', *BSHPF* 122 (1976), 77–86; Aymon, I, pp. 225, 279.

[33] Bourchenin, *Étude*, pp. 152–3, 467

from the sum allocated to the province of Bas-Languedoc.[34] The rest of the income for the Die academy came from the Protestant churches in the provincial synod and from the city authorities.[35]

Clearly, the national synods recognized that the work of the Die academy should be supported, even if only minimally at first. Indeed, the financial involvement of the national synods in the academies is but one indicator of the hopes that were placed in these institutions to train young men to become the future leaders of the Huguenot church. Sought-after leaders included future professors, to ensure that the academies would continue to find qualified and trained teaching staff. For example, the academy of Saumur suggested to the provincial synod in 1617 that each region set aside 400 *livres* for the preparation of two young men in each academy for careers as theology professors. However, this suggestion was never implemented.[36] As for the importance of the academies as training centres for ministers, in 1604 the duc de Bouillon wrote that he had established the academy of Sedan in his lands as 'an academy and school of faith, which has been providing a number of pastors over the last five years, to restore twenty-five or thirty churches'.[37]

By offering both theological training for future pastors and the standard philosophy curriculum, the academies hoped to become a 'one-stop resource' for Calvinist students, and the presence of the *collèges* also contributed to this integrative approach to education. The intention was to have students follow the entire curriculum, from the first years of the *collège* through the classes of the academy. To ensure that oversight and teaching were as uniform as possible across the academies and to deal with complaints about students' behaviour and lack of interest in their studies, by 1603 the national synods began to call for common statutes for these institutions.[38] These regulations finally appeared in the records of the national synod of Alès in 1620.[39] These statutes are of interest as they show both the intended structure and operation of the academies and the national synods' priorities regarding higher education. In terms of

---

[34] Aymon, I, p. 438. Aymon's text reads 3,000 *livres*, but this seems to be a mistake, as the next synod refers to 1,000 *livres*, as do all the secondary sources.

[35] A. Rochas, 'L'Académie de Die et quelques-uns des Professeurs qui y ont enseigné (1604–1684)', *BSHPF* 5 (1857), 299–300. On 28 October 1604, the consuls and pastors set up a contract specifying that the city would pay 1,400 *livres* annually for the academy taken from income from the public weights, and the churches of Dauphiné would pay 3,000 *livres* annually.

[36] Bourchenin, *Étude*, p. 350.   [37] *Ibid.*, p. 121.

[38] Aymon, I, p. 275. For complaints about the students and the synod's call to improve behaviour and standards, see *ibid.*, II, p. 124.

[39] *Ibid.*, II, pp. 36, 209–12.

supervision, the synodal regulations called for two academic councils to be created for each academy. The first was the ordinary council, whose members were the pastors, professors and regents of the highest classes in the *collège*. This council was to meet weekly and deal with the day-to-day affairs of the academy and the rector of the academy was answerable to this body. The second was the extraordinary council, whose members were to be leading figures of the local church, appointed by the magistrates in fully Protestant areas and by the consistory elsewhere.[40]

At a local level, therefore, the national synods ratified the communal control of the academies' operations, concentrated in the hands of church members. Unlike the case of the Genevan academy, the synodal regulations left no room for the civil authorities to do more than appoint members of the extraordinary council. By preserving the oversight of the academies in church hands, the French synods implicitly underlined the very different political realities of France. Entrusting the control of the academies to members of the Calvinist churches was one way to make sure that these institutions would not lose their confessional character.

Apart from strong administrative procedures, the statutes also focused on other ways to attract students. One key aspect of the academies' drawing power was their curriculum. The strengths of this programme did not lie in its innovative content: in many ways the French Calvinist academies were no different from their counterparts in the Swiss lands, Geneva or the German territories. In fact, the broad similarity in approach served to integrate the Huguenot centres of learning into the network of Protestant academies and universities visited by a stream of young men from across Europe.[41] As previously noted, most of the academies focused primarily on philosophy, the ancient languages, and theology. Indeed, theology and theological training remained the goal of these institutions: the majority of the statutes of Alès in 1620 dealt with theological studies, as ten of the seventeen articles specified the content of the courses, coursework and conduct of the theology students.[42] The Alès statutes called for at least two theology professors, one focusing on Scripture and the other

[40] *Ibid.*, II, pp. 209–10.
[41] On the Huguenot academies' attractiveness for foreign students, see J.-P. Pittion, 'Les Académies réformées de l'Édit de Nantes à la Révocation' in R. Zuber and L. Theis (eds.), *La Révocation de l'Édit de Nantes et le protestantisme français en 1685* (Paris, 1986), p. 200.
[42] Although the pastorate was not the only career intended by the students in the Huguenot academies, the weight of scholarship does agree that the academies' main goal was indeed the training of future pastors. See Deyon, 'Les Académies protestantes en France', 81–2. Sedan and Nîmes, however, did appoint professors of law. None of the academies managed to have more than intermittent instruction in medicine: Bourchenin, *Étude*, pp. 233, 463–72.

on doctrine. If possible, three professors should be found, two of them dividing the study of the Old and New Testaments between them.[43] Although the theological position of each academy differed somewhat, with Saumur considered as the more liberal and Sedan as the more theologically conservative, all these academies shared a common focus on the understanding of the biblical text as the foundation of theological discourse.[44]

Once again, this approach was the norm in Calvinist centres of learning.[45] The interesting feature of the national synods' oversight of theology, however, is the care they took over the professors' methodology. The synod of Alès specified that 'the professors of theology will abstain as much as possible from arcane topics and the vain scholarship of Catholic scholastics. Except where necessary in interpreting passages of Holy Scripture, they will not deal at length with the refutation of heresies which have never surfaced here. Their explanations in dogmatic instruction should be serious and straightforward, following the tone in the writings which God has used in these recent times to rekindle the flame of the Gospel.'[46] The fact that the national synod insisted on warning professors about their approach suggests that the church authorities felt that professors were in danger of preferring form over content. In an era in which oral and written debates between Catholics and Protestants in France still took place, the training centres of the Huguenot church had to tread cautiously. On the one hand, they had to prepare their students for such encounters and on the other make sure the future pastors were sufficiently grounded not only in polemic but also in the knowledge and abilities needed to sustain their ministry.[47] Here the Huguenot academies' authority to confer degrees was significant, since a degree enabled Protestant graduates to compete on a more equal footing with their Catholic rivals. With a doctorate in theology, Huguenot pastors could match the qualifications of their Catholic opponents when engaged in oral or written controversies. Conferring theological degrees on its future pastors also enabled the Huguenot church to underline the seriousness of the academic preparation undertaken by these young men, and allowed the synods to refer to the academies as 'universities' in their records.

---

[43] Aymon, II, p. 210.   [44] See Pittion's helpful analysis, 'Les Académies réformées', pp. 194–9.
[45] L. Brockliss, 'Curricula' in de Ridder-Symoens, *A History of the University*, II, pp. 595–6.
[46] Aymon, II, p. 203.
[47] Pittion argues convincingly that the academies were relatively successful in generating an esprit de corps among the students: see Pittion, 'Les Académies réformées', pp. 197–9.

Because of their wish to see these academies flourish, their academic councils also made strenuous efforts to employ professors who would enhance the institutions through their lectures and contribution as scholars. Although talented professors were at times hard to find, the Huguenot academies did their best to attract men of high calibre, who contributed significantly to the drawing power of the academies. The most renowned professors included men such as Moïse Amyraut at Saumur, Pierre du Moulin at Sedan and Daniel Chamier at Montauban.[48] At times, the same professor taught in different academies, such as John Cameron, who taught philosophy in Sedan from 1602 to 1604, theology at Saumur from 1618 to 1622 and at Montauban between 1624 and 1625.[49] Cameron's career and that of others shows both how mobile professors were and how permeable academic disciplines could be, since it was possible for some individuals to teach in a variety of fields. Cameron was also only one of a number of foreign-born professors teaching in the Huguenot academies, indicating once again how well these institutions were integrated into the European Reformed world of higher education.[50] Indeed, the academies contributed to the development of a Europe-wide Protestant culture, as they served as both training centres and focal points of intellectual and scholarly activity. Men such as Pierre Bayle, the eminent philosopher and editor of the *Dictionnaire historique et critique*, the theologian and hebraist Louis Cappel, and the Cartesian philosopher Jean-Robert Chouet all taught in the Huguenot academies. Their influence spread not only among their students but also throughout Europe, through their writings, correspondence and contacts with other scholars.[51]

The fame of these professors was clearly one of the drawing points for students to enrol in the Huguenot academies. However, any analysis

[48] On Amyraut, see B. Armstrong, *Calvinism and the Amyraut Heresy: Protestant Scholasticism and Humanism in Seventeenth-century France* (Madison, WI, 1969). On du Moulin, see Frans Pieter van Stam, *The Controversy over the Theology of Saumur, 1635–1650* (Amsterdam, 1988). On Chamier, see C. A. Read, 'Daniel Chamier, nouvelles recherches et informations nouvelles, généalogiques, biographiques, bibliographiques', *BSHPF* 35 (1886), 160–8, 227–40, 364–75, 410–22, 557–65.

[49] On Cameron's career, see Bourchenin, *Étude*, pp. 463–8. On Cameron's significance for theology at Saumur and in France, see Armstrong, *Calvinism and the Amyraut Heresy*, pp. 42–70.

[50] Scottish professors in particular were very prevalent: see David Murray, 'Ninian Campbell, Professor of Eloquence at Saumur, Minister of Kilmacolm and of Rosneath', *Scottish Historical Review* 18 (1921), 183–98. Deyon speaks of around forty foreign professors, from Scotland but also from the Netherlands, Zurich, Basle and Geneva: Deyon, 'Les Académies protestantes', 84.

[51] On the academies' contribution to Protestant learning and culture see Bourchenin, *Étude*, pp. 395–441. The theological debates opposing conservative Sedan to the more liberal Saumur would go beyond the scope and remit of this contribution. Interested readers should consult Armstrong, *Calvinism and the Amyraut Heresy* as a starting point.

of the number of students, their aims and the impact of the education they received will be partial at best, given that no complete matriculation records have survived for any of the academies. There is some anecdotal evidence of the overall enrolment in some of the academies: in 1610, the academy of Die noted that it had 28 students enrolled, while 106 were in the *collège*. In 1618, this number had risen slightly to 34 in the academy but dropped to 73 in the *collège*.[52] Die was one of the smallest academies. In 1608, Philippe Duplessis-Mornay wrote to the duchesse de La Trémouille that there were no fewer than 400 students in Saumur's academy, although this number undoubtedly included both those in the *collège* and in the academy itself.[53] Other information from Saumur's records suggests that there was an average of about twenty-five students in philosophy and six to ten in theology every year between 1607 and 1661.[54] Charles Garrisson, in his account of Montauban's academy between 1659 and 1661, claims that the *collège* and academy together had more than 500 students, although he does not specify how many students were in each section, nor does he provide a source for this figure.[55] Information on student enrolments in the other academies is largely lacking. The numbers were small, however, compared with the attendance at other institutions across Europe, and indicate something of the difficulties facing the Huguenot academies in finding a secure and sustained level of student matriculations.[56]

One of the reasons for low enrolments by the later seventeenth century was the growing pressure on the Huguenot academies from the king and the Catholic church in France. By 1685, at the Revocation of the Edict of Nantes, the last of these academies was shut down. However, the official order to close was the final nail in the coffin, rather than a bolt out of the blue for Huguenot higher education. For years, the academies had been suffering under the double burden of internal problems and external pressures. When Louis XIV proclaimed the closure of the academies, he was ordering the shut-down of institutions that were already ailing.

The main problem facing the academies was the concerted opposition of both the crown and many of the leading forces in the Catholic church to the existence of Protestantism in France in general, and specifically to the presence of the academies. The bases of opposition are not

[52] A. Roux, 'L'Académie de Die, en Dauphiné (1604–1684)' in Boisset, *La Réforme et l'éducation*, pp. 113–14.
[53] Patry, *Philippe Du Plessis-Mornay*, p. 439. [54] Pittion, 'Les Académies réformées', p. 195.
[55] C. Garrisson, 'Les Préludes de la Révocation à Montauban (1659–1661)', *BSHPF* 42 (1893), 8.
[56] For comparisons with Geneva and the university of Heidelberg for the first two decades of the seventeenth century, see Maag, *Seminary or University?*, p. 82.

hard to find. First, for the tidy-minded royal officials and seemingly for the king himself, French Protestantism and its official institutions presented an anomaly and hindered the effective and efficient control of the entire country.[57] Secondly, the academies provided training to the young Huguenot elite, reinforcing their beliefs, and provided leaders for the Huguenot church. While the national synods and others viewed the academies as *pépinières*, or nurseries for the next generation, Catholic leaders described the situation differently. In a letter to Cardinal Mazarin in 1659, the bishop of Montauban, Pierre de Bertier, wrote 'Your eminence should shut down the *collège* and academy which are the source of all sedition, and if the Huguenots must have such institutions, let the king place them in towns where the violence of the *proposants* and students studying for the ministry can be better contained. The students here are learning rebellion and disobedience.'[58] It should be noted, however, that even when the Catholic authorities got their wish and the academies were closed, this did not necessarily end all pastoral training. In Nîmes, for example, even after the academy was shut in 1664, young men who had completed their academic studies elsewhere returned to the city to gain covert practical experience before being ordained.[59]

Apart from calling for closure of the Calvinist centres of learning, various groups within the Catholic church also tried to limit these academies' impact by establishing competing Catholic *collèges* in the immediate vicinity, attempting to draw away the students in the Protestant institutions. As the *collèges* fed into the academies, the longer-term consequence of a decline in attendance at the former would lead to enrolment problems in the academies. The Jesuits were the leading Catholic educators in France, specializing in the creation of *collèges*, which followed a similar curriculum to the Huguenot ones, apart from the confessional approach.[60] Indeed, the two systems were so similar that the Jesuits' schools were attractive even to Calvinist families, who were willing to put aside their confessional allegiance in order to have their sons benefit from attending the schools of the majority. The national synods did all they could to prevent parents from sending their children to Jesuit *collèges*. In 1578, the national

57 Pittion, 'Les Académies protestantes', pp. 200–1.
58 *Proposants* were theology students intending to become pastors and often supported financially by the churches. They were called *proposants* because they were required to give practice sermons as part of their training. See Garrisson, 'Les Préludes', 12.
59 See Chareyre, 'Les derniers feux', pp. 285–6.
60 See E. Labrousse, *Une foi, une loi, un roi? Essai sur la Révocation de l'Édit de Nantes* (Geneva, 1985), p. 143 for her comments on the curriculum. On Jesuit *collèges*, see A. Lynn Martin, *The Jesuit Mind: The Mentality of an Elite in Early Modern France* (Ithaca, NY, 1988), pp. 43–63.

synod of Sainte-Foy stated that parents who sent their children to the schools run by priests, Jesuits or nuns were to be strongly condemned. These strictures were repeated in 1601 and by 1609, delegates to the national synod of Saint Maixent went as far as to ask at which point parents should be excommunicated for sending their children to Jesuit schools.[61] However, the Calvinists found it more and more difficult to compete with the Jesuits, especially as the latter received official support in their efforts to take over the Huguenot *collèges*. By 1633, the *collèges* of Montpellier, Nîmes and Montauban had all become *mi-partie* – that is, half the regents were to be Protestant and the other half Catholic.[62] As these were institutions that had been set up by the Huguenots at their expense for their own children, the Calvinists resented the Jesuits' presence: in Nîmes, for instance, the consistory urged parents to boycott the classes taught by the Jesuits, and to send their sons elsewhere for those years.[63]

Such moves by the Jesuits received the support of Louis XIII and Louis XIV and their advisors. However, these kings also took measures to limit the scope of higher education among French Huguenots. Increasingly, laws were put in place limiting contacts between French Calvinists and their counterparts elsewhere in Europe. A policy of isolation, it was hoped, would weaken the movement. Hence, no French delegates were allowed to attend the synod of Dordt in 1618, which discussed many central doctrinal matters for Calvinism.[64] Furthermore, royal commissioners attending the national synods informed the Huguenot leadership that they could not correspond with churches or individuals outside France; they could not select foreign-born ministers for French parishes; French pastors could not travel outside France or take up posts in other countries.[65] Finally, by 1644, the royal commissioners ordered the national synods to forbid foreign study to theology students intending to become pastors. The banned study locations included Geneva, the Swiss lands, the Netherlands and England. According to the commissioners, the danger of these locations lay in their republicanism.[66] At the same

---

[61] Aymon, I, pp. 130, 239, 360. The national synod decided that any excommunication penalty should be considered by the local consistories.

[62] Bourchenin, *Étude*, pp. 444–5. Montpellier was already *mi-partie* by 1604. Nîmes's *collège* retained a few Calvinist regents until 1668, but they were vastly outnumbered by Jesuit teaching staff, and thus had only a minimal influence. See Moreil, 'Le Collège et l'Académie réformée de Nîmes', 82–5.

[63] For Nîmes, see Chareyre, 'Les derniers Feux', p. 259.

[64] Labrousse, *Essai sur la Révocation de l'Édit de Nantes*, p. 47. [65] Aymon, II, pp. 334, 455, 535–6.

[66] *Ibid.*, II, p. 633. Clearly the unstated reason for royal opposition to study in these locations was not only political but religious, as these lands had the largest number of Calvinists. Interestingly, Scotland did not appear on the banned list.

time, the measures kept the Huguenot academies, their professors and students, from participating in the international exchange of ideas in the wider Reformed world.

Thus the crown increasingly limited the choices of young Huguenots, leaving their own academies as the only possible option for higher studies. These institutions, however, were simultaneously put under increasing pressure, both by the Jesuit establishments, as previously mentioned, but also by the drastic drop in funding provided by the crown to the Reformed church. In 1598, Henri IV had begun paying a yearly subsidy to the Huguenot churches, to compensate them for the church taxes which Huguenot citizens continued to have to pay to maintain the Catholic church. This subsidy, known as the *deniers du roi*, was divided up among the academies and the various churches, to help pay for the salary costs of the professors and pastors.[67] In the late sixteenth and early seventeenth centuries, this income, combined with the money donated by Huguenot congregations, was sufficient to run the academies and the churches. Once the money from the crown stopped being paid regularly or at all, the situation of the French Calvinists drastically worsened.

By 1631, the national synods concluded that the money from the king was no longer paid with any regularity, and decided to take steps to find funds themselves.[68] Various provincial synods suggested repeatedly that one way to ensure the continuation of at least some form of Huguenot higher education was to rationalize the number of academies by consolidating them into one or two flourishing institutions, rather than several weak ones.[69] The national synods, however, consistently rejected any attempt to reduce the academies' number or to move them to other locations.

Instead, to keep the academies going, the national synods decided to have each provincial synod pay a share of the total cost of maintaining the academies. The national synod of Charenton in 1631 declared, 'until we can receive the fruits of His Majesty's generosity, we will put aside a fifth of all offerings, from which sum a certain amount will be taken to maintain our universities and *collèges*. This will be an advance, or a loan, which will be paid back as soon as we receive the money granted to us by His Majesty.'[70] Thus the national synods hoped to fund higher education

---

[67] Bourchenin, *Étude*, p. 301.   [68] Aymon, II, pp. 511–12.

[69] This suggestion appeared and was examined at the national synods of Vitré in 1617 (*ibid.*, II, p. 122), Charenton 1623 (*ibid.*, II, p. 286), Castres 1626 (*ibid.*, II, pp. 401–2), and Charenton in 1631 (*ibid.*, II, p. 511).

[70] *Ibid.*, II, p. 512.

by using a part of the donations provided by each congregation for the work of the church. While this strategy may have given the Huguenots an increased sense of ownership of these establishments, the authorities did run into some problems. First, it was difficult to get each province to pay its share in full and on time. Instead, payments were late, partial or non-existent. Some provinces claimed they could not pay their share because of destitution resulting from war, as was the case for Provence in 1631.[71] Others simply did not see the payments as a high priority and refused to contribute, leading to severe censure from the national synod, as was the case for the Île de France in 1637.[72]

The second major problem with relying on donations from the churches to support higher education was that even if the congregations did pass on a fifth of their offerings, this money was not necessarily enough to cover the expenses of the academies, in particular the salaries of the professors. Significantly, student academic fees played only a minimal role in bringing in income to the academies: attendance was free, except for a yearly enrolment fee, known as a *minerval*, which varied between 3 and 12 *livres* per student. Poor students were exempt from these fees altogether.[73] Given the relatively low enrolments in the academies, it is not surprising that professors' salaries could not be paid from this source. The combination of minimal support from the crown, the churches and the students meant that the professors could have to face being paid considerably less than they were meant to receive, or were in danger of receiving nothing at all. This was the case, for instance, at the academy of Die in 1636, where several professors had not been paid in over three years.[74]

The final blows to the academies came one at a time over the course of sixty years, as the royal power increasingly hardened its approach to Protestantism. By 1617, at the request of the provincial synod of Bas-Languedoc, the national synod of Vitré decided to close Montpellier's academy and amalgamate it with that of Nîmes. The continued pressure of Catholics in Montpellier made it difficult for its Huguenot academy to flourish, and hence the national synod decided that a merger was the best option.[75] The academy of Orthez was closed down when the territory was occupied by French troops in 1620.[76] It is clear that the crown deliberately targeted institutions that might have provided a focus for continued non-assimilation. In Montauban, the Jesuits' presence in

[71] *Ibid.*, II, p. 513. [72] *Ibid.*, II, p. 583. [73] Bourchenin, *Étude*, pp. 307–21. [74] *Ibid.*, p. 322.
[75] Aymon, II, p. 122. [76] Bourchenin, *Étude*, p. 443.

the *collège* and a dispute over a play which the Catholic students were to perform led to a riot, which then gave the Catholic leaders in Montauban the grounds to urge the king to move Montauban's academy out of the city. In 1659, it was transferred to the small and remote town of Puylaurens.[77] Nîmes's academy closed in 1664, Sedan followed in 1681 after France sent occupying troops into the principality, and that of Die folded in 1684. The closure of the academy of Montauban and that of Saumur, both in 1685, reflect again the aim of the king and his advisors to leave no possible ember that could later grow into a fire of resistance.[78]

In terms of its academic content, the syllabus of the Huguenot centres of higher education was not unusual in its day. Instead, the curriculum modelled itself on those of other academies or universities, such as Geneva and Leiden. Several of the French academies had eminent professors and a strong international reputation, but again other European centres of learning were equally renowned, if not more so. The uniqueness of the Huguenot academies lies specifically in their creation and survival through the seventeenth century, in spite of the lack of support and, indeed, growing opposition of civil and ecclesiastical powers in France. The Huguenot churches went to considerable lengths to fund and maintain these institutions, in spite of the endemic financial pressures they faced. In their heyday in the early part of the seventeenth century, these academies provided one of the poles of attraction for Calvinist learning across Europe. Yet they were equally important at a local and regional level, ensuring that young Huguenots received a high-calibre education that enabled them to become intellectually influential figures in their communities in France and later in exile, following the Revocation of the Edict of Nantes.

---

[77] See Garrisson, 'Les Préludes', 10-17.   [78] Bourchenin, *Étude*, p. 443.

10. *Huguenot poor relief and health care in the sixteenth and seventeenth centuries*

Martin Dinges

In the decades prior to the Revocation of the Edict of Nantes, France became a battleground of religious beliefs. This was especially true for the diocese of Grenoble where the Compagnie du Saint Sacrement had been active for many years.[1] These Catholic enthusiasts tried to entice poor Protestants to Roman Catholicism; among their many efforts, they collected alms, revitalized hospitals and opened special institutions for poor children to be educated in the Catholic religion.[2] Poor relief soon became an arena for fierce confessional competition, which sharpened when in 1671 Etienne Le Camus was appointed bishop of Grenoble. He was the founder of the *caisse de conversion*, which sought to win over the souls of impoverished Huguenots by offering them monetary assistance.[3]

It was against this background that the consistory of L'Albenc met in the minister's house on 1 January 1675; the village on the Isère, to the west of Grenoble, had a population of some 700, of whom 30 per cent were Calvinist. The four elders and two heads of households met to discuss the financial crisis that faced their community because the church's revenue had not been collected in the previous year and so the minister could not be paid. They also discussed the successful conclusion of the ' enlèvement des filles de Magdelaine Bergerand'. A detailed record of the events surrounding this perceived kidnapping, which took place during the autumn of 1674, was made by sieur Guillaume Combet de Varcis, an *avocat* of the *parlement* of Grenoble and an elder of the church.[4]

---

[1] J. Garrisson, *L'Édit de Nantes et sa Révocation. Histoire d'une intolérance* (Paris, 1985), pp. 94–6, 137–9, 142.

[2] K. Norberg, *Rich and Poor in Grenoble, 1600–1814* (Berkeley, 1985), pp. 65–7; C. Jones, *The Charitable Imperative. Hospitals and Nursing in the Ancien Régime* (London, 1989), pp. 129–31; M. Dinges, 'Health Care and Poor Relief in Regional Southern France in the Counter-Reformation' in O. Grell, A. Cunningham and J. Arrizabalaga (eds.), *Health Care and Poor Relief in Counter-Reformation Europe* (London, 1999), pp. 240–79.

[3] D. Ligou, *Le protestantisme en France de 1598 à 1715* (Paris, 1968), p. 225.

[4] F. Francillon (ed.), *Livre des délibérations de l'Église réformée de l'Albenc (1606–1682)* (Paris, 1998), p. 247.

On 3 October 1674, a notary, Champel, arrived at the château of the Catholic sieur Pollemieu with a legal document concerning Magdelaine Bergerand. She had been widowed five years earlier and though she worked as a *domestique* in Lyon, Bergerand was unable to care for her three daughters, aged eleven, nine and six years. Accordingly, she had entrusted them to her parents-in-law. The notarial instrument asked Pollemieu to return Bergerand's two daughters Isabeau and Olimpe who were living and possibly working in his household. Pollemieu refused because the girls' grandfather, Samuel Poutet, who was also their legal guardian, had entrusted them to him. Poutet had two months earlier converted to Catholicism and Pollemieu, as a Catholic nobleman, had agreed to help his new co-religionist. Poutet reproached his daughter-in-law Magdelaine, alleging that she had not properly cared for her children and had abandoned them to poverty.[5] He even claimed that this was well known throughout the neighbourhood. During the past few years, he had asked Bergerand several times to take the children back, because he did not want to feed them. On the other hand, Poutet's wife wished to continue providing care for them.

After his conversion to Catholicism, Poutet saw a means to resolve the problem. In the summer of 1674, he began working on repairs to Pollemieu's château and took two of the three children with him; the third daughter was ill and so remained at the family's home in L'Albenc. Arriving at the château, Samuel Poutet spoke with Pollemieu about the problems he was having with his granddaughters. The nobleman and his wife saw an opportunity for charity and religious education. They agreed to care for one of the girls; the second child was later placed with Madame d'Albenc, with the similar aim of educating the young girl in a Catholic manner. Thus the grandfather rid himself of two of his impoverished grandchildren while the Catholic nobles found a suitable outlet for charity and proselytization.

The Calvinist mother and the grandmother strongly disputed this version of events. Magdelaine Bergerand declared that she had cared for her daughters through her own 'industry' and the 'revenues' belonging to her and their deceased father.[6] Although her means were probably insufficient, as she worked as a servant, Bergerand sought to demonstrate that she had not abandoned her children. She had tried earnestly and this gave her the right to recover the 'fruit of her womb' from the Catholic nobles.[7]

---

5 *Ibid.*, p. 263.   6 *Ibid.*, p. 264.   7 *Ibid.*, p. 254.

After an unsuccessful first attempt, Bergerand enlisted the assistance of the consistory. She and her mother-in-law also feared that the third daughter, once recovered from her illness, would be placed under the control of the now Catholic grandfather. The consistory immediately understood the significance of the matter, at a time of increasingly sharp confessional competition, and took legal steps to recover the children and their souls for the Calvinist community. These efforts were impressive and ultimately occupied officials at the highest level. The consistory sought to have a summons issued against the Catholic nobles; its members made several journeys to Grenoble for advice from the '*conseil des Églises*'; and they brought charges before the provincial governor in an attempt to circumvent the *chambre de l'Édit*, which they considered hostile. The governor, in turn, petitioned the *conseil privé* for a decision.

The final outcome was favourable for the Protestants, who saw this as another reason to record the events. The resistance of the Catholic nobles around L'Albenc and their attempts to modify the king's *lettre de cachet* were fruitless; eventually the girls were returned to their mother. The legal reasoning for this was that, because the children were minors, they could not yet decide their faith independently and secondly, the grandfather – although their guardian – had no right to make such decisions in place of their mother. This story of three innocent daughters, a Calvinist widow and a Catholic grandfather using and abusing his responsibility for the children in the light of his new confessional position, serves to illustrate a number of aspects of Huguenot poor relief at a time of enormous confessional tension.[8]

The Protestants carefully recorded and preserved this narrative because they wanted to document judicial decisions, which they saw as important to the entire Reformed community, and secondly to commemorate a 'consolation to the church and to a poor mother which came from God alone'. It was a useful example to fortify people's faith.[9] While there is a strong confessional bias in the description, it also offers valuable information about poor relief – providing insights that most Huguenot parish registers lack. These records typically refer to the organization of social welfare and financial expenditure, but are less informative about particular motives and circumstances.

[8] There are surprisingly few references to poor relief at L'Albenc, other than those concerning wills: *ibid.*, pp. 108, 144, 165, 185.
[9] *Ibid.*, p. 266

There are studies of Protestant poor relief for many parts of Europe, but the matter has not been fully examined for France.[10] This essay draws upon a range of sources from the 1560s up to the eve of the Revocation, from Protestant strongholds in the south and communities where the Huguenots were a minority, as well as from rural areas and large Catholic cities, such as Bordeaux with its detailed records of Huguenot poor relief.[11] These efforts were usually noted in the general administrative records of the church, but sometimes specific registers were kept and a few of these have survived.[12] These sources and secondary literature allow a thorough inquiry into Huguenot charity.

Poor relief was an important concern from the beginnings of the Huguenot movement; the deacons at Le Mans, Nîmes and elsewhere had the task of visiting the poor, the sick and those in prison and to provide comfort and succour.[13] Furthermore, confessional propaganda and catechizing was a significant feature of these visits. The deacons at, for instance, Nîmes during the 1560s and Aubenas in the 1570s called on persons of both faiths, but made distinctions between the poor 'not from the church' and the 'believing faithful'. At Nîmes, those 'de la foy' received preferential treatment.[14] This relationship between social welfare and confessional propaganda was still evident in the 1660s at Bordeaux.[15] The possible conversion of a man from Normandy was reason enough

[10] The exception is J. Garrisson, *Protestants du Midi 1559–1598* (Toulouse, 1980). Studies for cities outside France include J. Olson, *Calvin and Social Welfare. Deacons and the Bourse Française* (London, 1989); C. H. Parker, *The Reformation of Community: Social Welfare and Calvinist Charity in Holland, 1572–1620* (Cambridge, 1998); T. Fehler, *Poor Relief and Protestantism: The Evolution of Social Welfare in Sixteenth-century Emden* (Aldershot, 1999).

[11] Francillon, *Livre des délibérations*; H. Chardon (ed.), 'Papiers et registre du consistoire de l'Église du Mans réformée selon l'Évangile 1560–1561' in Anjubault and H. Chardon (eds.), *Recueil de pièces inédites pour servir à l'histoire de la Réforme & de la ligue dans le Maine* (Le Mans, 1867); A. Leroux, E. Molinier *et al.* (eds.), 'Extraits du premier registre consistorial de Rochechouart (1596–1635)' in their *Documents historiques bas-latins, provençaux et français concernant principalement la Marche et le Limousin*, 2 vols. (Limoges, 1885), II, pp. 63–132; M. J. Pellisson (ed.), 'Registre des délibérations du consistoire de Barbezieux (1680–1684)', *Bulletin de la Société archéologique et historique de la Charente* I (1876), 3–52; and AD Gironde, Bordeaux, 3 JI 3 'Registre des délibérations du consistoire protestant (1660–1670)', (hereafter RCPB).

[12] AN, TT 232, 'Administration de la Caisse des Pauvres d'Aubenas'; AN, TT 276A, 'Recepte et dépenses pour les Pauvres de Villeneuve-de-Berc'; S. Bertheau, 'Le consistoire dans les Églises réformées du Moyen Poitou au XVIIe siècle', *BSHPF* 116 (1970), 542–3; R. A. Mentzer, 'Organizational Endeavour and Charitable Impulse in Sixteenth-century France', *French History* 5 (1991), 1–29.

[13] Mentzer, 'Organizational Endeavour', 8; Chardon, 'Papiers et registre du consistoire', pp. 7, 12, 18.

[14] Garrisson, *Protestants du Midi*, p. 258; Chardon, 'Papiers et registre du consistoire', p. 28.

[15] T. Wanegffelen, *Ni Rome, ni Genève: des fidèles entre deux chaires en France au XVIe siècle* (Paris, 1997), pp. 362–5.

for the consistory to pay him 3 *livres*; a monk with similar intentions received 83 *livres*, although the secretary did consider this excessive.[16] Confessional choices in almsgiving were necessary not only to preserve the limited resources of the Calvinists, but also as a way of emphasizing the benefits of church membership.

Poor relief placed a serious strain upon the financial resources of Huguenot communities. Apart from the exceptional case of Béarn, where confiscated ecclesiastical property could be exploited, the majority of Reformed communities had to raise their funds from the congregation. This distinction between the Huguenots, who had to collect money from amongst themselves, and the Catholics, who could draw upon the accumulated wealth of the established church, meant that to be a Huguenot was financially demanding. Money had to be found for various expenses, ranging from the pastors' salaries to the construction of temples, without the benefit of medieval ecclesiastical property and traditional tax structures. Funds were raised through Sunday collections and regular contributions to the church for the poor.[17] Although the accounts for the poor and the church were meant to be separate, this was not always the case. The same official often maintained both funds.[18] Still, early records at Le Mans, for example, distinguished between the 'collecteurs des deniers des pauvres' and those for the 'affaires de l'église'.[19]

It is not easy to chart the change from traditional forms of almsgiving, such as contributing to the poverty-stricken in the streets and during funerals, to the exclusive practice of donating money to the *bourse des pauvres* as encouraged by Calvinist theologians.[20] Organized forms of poor relief meant that, in keeping with other early modern ideas on reform, charity could be directed towards the worthy poor and traditional direct forms of giving could be suppressed.[21] Older practices could also be discouraged through systematic preaching which recommended almsgiving to the poor but with deacons collecting contributions from

---

[16] RCPB, fos. 11, 15.

[17] F. Labrousse, 'L'Église réformée du Carla en 1672–1673', *BSHPF* 106 (1960), 28–33; Garrisson, *Protestants du Midi*, p. 261.

[18] Garrisson, *Protestants du Midi*, p. 80. A complaint about 'charité presque entièrement refroidie' may concern the general collection for the church or the particular almsgiving, cf. Pellisson, 'Registre des délibérations', 30; it concerns the poor in Bordeaux, RCPB, fo. 11 and in Francillon, *Livre des délibérations*, p. 251. In L'Albenc the minister kept the accounts for a considerable time, which seems exceptional: *ibid.*, p. 214.

[19] Chardon, 'Papiers et registre du consistoire', p. 5.

[20] Garrisson, *Protestants du Midi*, p. 250; R. Jütte, *Poverty and Deviance in Early Modern Europe* (Cambridge, 1994), pp. 100–1.

[21] Cf. Olson, *Calvin and Social Welfare*, pp. 116–17.

the congregation after the service.[22] The consistory considered and approved the expenditure of alms at its regular meetings, restricting the amount that the deacons could dispense to the poor. The deacons kept lists of the poor as well as the payments made to them, a practice that was particularly important when large numbers were involved. Sometimes the administration was more closely organized with a deacon assigned to each district within a town. The deacons' lists allowed for weekly reports to the consistory regarding expenditures.[23] In cities such as Lyon and Nîmes, where Protestants temporarily took over municipal government, poor-relief schemes with compulsory taxes were established.[24]

Beyond the collection of alms, more substantial and stable resources were needed for times of exceptional hardship. To raise the requisite capital, Huguenots were encouraged to bequeath money in their wills, even though the new religious understanding meant that this gesture did not convey spiritual benefits on the donor. However, theological differences helped the Huguenots, for while the Catholics faced a range of potential beneficiaries – money earmarked for the parish church, mendicant orders, parish masses, candles or votive offerings to the saints – in the Reformed world, the sole competitor for pious bequests to the poor was the church itself. Calvinists had abolished all the other costly religious practices, which had absorbed substantial resources in people's wills.[25] At Aubenas, the poor were mentioned in at least every other will; in other communities, they appeared more frequently and sometimes were the exclusive beneficiaries.[26] The remarkable rate of bequests in Nîmes might even be the result of the specific local confessional competition.[27]

Generally, Catholic theologians insisted on the obligation of the rich to donate, while the Calvinist ministers preached on the general responsibility of all members of the church to look after the poor. It is therefore not surprising that the practice of giving was more widespread within Calvinist communities than in the Catholic ones. For example,

[22] Chardon, 'Papiers et registre du consistoire', pp. 22, 24, 25; Leroux *et al.*, 'Rochechouart', p. 86.

[23] Chardon, 'Papiers et registre du consistoire', pp. 18, 23, 45; Bertheau, 'Le consistoire', 543; RCPB, fo. 267. Cf. Olson, *Calvin and Social Welfare*, p. 94; Mentzer, 'Organizational Endeavour', 9.

[24] W. J. Pugh, 'Social Welfare and the Edict of Nantes: Lyon and Nîmes', *French Historical Studies* 8 (1974), 351, 364–6; Garrisson, *Protestants du Midi*, p. 104.

[25] M. Dinges, *Stadtarmut in Bordeaux (1525–1675) – Alltag, Politik, Mentalitäten* (Bonn, 1988), p. 484.

[26] Garrisson, *Protestants du Midi*, p. 261; RCPB, fos. 193, 201; Leroux *et al.*, 'Rochechouart', p. 73.

[27] W. J. Pugh. 'Catholics, Protestants and Testamentary Charity in Seventeenth-century Lyon and Nîmes', *French Historical Studies* 11 (1980), 493–5.

at Grenoble between 1620 to 1690, the poor appear in 59 per cent of Calvinist wills compared to 39 per cent of Catholic wills.[28] Yet the average sum donated by Protestants at Grenoble was five times less; it is possible that the more egalitarian Calvinist practice resulted in smaller bequests.[29] However, it is not possible to establish an overall trend for Calvinist testamentary donations as they varied greatly from one city to another, in part due to differing economic development. The trends at Lyons and Nîmes, moreover, do not reveal anything comparable to the surge in Catholic charitable bequests during the seventeenth century, and Grenoble even shows a decline after the 1660s.[30]

It seems that it was easier during the 1560s and 1570s than during the 1580s and 1590s for the church to secure money that testators had bequeathed.[31] Was the change, as Janine Garrisson suggests, the result of growing criticism of the (theologically contested) beneficial effects of pious works by the second or third generation of Calvinists? The existence of anonymous donations at Bordeaux, for instance, might also be interpreted as a wish to avoid ostentatious almsgiving.[32] The growing difficulties in obtaining legacies might also have much to do with the worsening economic environment of the later sixteenth century. No doubt there was always a certain difference between the generosity of testators and the interests of their heirs.[33]

It is difficult to assess the overall solvency of Huguenot poor relief as it varied according to time, economic fluctuations, and the size and wealth of individual communities. For most of the period the *bourse des pauvres* seems to have run a surplus, as was evident during the early years at Le Mans and also at Montauban and Nîmes during the 1590s.[34] Nevertheless, the consistories of the latter communities found it necessary to summon the city's notaries and exhort them to encourage people to make testamentary bequests.[35] Churches in Poitou during the seventeenth century also mention a surplus, but even where the records survive, it is difficult to assess the exact size of the surplus.[36] Sometimes the ratio between income and expenses is given; poor-relief

[28] Norberg, *Rich and Poor*, pp. 142–4; Pugh, 'Catholics, Protestants and Testamentary Charity', 482.
[29] At Bordeaux, Protestant donations varied between 50 and 1,000 *livres*, with many between 100 and 200 *livres*; in L'Albenc sums up to 100 *livres* were usual: Francillon, *Livre des délibérations*, pp. 108, 144, 165, 185. Cf. the list from Leroux *et al.*, 'Rochechouart', p. 74.
[30] Dinges, 'Health Care and Poor Relief', pp. 266–7; Norberg, *Rich and Poor*, p. 141.
[31] Garrisson, *Protestants du Midi*, p. 104.   [32] RCPB, fos. 90v, 201.
[33] Cf. for example Francillon, *Livre des délibérations*, pp. 223, 227, 232, 250; RCPB, fos. 66, 90v, 214.
[34] Chardon, 'Papiers et registre du consistoire', p. 62; Mentzer, 'Organizational Endeavour', 10.
[35] Garrisson, *Protestants du Midi*, p. 61; Mentzer, 'Organizational Endeavour', 8.
[36] Bertheau, 'Le consistoire', 544.

expenditures amounted to two-thirds of income at Le Mans in the 1560s, but only one-third at Le Carla in 1672–3.[37] At Bordeaux, the community's accounts show an annual surplus of over 20 per cent during the 1660s, but poor relief accounted for between 13 and 25 per cent of total expenditure.[38] Overall, it seems that French Protestants succeeded in creating a strong financial base for social-assistance programmes, which underwent real strain mainly after periods of religious unrest.[39]

A surplus could also lead to problems. Investing the sum in *rentes* was forbidden by the national synod in 1596,[40] but throughout the sixteenth and seventeenth centuries, funds were transferred from the *bourse des pauvres* for purposes other than poor relief.[41] This was particularly true when there were serious problems in meeting the minister's salary or when a church was too poor to pay for an elder to accompany the minister to the synod.[42] Synodal prohibitions notwithstanding, the practice of loaning money assigned for the poor continued throughout the seventeenth century as there was frequently a surplus in the *bourse des pauvres*. Another solution was to use the funds to purchase real estate or houses.[43] In periods of economic difficulty the financially sound *bourse des pauvres* was always the first recourse to cover deficits in other areas. It appears that spending for the poor was considered a less pressing need in comparison to other goals. Perhaps this is not surprising, as the needy had little opportunity to protest.[44]

Poorer communities, however, were occasionally overburdened by the demands of social assistance. The elders at L'Albenc drew up their narrative of the kidnapping in the hope of being reimbursed for their travel expenses and the costs for the lawsuit. Their expectations were based on the practice of reimbursement for activities carried out in the interests of the Protestant provincial synod. But they were to be disappointed. In 1675 the Calvinist churches of Dauphiné were financially exhausted; the elders of L'Albenc themselves had not paid their contribution to the

---

37 Chardon, 'Papiers et registre du consistoire', p. 62; Labrousse, 'L'Église réformée du Carla', 38.

38 This may have been higher because there were three poor rolls, possibly with more detailed and higher expenditures, than recorded in the general account. M. Dinges, 'L'Assistance paroissiale à Bordeaux à la fin du XVIIe siècle – l'exemple du consistoire protestant', *Histoire, Economie et Société* 5 (1986), 501.

39 Cf. Mentzer, 'Organizational Endeavour', 14–15.   40 Garrisson, *Protestants du Midi*, p. 261.

41 Labrousse, 'L'Église réformée du Carla', 49; Francillon, *Livre des délibérations*, p. 216; Chardon, 'Papiers et Registre du Consistoire', pp. 39, 66, 71.

42 Francillon, *Livre des délibérations*, p. 104.   43 RCPB, fos. 10v, 22, 86.

44 Garrisson, *Protestants du Midi*, p. 104; RCPB, fos. 121v, 122.

regional fund.[45] The poverty of the provincial church was closely linked to the ability of local communities to support the indigent. The system of mutual regional assistance was an important aspect of Calvinist charity programmes. It underscores the fact that the Huguenots understood that inadequate poor relief might endanger their confessional cohesion, for impoverished members of the church might be tempted to change their faith or collaborate with Catholics. Hence, well-organized poor relief had a vital role for the Reformed community.

The kidnapping story also hints at other important aspects of poor relief. Confessional solidarity within the family was crucial, especially for the next generation. The ideal was for households in which all members shared the same faith. Contemporaries supposed that where all household members worshipped and prayed together, the family would ensure that the children were brought up with strong Protestant beliefs and values. For that reason, consistories worked assiduously to discourage confessionally mixed marriages and to assist families in economic trouble; financial distress could expose a family to dangerous outside influences.

Illness was just such an instance as this. It constituted a moment of physical and psychological weakness and could lead an individual to reconsider his or her confessional position. Visiting the sick was therefore important to fortify a person's spirit and strengthen the determination to resist the temptation to despair or convert to Catholicism. Both faiths emphasized the importance of helping the sick, following the biblical insistence on performing works of charity, but they also used the occasion for catechizing.[46] Daily visits were the norm in Catholic as well as Huguenot communities. In Bordeaux, each of the twenty members of the consistory had to visit every sick person once a fortnight, which theoretically assured more than one visit a day.[47]

For the needy and the sick, self-help was the principal strategy, but when an individual's resources and those of the family or other support networks were exhausted, external poor relief became necessary.[48] The consistories helped regularly by providing treatment and medicines free of charge. Often barber surgeons or physicians were members of the

---

[45] Francillon, *Livre des délibérations*, pp. 251, 270.
[46] In the case of Catholic parish assistance it seems that sometimes this was the primary goal. Cf. the statutes of these societies in *Ordonnances et constitutions synodales, decrets et reglements. Donnez au dioceze de Bourdeaux* (Bordeaux, 1639), pp. 297–307, see Dinges, *Stadtarmut in Bordeaux*, p. 438.
[47] RCPB, fo. 266.
[48] M. Dinges, 'Self-help and Reciprocity in Parish Assistance' in P. Horden and R. Smith (eds.), *The Locus of Care: Communities, Caring and Institutions in History* (London, 1997), pp. 111–25.

consistory. In other cases the consistories had physicians or apothecaries under contract and paid them directly for their services.[49] Medicine was a heavy budgetary burden and might amount to 40 *livres* in a single case.[50] The references to these illnesses tend to be very general, such as a 'blow with a sword to the face' or a recurrent 'pain at the leg'. Other records refer to a broken thigh, a dislocated shoulder, or the 'stones'; more exceptional is the treatment of mental illness.[51] None the less, sickness was an important area of poor relief, accounting for 37 per cent of the 524 cases in Bordeaux and almost a quarter of those at Nîmes.[52]

Usually the ill received relief through the household, with the consistory providing a single payment or regular weekly subventions to an individual or family. Only a wet nurse or a person 'gravely ill' received payments for an entire quarter or whole year.[53] In Bordeaux, the concept of a socially stratified level of consumption was the consistory's guiding principle; neither the size of the family nor the age of the recipient or any other factor played a role in the level of the aid.[54] The consistory arranged for sick or poor people who could not stay in their own homes to be placed with other families. At Bordeaux, the consistory provided a pension for households that took in poor Huguenots. These host families were often at some point themselves recipients of poor relief. In line with experiences at Geneva and Nîmes, the consistory thereby created bonds of mutual obligation between itself and households as well as between Huguenots of different social status. Although there were at times conflicts between recipients and donors, the social cohesion that the arrangements fostered became an important aspect of the Huguenot system of relief.[55] In addition, it demonstrated to the less fortunate who applied for help that they would be obliged to provide aid, if and when they were able to do so.

The system of helping households allowed Protestants to avoid municipal hospitals, which were generally controlled by the Catholic majority, even though they were obliged by law to accept Calvinists. A minister was assigned to care for the spiritual welfare of Protestants who were, if possible, to be placed in a separate ward. There were even religiously

---

[49] Pellisson, 'Registre de délibérations', pp. 24, 29, 38; for Bordeaux see Dinges, *Stadtarmut in Bordeaux*, p. 445; Leroux *et al.*, 'Rochechouart', p. 121; Chardon, 'Papiers et registre du consistoire', pp. 19, 40; RCPB, fo. 103v; Olson, *Calvin and Social Welfare*, pp. 98–100.

[50] RCPB, fos. 49v, 136v, 140v.

[51] RCPB, fos. 13v, 20v, 34v, 88, 89v, 101, 107, 195, 245v, 252, 253, 258.

[52] Mentzer, 'Organizational Endeavour', 16.   [53] RCPB, fo. 256v.

[54] For a detailed discussion on this point see the list in Dinges, 'L'Assistance paroissiale', 487.

[55] Olson, *Calvin and Social Welfare*, pp. 104, 172–3; Mentzer, 'Organizational Endeavour', 25.

mixed commissions to administer the hospitals in biconfessional cities.[56] In Catholic-dominated Bordeaux, the Protestants made a financial contribution to the Saint André hospital; they even gave to the collections of Catholic preachers for the city's workhouse created by the Counter-Reformation elite. The Calvinists approved of the programme of reforming idle people through hard work, but they also wanted to avoid possible aggressive street confrontations following provocative sermons. It is unclear how many Protestants received care at Saint André but the consistory clearly tried to remove Protestants from the hospital. For example, in 1667, the elders offered a man adequate assistance on condition that he brought his wife home. However, the death of a Protestant shoemaker in the Catholic hospital shows that they were not always able to separate the two denominations.[57]

Hospitals became a focus of contention as confessional and political stridency increased. The Catholic revival at Montpellier after 1628 led by the late 1660s to the introduction of the *filles de la charité* as new personnel in the municipal hospital. This Catholic nursing order explicitly welcomed the Calvinist poor at Gex and Alès, as they sought to convert destitute Protestants, allowing them to 'die as good Catholics'.[58] These confessional dynamics make clear why the Huguenots were interested in keeping their co-religionists out of Catholic-dominated institutions. The civic right to be admitted to the hospital had been transformed into a confessional threat. Unfortunately, little is known about the treatment of the Catholic minority in the hospitals of the Protestant-dominated cities of southern France.

Legally, the Huguenots could only open new hospitals with the permission of the king or bishop. This restriction led to the creation of what might be termed 'crypto-hospitals'. At Rochechouart, money was given to the hospitalier Jean de Lybersac for a foundling; at Bordeaux, the Reformed community maintained a small hospital with an elderly couple to run it. Still, the Chambre de Sainte Croix was little more than a room with several beds in a private house. Between one and three patients from outside Bordeaux were cared for in this 'hospital'.[59] It is possible that comparable institutions existed elsewhere – the consistory of L'Albenc,

---

[56] J. Imbert, 'L'Hospitalisation des protestants sous l'ancien régime', *BSHPF* 131 (1985), 178; Bertheau, 'Le consistoire', 545; J. Imbert, *Le droit hospitalier de l'ancien régime* (Paris, 1993), pp. 135, 181–3.

[57] *Inventaire sommaire des registres de la Jurade 1520–1783*, 9 vols. (Bordeaux, 1896–1947), IX, p. 379; RCPB, fos. 11v, 61, 169v.

[58] Jones, *The Charitable Imperative*, pp. 129–31, 190–2.

[59] Leroux *et al.*, 'Rochechouart', p. 68; RCPB, fos. 222v, 130, 153–6.

for example, complained about the expense of transporting sick people from the immediate vicinity to Grenoble.[60]

Another important facet of poor relief focused on employment issues. They were the second most prevalent reason for assistance at Bordeaux, accounting for over 30 per cent of the relief. In 45 of the 160 cases, women were willing to work in a household but lacked appropriate clothing. The consistory paid for forty-four apprenticeships and sought suitable employers, so that poor Protestants could work within Huguenot households and thereby avoided pressure to convert to Catholicism. It was a question of maintaining the community's strength.[61] Poor artisans were helped by loans or the purchase of tools and stocks of materials. The consistory also offered temporary help for basic subsistence. In nearly 30 per cent of all cases, it sought to relieve misery with monthly or annual subventions or paid rents and subsidized the acquisition of tools, furniture and clothing.[62]

The impression left by the kidnapping case about the status of widows cannot be generalized. Obviously, a couple would have greater resources than a single mother, but in the case of the recipients of poor relief at Bordeaux a gender gap is not evident. There are more men than women receiving help. This reflects the reality that the public demand for money was more often expressed by the – normally male – head of the household, who eventually distributed the money to all members of the household.[63] Another aspect of the kidnapping case, however, is worth close consideration. The Catholic grandfather's argument possessed a certain familiar logic when he contended that those who supported the children financially should be able to decide their faith. This particular case could be interpreted as a gender conflict between a financially potent patriarch imposing his will on a widowed daughter-in-law and his own spouse. The more general problem of a confessional division between parents and children arose from time to time in the consistory's deliberations. At L'Albenc, the elders paid for the maintenance of two girls after the conversion of their parents to Catholicism lest the Huguenot community lose the children too.[64] In a similar way a young man who had been abandoned by his parents for confessional reasons

---

[60] Francillon, *Livre des délibérations*, p. 271.

[61] RCPB, fo. 68; cf. a similar case in L'Albenc, p. 42; E. Labrousse, 'Conversion dans les deux sens', in her *Conversion et conviction. Études sur le XVIIe siècle* (Paris, 1996), pp. 96–112.

[62] Chardon, 'Papiers et registre du consistoire', p. 66.

[63] 300 men, 217 women, 29 explicit cases of families. These 546 persons received relief in 948 cases; cf. Mentzer, 'Organizational Endeavour', 16 for a more balanced gender ratio.

[64] Francillon, *Livre des délibérations*, p. 271.

received help at Le Mans in the early 1560s.[65] Religious dissent inside the household could destroy blood ties and oblige Reformed elders to assume certain economic functions of the family. In these exceptional cases, it seems that the elders were obliged to overturn paternal authority in favour of women and children; they did so for confessional reasons. Clearly, they otherwise shared the values concerning the family with the surrounding Catholic society.

One might even suppose that the specific culture of a confessional minority strengthened the sense of the church as a community of families that had to help themselves even as they helped each other.[66] This trait was emphasized above in discussing assistance to those ill persons without a proper household in the Bordeaux community. Most of them were placed with other families to avoid the (Catholic) hospital. Placing boys as apprentices and girls as household servants within the Protestant community served the same aim.

The eventual fate of the kidnapped girls from L'Albenc underscores these communal links. Once the daughters returned from the households of the Catholic nobles, new homes had to be found. Magdelaine Bergerand probably did not have any other relatives and so asked the consistory for help in raising her children. Her appeal prompted a wave of almsgiving and practical charity: nine-year-old Olimpe was accepted into the household of a fifty-seven-year-old prosperous widow, eleven-year-old Susanne by a couple in nearby Saint Etienne. It was more difficult to place the six-year-old Isabeau; perhaps her age made her less useful.[67] Initially the consistory decided to pay for her upkeep for a year until the mother had found an alternative solution. Several members of the consistory contributed a *livre* each to start a special fund, until two elders offered to take her in for half a year each and provide an annual pension of 30 *livres*.[68] Thus, the consistory provided for the children and thereby acknowledged the widow's inability to be self-reliant.[69]

But such activism in the face of disaster, as demonstrated in this case, was seen as the temporary provision of poor relief and only

[65] Chardon, 'Papiers et registre du consistoire', p. 57.

[66] V. Cousseau, 'Sociabilité, parenté baptismale et protestantisme: l'exemple de Preuilly (1590–1683)', *BSHPF* 141 (1995), 221–46.

[67] E. Wolff, '"Der willkommene Würgeengel". Verstehende Innenperspektive und "genaue" Quelleninterpretation – am Beispiel des erwünschten Kindstodes in den Anfängen der Pockenschutzimpfung' in M. Dinges and T. Schlich (eds.), *Neue Wege in der Seuchengeschichte* (Stuttgart, 1995), pp. 105–42.

[68] Francillon, *Livre des délibérations*, p. 266.

[69] On social capital, see Dinges, 'Self-help and Reciprocity', p. 113 and Jütte, *Poverty and Deviance*, pp. 83–6.

supplementary to self-sufficiency. The admonitory role of the elders is clear from the very beginnings of Huguenot social welfare. The elders of Le Mans were willing to grant a pittance to a poor man but counselled him to maintain a modest lifestyle; the elders further insisted that his brothers help him.[70] This logic also prevailed at Bordeaux. A systematic analysis of the weekly and monthly payments indicates that they were only a supplement; the monetary assistance was insufficient to meet all the expenses of a poor person or an impoverished household.[71] The indigent were expected to take up work whenever they could. Only when individuals fell ill did they receive sufficient assistance to live entirely from it.

Another important example of confessional solidarity was the aid provided to Protestants who were passing through the community. At Geneva, for example, assistance to religious refugees was the basic reason for establishing the *bourse française*.[72] In France, a single cash grant, a so-called *passade*, was made on condition that the recipient moved on to another place. The practice allowed the consistory to bestow charity while minimizing expenses.[73] This type of relief was common in cities along major trade routes. At Nîmes, the passing poor received money and instruction in catechism already in 1560, and by the 1590s they accounted for 14 per cent of social-welfare expenditures.[74] In the well-documented case of a large city like Bordeaux with its important function as a transit point during the 1660s, it represented a sizeable outlay. Relief for the resident poor varied during the decade; it was between 66 and 80 per cent of the consistory's total budget for poor relief. The amount for the *passades* fluctuated between 5 and 10 per cent. By way of comparison, this was similar to the amount allotted to help prisoners; between 1 and 10 per cent for legal assistance and just under 10 per cent to assist young men studying theology.

On average forty-eight *passades* were issued each year. This figure increased between May 1662 and April 1663. The number of *passants* then doubled in 1668–9, which coincided with a period of rising cereal prices; in addition, it probably relates to a desperate search for employment during hard times.[75] Three-quarters of the *passants* were men, reflecting the fact that ministers, soldiers, artisans and the like travelled, more than women, for professional reasons. This over-representation of men may

[70] Chardon, 'Papiers et registre du consistoire', p. 50.
[71] Dinges, 'L'Assistance paroissiale', 490; Labrousse, 'L'Église réformée du Carla', 33–5.
[72] Olson, *Calvin and Social Welfare*, pp. 37–40.
[73] RCPB, fos. 23v, 25v, 36, 36v, 92; Garrisson, *Protestants du Midi*, p. 259.
[74] Garrisson, *Protestants du Midi*, p. 260; Mentzer, 'Organizational Endeavour', 13.
[75] Dinges, 'L'Assistance paroissiale', 480.

also be partly explained by the longer distances of their journeys, which made them economically more vulnerable. Male immigrants were also less likely to work in households that could care for them in the case of illness at their own expense. The passing poor also reveal the international character of the Protestant community. Of 460 recorded places of birth or residence, 50 were from outside the realm; among them, 25 were from Switzerland (14 from Geneva alone) and 10 from the Netherlands. For France, the distribution reflects the geographical distribution of the 'Protestant crescent', as do the 102 destinations for the travellers.[76]

The consistory did not provide itinerant Protestants a place to sleep or something to eat, which had been the traditional gifts of hospitality in Catholic monasteries. Instead, they received between 15 and 30 *sous*, which allowed them to buy simple meals for a week or two. Allowing for the other Protestant communities around Bordeaux, one might imagine a network of beneficent consistories, which made it possible for less fortunate persons to travel from one point to another inside a 'Protestant world'. Thus, they maintained independence from Catholic charitable institutions, which might have had a bad influence on them. But this generosity presupposed control measures to guard against poor Catholic travellers who were attracted by the alms and pretended to be Protestant. The synods prescribed special certificates from the poor traveller's home congregation. They were intended to help in the identification of members of the Reformed community. None the less, the evidence suggests that the system was far from perfect.[77]

On the other hand, these travellers sometimes had something to offer. They could function as informants, providing details about the situation of Calvinists in other places. Two master bakers, banned from Montauban and passing through Bordeaux on their way to Paris, received the substantial aid of 24 *livres*. In exchange they gave valuable information on the confessional situation at an important Protestant town. Such informal exchange of news was crucial for the coherence of a minority.[78]

In many cases, the consistory provided legal aid. Protestant *avocats* on the higher courts – sometimes members of the consistory – made it possible for Huguenots from other places to undertake lawsuits and economize on travel expenses, which otherwise would have been charged

---

[76] S. Mours, *Essai sommaire de géographie du protestantisme français au XVIIe siècle* (Paris, 1966); Dinges, 'L'Assistance paroissiale', 483–5.

[77] Garrisson, *Protestants du Midi*, p. 261; Labrousse, 'L'Église réformée du Carla', 34; Bertheau, 'Le consistoire', p. 543; RCPB, fo. 93v. P. El Bounia-Rondet, 'Les protestants de Tonneins sous le règne de Louis XIV (1661–1715)', *BSHPF* 135 (1989), 209.

[78] RCPB, fo. 91v. See also Mark Greengrass's essay in this volume, chap. 6.

on the *bourse des pauvres*. Money was provided, but the register does not tell us much about the nature of the lawsuits.[79] The kidnapping at L'Albenc provides a clear example of how a widow, with the support of the consistory, could seek redress by appealing to the law. The use of the judicial system serves to demonstrate further how the Huguenots were prepared to resort to the courts to defend their rights. By the late seventeenth century, specific problems such as the growing exclusion of Protestants from certain professions became the background for a number of lawsuits.[80] An example is the lengthy, expensive affair of a pharmacist; it reminds us that Huguenots faced severe repression in the medical profession and that it adversely affected their capability for self-help in the health sector.[81] Judicial assistance always played a role in poor relief, but its importance probably grew after 1661 and the king's assault on Protestants. A more traditional form of assistance involving the legal system consisted of visits to prisoners and weekly payments to allow them simple meals. An annual gift to the guardian of each prison in Bordeaux probably facilitated the visits. Negotiations with the city council even led to the release of a prisoner.

The consistory subsidized elementary schooling for poorer boys. It created opportunities for economic stability; better-educated Huguenots would be better able to provide for their families in later life. There was also a religious dimension; literacy meant the capacity to read Scripture. Teachers received a part of their salary from the consistories at Nîmes and Le Mans.[82] Similar organizational attempts were undertaken from time to time in other towns;[83] the register of Bordeaux mentions starting a fund for a course to teach the lute. In any case, confessional schooling was another means to keep children from falling prey to Catholicism.[84]

Although not strictly charity, spending on ministerial training could sometimes be linked to it.[85] Theology students were occasionally

---

[79] RCPB, fos. 7v, 9.

[80] B. de Coulon de Labrousse, 'Le Statut juridique du protestantisme à Bordeaux (1558–1787)', law dissertation, Université de Bordeaux I, (1974). See also Penny Roberts's essay in this volume, chap. 5.

[81] P. Bert, 'Histoire de la Révocation de l'Édit de Nantes à Bordeaux et dans le Bordealais (1653–1715)', *Revue historique de Bordeaux* 1 (1908), 99–100, 169; concerning Montpellier see L. Brockliss and C. Jones, *The Medical World of Early Modern France* (Oxford, 1997), p. 190.

[82] Garrisson, *Protestants du Midi*, p. 259; Chardon, 'Papiers et registre du consistoire', pp. 39, 56, 66, 71.

[83] Francillon, *Livre des délibérations*, p. 231; Leroux *et al.*, 'Rochechouart', pp. 108, 112; RCPB, fo. 19v.

[84] Francillon, *Livre des délibérations*, p. 52.

[85] Olson, *Calvin and Social Welfare*, p. 168; Leroux *et al.*, 'Rochechouart', pp. 76, 78, 126.

recorded in the registers as travellers, but the main expenditure concerned regular stipends for their education. The students were often the
sons of ministers, and their families were unable to finance study at the
academies of Puylaurens or Geneva, for example.[86] More exceptional is
the case of a poor son of a widow, who had already received consistorial assistance for his secondary schooling.[87] He seemed disinterested in
returning to Bordeaux and the consistory promised support only at the
moment of his arrival in the city. Here the objectives of poor relief and
confessional survival were intermingled.

Finally, the Reformed efforts in the area of poor relief displayed an
interregional solidarity. Payments to impoverished Calvinist churches,
some as far away as Poland, were part of the greater effort by the
Huguenots to keep their community together.[88] These practices and the
broad accompanying notions of poverty suggest that, for the consistory,
poor relief covered a wide range of aid.

Poor relief was a defining aspect of Huguenot culture in France as elsewhere in Europe.[89] It provided a framework in which the members of the
church, both donors and recipients, fulfilled the basic ideal of Christian
love and the more straightforward necessity to maintain solidarity with
the weak. These interactions reinforced the coherence of the church and
strengthened the inner bonds between families and individuals, between
the poor and the better off, and even between churches in different regions of the kingdom as well as abroad. It established, moreover, the
external limits of the Calvinist church in relation to the Catholic community in a large number of fields, ranging from illness to employment,
schooling and travel assistance. On the level of everyday practices for
most Huguenots it became routine to turn in times of sickness to their
own deacons for relief and not to the hospital, especially if it was dominated by the Catholic majority. Assistance was a communal undertaking.
Huguenot households offered employment opportunities; the church arranged and often paid master artisans and teachers for apprenticeships
and schooling to benefit poor boys; travel by the less fortunate became, in

---

[86] Garrisson, *Protestants du Midi*, on recruitment (p. 129) and salaries (p. 141) during the second half
of the sixteenth century.
[87] RCPB, fos. 13, 40v, 44, 169.   [88] Francillon, *Livre des délibérations*, p. 249; RCPB, fo. 13v.
[89] A. Spicer, 'A Process of Gradual Assimilation: The Exile Community in Southampton, 1567–
1635', *Proceedings of the Huguenot Society* 26 (1995), 194; R. Jütte, *Obrigkeitliche Armenfürsorge in
deutschen Reichsstädten der Frühen Neuzeit* (Cologne, 1984), p. 198; P. Bonenfant, 'Un aspect du
régime calviniste à Bruxelles au XVIème siècle: la question de la Bienfaisance', *Bulletin de la
Commission Royale d'Histoire* 89 (1925), 277.

some cases, the occasion to meet brethren in the faith. Easing the financial burden was also invoked to win new hearts and souls, but had to be kept within a certain judicial framework, which limited the opportunities for zealots of both confessions to influence people's minds.

Charity was likely less important for the implementation of the Huguenot moral order. No doubt there were attempts to combine assistance payments with admonitions to live properly and, for example, to stop drinking.[90] Occasionally the consistory cut off relief payments due to bad behaviour, but more often assistance ceased for strictly financial reasons.[91] The inherent limits on providing help for the poor meant that this aid was not a strong lever for consistories to use to enforce social discipline.

If confessional culture is defined as a net of interrelated practices and beliefs it is evident that poor relief contributed enormously in creating, re-creating and stabilizing this particular confessional culture. Beyond these practices, the Huguenot system was marked by a high level of direct personal engagement. There were strong links to family and household. At the same time, it had a unique organizational scheme, which had to supplant the social welfare institutions of the Catholic majority.[92] Within a close community, this also allowed the opportunity for a high degree of collective social control and, as such, is a trait shared by minority cultures throughout early modern Europe.

By the second half of the seventeenth century, Huguenot poor relief suffered under relentless pressure. What had begun in the 1660s as a campaign to exclude Protestants from medical professions, such as pharmacy, and continued with the closing of Huguenot hospitals in 1675,[93] ended with the complete dismantling of all forms of Calvinist poor-relief after 1685. This left a million Protestants without proper means to help themselves and led to the overcrowding of the remaining poor-relief institutions, especially in those regions, such as the vicinity of Montpellier, where the Protestants were a strong minority.[94] This development might be taken as final proof of the important contribution made by Huguenot poor relief toward alleviating the situation of the indigent.

---

[90] Chardon, 'Papiers et registre du consistoire', p. 50; Garrisson, *Protestants du Midi*, p. 259.

[91] RCPB, fo. 7v; Olson, *Calvin and Social Welfare*, p. 177; see Mentzer, 'Organizational Endeavour', 25.

[92] Similar to the English case, see A. Spicer, 'Poor Relief and the Exile Communities' in B. A. Kümin (ed.), *Reformations Old and New* (Aldershot, 1996), pp. 237–55.

[93] Brockliss and Jones, *Medical World*, pp. 190, 685.

[94] Jones, *The Charitable Imperative*, pp. 136, 242.

11. 'Qui est de Dieu oit la parole de Dieu': the Huguenots and their temples

Andrew Spicer

In the almanacs for 1686, Louis XIV was proclaimed 'Louis le Grand, la Terreur et l'Admiration de l'Univers' and his achievements of the previous year were illustrated and praised. Foremost amongst these achievements was the Revocation of the Edict of Nantes in October 1685; the almanacs depicted the destruction of the Huguenot temples and in particular the systematic demolition of the temple at Charenton, the place of worship for the Reformed community in Paris. Louis was hailed as the destroyer of heresy, enthroned and surrounded by the figures of Divine Zeal, Piety and Religion as well as the French Catholic hierarchy; the figure of Heresy was unmasked by Truth.[1] The Huguenots viewed the Revocation very differently. A crude drawing entitled 'The Henchman of Satan assembles for the destruction of the Temple of Charenton' saw it in more apocalyptic terms, relating it to the prophecies of the Book of Revelation. The destruction of the temple is overseen by Satan and the seven-headed hydra of the Catholic church, while a woman, representing the Reformed church, flies from the temple bearing the Tables of the Law. She has been given wings to escape to safety in the wilderness.[2] The use of the temple, and in particular Charenton, in these illustrations is not only a reflection of the reality but is also a metaphor for the ruination of the Reformed church in France. The depictions serve to underscore the importance that the temple had assumed within France as a symbol of French Protestantism.

From the earliest days of the movement, Reformed services had been subject to religious violence in, for example, the 'Affair of the rue St Jacques' and the Massacre of Vassy. The construction of temples, however, provided a clearer target for Catholic hostility. During the 1560s, Le Paradis in Lyon, La Calade at Nîmes and the temple at Meaux were

---

[1] Plates I and II: BN Estampes, 72 C 52482, 72 C 52499.
[2] Plate III: BN Estampes, 85 C 124974; Rev. 12.

Plate I. L'Hérésie démasquéé par la verité. While the king is surrounded by his clergy and the personifications of Zeal, Religion and Piety, the unmasking of Heresy is witnessed by a Huguenot minister with his Bible. In the cartouches at the bottom of the page, the consequences of this are seen with the abjuration of the people (left) and the demolition of the temples (right).

Plate II. Louis le Grand, la Terreur et l'Admiration de l'Univers. The central cartouche illustrates the demolition of the temple of Charenton with its bell being carted away in the foreground. The vignettes on the left-hand side show the triumph of Catholicism, with depiction of the missions, the repair of the churches and a grateful clergy.

LES SVPOST DE SATAN ASEMBLES POVR
LA DETRVCTION DV TEMPLE DE CHARANTON

Plate III. Les Svpost de Satan. The seven-headed hydra of the Catholic church accompanies Satan while the temple of Charenton is demolished. In the background a winged woman flies from the temple with the Table of the Ten Commandments.

all the victims of Catholic assaults.[3] The number of potential targets increased in the wake of the Edict of Nantes and some temples were the objects of repeated attacks. On the outskirts of Paris, Charenton was razed by fire in 1621; panic ensued following rumours of an approaching Catholic mob in 1645, and there was a further, but less destructive, fire in 1671.[4] One of the most unfortunate communities was at Rennes, where the temple at Cleuné was burnt down in 1613, 1654, 1661 and 1675.[5]

3 G. Gigue, 'Jean Perrissin: Peintre Lyonnais (1564–1608)', *Réunion des Sociétés des Beaux-Arts des Départements* 15 (1891), 433–6; M. Mousseaux, 'Implantation géographique et historique de la Réforme en Brie XVIe, XVIIe et XVIIIe siècles', *BSHPF* 119 (1973), 422; P. Chareyre, 'Le consistoire de Nîmes, 1561–1685', thèse d'État, Université de Paul-Valery Montpellier III, 4 vols. (1987), I, p. 295.
4 P. Benedict, '*Un roi, une loi, deux fois*: Parameters for the History of Catholic–Reformed Co-existence in France, 1555–1685' in O. P. Grell and B. Scribner (eds.), *Tolerance and Intolerance in the European Reformation* (Cambridge, 1996), pp. 86–7.
5 W. Beik, *Urban Protest in Seventeenth-century France: The Culture of Retribution* (Cambridge, 1997), pp. 161–2; B. Vaurigaud, *Essai sur l'histoire des Églises réformées de Bretagne 1535–1808*, 3 vols. (Paris, 1870), II, pp. 229, 287–91; L. Bastide, 'La Révocation de l'Édit de Nantes à Rennes', *BSHPF* (1928), 242–3.

For the Catholic church and its adherents the temple symbolized not only the religious concessions afforded by the Edict of Nantes but the presence of heretical worship within the midst of their community.[6] The bishop of Uzès denounced temples as 'chaires de pestilence, Synagogues de Satan, heresie, mensonge, audace, monstre et autres semblables' and similar attacks were made by other observers who derided the buildings as barns, theatres or rats' nests.[7] The hostility that these structures engendered must have been even more intense in cities where the Protestants were in the ascendancy: Bergerac, La Rochelle, Montauban, Montpellier, Nîmes and Uzès. These temples occupied prominent positions within the centres of the towns and in some cases were constructed in the latest architectural style.[8] Further provocation was caused by the inscriptions that were employed not only in the leading centres but also in smaller communities to proclaim to the world the buildings' function. In the village of Barre des Cevennes the inscription 'Qui est de Dieu, oit la parole de Dieu' [Who is of God, hears the Word of God] was erected over the door of the temple in 1608; similar sentiments were expressed in inscriptions that appeared elsewhere.[9] The bishop of Montpellier was so outraged by the inscription 'Verae religioni sacrum' on the Petit Temple that he protested to the king.[10] The temple therefore provided a focus for the hostility felt towards the Huguenot minority as a whole. The buildings and their inscriptions provided a visual challenge and affront to the Catholic hierarchy, which failed to recognize the legitimacy of the Reformed church.

For the Huguenots themselves the temple was the place where they regularly met as a community 'to listen to the Bible and to worship'. The minister was responsible for delivering the Word of God and the congregation, as active participants in the service, were to receive it with reverence. It was the place where they met four times a year to partake in the

---

[6] H. Phillips, *Church and Culture in Seventeenth-century France* (Cambridge, 1997), pp. 205–6.

[7] E. Benoist, *Histoire de l'Édit de Nantes*, 3 vols. (Amsterdam, 1693–5), III, pt 1, p. 204, pt 2, p. 36. See also BN Estampes, 56 E 11592; H. Guicharnaud, 'An Introduction to the Architecture of Protestant Temples Constructed in France before the Revocation of the Edict of Nantes' in P. Corby Finney (ed.), *Seeing beyond the Word. Visual Arts and the Calvinist Tradition* (Grand Rapids, MI, 1999), pp. 135, 143; M. Koch, 'Calvinism and the Visual Arts in Southern France, 1561 to 1685' in Corby Finney, *Seeing beyond the Word*, p. 182; Gigue, 'Jean Perrissin', 435.

[8] See below, p. 187. M. Chaleil (ed.), *La France Protestante. Histoire de Lieux et Mémoire* (Paris, 1992), pp. 360, 372; P. Cabanel, *Itinéraires protestants en Languedoc: XVIe XXe siècle*, 3 vols. (Montpellier, 1998–), II, pp. 262, 287, 377–8.

[9] J.-P. Chabrol, *La Cévenne au village: Barre-des-Cevennes sous l'ancien-régime (1560–1830)* (Aix-en-Provence, 1983), p. 175. For example the inscription 'Bienheureux sont ceux oyent la parole de Dieu et qui la gardent' came from the temple at Castelmoron. H. Gelin, 'Inscriptions Huguenotes (Poitou, Aunis, Saintonge, etc.)', *BSHPF* 43 (1894), 104, 157–8.

[10] P. Corbière, *Histoire de l'Église réformée de Montpellier* (Paris, 1861), p. 131.

Lord's Supper; it was where they gathered at times of crisis for special prayers, sermons and fasts. Couples came to the temple to be married, brought their babies there to be baptized, and their young children to be instructed in the catechism. Money collected at the sermons contributed towards the maintenance of the poor, the sick and the welfare of the community. The temple, particularly in the smaller communities, was often the place where the consistory held its meetings and exercised jurisdication over the lives of members of the Reformed community. For Catholics, the parish church represented just one (albeit often the most important) focal point of their religious life; for the Reformed, the temple stood at the centre of their religious, if not daily, lives.

Huguenot temples are generally characterized as buildings which were erected in the wake of the Edict of Nantes and were subsequently de-molished during the reign of Louis XIV. This somewhat simplistic view negates the continuing programme of construction which began in the 1560s and continued until the eve of the Revocation itself. The le-gal framework that permitted the establishment of Reformed places of worship, of course, dated back to the very beginnings of the wars of religion. In January 1562, the Edict of St Germain had granted the Huguenots freedom to worship outside the walled towns, but it also ordered the restitution of the church property that had been oc-cupied by the Protestants. The edict went on to prohibit specifically the building of temples either within or outside the towns.[11] The con-cessions over where worship could take place were somewhat circum-scribed and more closely defined by the Edict of Amboise in the wake of the first war of religion. This permitted Reformed worship on the estates of nobles holding rights of *haute justice* and in the homes of other nobles, one location within each *baillage* or *sénéchaussée* and in places where the Huguenots had worshipped freely until 7 March 1563.

Subsequent edicts also sought to refine the designation of the places where the Huguenots were permitted to worship, but a significant ad-vance was made in 1577. According to the terms of the Conference of Nérac in 1579, the Peace of Bergerac and separate letters patent later in 1577, the Huguenots were permitted 'to buy, make, develop and construct places for the said exercise of the Religion in the sub-urbs of towns, market towns and villages that have been authorized in each *baillage, sénéchaussée* or *gouvernement*, and the places where the exercise

---

[11] A. Stegmann, *Édits des guerres de religion* (Paris, 1979), pp. 9–10, 15.

of the said Religion is permitted by the Edict'.[12] In 1598, the Edict of Nantes repeated this article, allowing the Huguenots to 'build places for the exercise'.[13] The failure of the edicts to permit the construction of temples prior to 1577 clearly did not constrain the Huguenots. The official designation by the royal commissioners of authorized places of worship for the Huguenots outside the towns, often in places where there was inadequate accommodation, led communities to construct some form of shelter from the elements. As early as 1561, the Huguenots in Toulouse had erected a covered barn to house worshippers.[14] In a few cases the crown granted permission for the erection of a shelter and some individual communities even received letters patent or specific authorization from Charles IX to build a temple.[15]

The Edict of Nantes in 1598 was the culmination of these earlier agreements and concessions between the Huguenots and the crown about the places where Reformed worship was permitted and it reiterated permission for the construction of temples. The edict identified three main locations in which the Huguenots were permitted to worship freely: first in places where the Reformed church had already been established, demonstrated through regular and public worship in 1596 and 1597. These became known as the *culte de possession*. Secondly they were permitted to worship in the suburbs of towns in each *baillage* or *sénéchaussée* identified by the royal commissioners, the *culte de concession*. Finally there were the *culte de fief*, where worship was permitted on the estates of nobles with rights of *haute justice*. The edict also excluded certain areas of the kingdom, such as episcopal cities, from these provisions; most notably the Huguenots were not permitted to worship within five leagues of Paris.[16]

Against the background of the emerging legal structure and the continued conflict of the wars of religion, the Huguenots did begin to build their own places of worship. During the 1560s, communities where the Protestants formed the majority of the population, such as Nîmes and

---

[12] *Ibid.*, pp. 158–9; *Les Articles resoluz et accordez a Nerac en la Conference de la Royne ... avec le Roy de Navarre* (Tours, 1581).

[13] J. Garrisson (ed.), *L'Édit de Nantes* (Biarritz, 1997), p. 35.

[14] D. Nicholls, 'Protestants, Catholics and Magistrates in Tours, 1562–1572: The Making of a Catholic City during the Religious Wars', *French History* 8 (1994), 24; P. Roberts, 'The Most Crucial Battle of the Wars of Religion? The Conflict over Sites of Reformed Worship', *ARG* 89 (1998), 260; M. Greengrass, 'The Anatomy of a Religious Riot in Toulouse in May 1562', *Journal of Ecclesiastical History* 34 (1983), 372.

[15] Roberts, 'Most Crucial Battle', 261; Benoist, *Histoire de l'Édit de Nantes*, III, pt 1, p. 595; Chareyre, 'Le consistoire de Nîmes', I, p. 295; G. Gillier, 'Les protestants de Haute-Provence XVIe–XVIIIe siècles', *BSHPF* 125 (1979), 416.

[16] Garrisson, *L'Édit de Nantes*, pp. 31–5.

Uzès, built temples that lasted into the seventeenth century. Even in communities where the Huguenots were not dominant, such as at Lyon and Meaux, temples were erected but were soon cast down by hostile opponents.[17] The Edict of Bergerac provided the impetus for further construction; the foundation stone for a new temple was laid at La Rochelle in 1577 and the temple at Alès also dates from then.[18] However, it was during the 1580s and 1590s that construction increased with new temples begun, for example, in Bergerac and Montpellier.[19]

None the less, construction in the period before the Edict of Nantes was constrained in part by the competing demands for funds during the second half of the sixteenth century. The military costs of the wars, the maintenance of the ministry as well as relief for those suffering from the effects of the conflict all proved to be more pressing needs.[20] As a result some communities were forced to seek temporary solutions and to seek makeshift accommodation for their place of worship. At Sainte-Foy the construction of a temple was seen in such circumstances to be an act of faith: 'in the year 1587 the civil war is continuing and coming to the end of the plague which started in this town on 22 July 1586 and the famine beginning to pursue us, we have resolved in recognition that it has pleased our God to show mercy on us during the late plague sickness to build the temple'.[21]

There was, however, a further reason for the limited construction of temples in the period before 1598. As Elie Benoist pointed out at the end of the seventeenth century, most of the temples dated from after the Edict of Nantes, rather than from the Peace of Bergerac. This was not because the Huguenots were prevented from building, but because they had no need to do so as they already occupied buildings where they could worship. These belonged either to the Catholic church or to the community.[22] From the beginnings of the movement the Huguenots had

---

[17] Cabanel, *Itinéraires protestants en Languedoc*, II, pp. 287, 377–8; Mousseaux, 'Implantation géographique et historique', 422; Gigue, 'Jean Perrissin', 433–6.
[18] Médiathèque, La Rochelle, MS 158 'Comptes municipaux, 1580–81', fo. 21; MS 160 'Comptes municipaux, 1598–99', fo. 9; MS 153 R. Collin, 'Annales de La Rochelle', p. 9; R. Laurent, *Promenade à travers: les Temples de France* (Montpellier, 1996), p. 411.
[19] Corbière, *Histoire de l'Église réformée de Montpellier*, pp. 106–8; J. Valette, 'Étude historique et archéologique sur le Temple de Bergerac (1636–1682)', *Congrès national des sociétés savantes, Lille, 1976, archéologie*, p. 379.
[20] On the funding of the Huguenot movement, see M. Greengrass, 'Financing the Cause: Protestant Mobilization and Accountability in France (1562–1589)' in P. Benedict, G. Marnef, H. van Nierop and M. Venard (eds.), *Reformation, Revolt and Civil War in France and the Netherlands 1555–1585* (Amsterdam, 1999), pp. 233–54.
[21] Quoted in S. Dubreuilh, 'Construction du Temple de Sainte-Foy (1584–1587)', *BSHPF* 81 (1932), 360.
[22] Benoist, *Histoire de l'Édit de Nantes*, II, pp. 544–5.

been prepared to seize existing religious buildings and to adapt them for Reformed worship; church takeovers had become commonplace by the summer of 1560.[23] The Huguenots at Nantes even suggested that the collegiate church of Notre Dame should be divided, allowing them to occupy the nave while the canons continued to use the choir. In Montpellier the Huguenots contracted with the ecclesiastical authorities in November 1561 to use three churches, in defiance of the king's order for the restitution of church property.[24] With the outbreak of the first war of religion and during the course of the conflict, the Protestant seizure of cities was often associated with the appropriation of the churches, outbursts of iconoclasm, and the proscription of Catholic worship.[25] In some cases the extent of the iconoclasm meted out on the churches meant that they were no longer fit to use as places of worship and so instead served as quarries for urban defences.[26]

The Edict of Amboise in 1563, and the subsequent seven peace agreements negotiated during the course of the religious wars, ordered the restitution of the churches that the Reformed had occupied.[27] None the less, where the Protestants remained in the ascendency they continued to utilise the church buildings. At Sancerre the Huguenots worshipped in the church of St Jean until the city capitulated to Catholic forces in August 1573. In strongholds such as Montauban and La Rochelle, they defiantly retained possession of these churches throughout the wars.[28] This continued occupation was not confined to the cities but was also true of the villages in the Protestant heartlands of the south. In these communities, where the majority of the population had embraced the Reformed faith, the parish church was seized and purged of the trappings of Catholicism during the 1560s and served as the Huguenot temple, in some cases, for the remainder of the century.[29]

---

[23] P. Benedict, 'The Dynamics of Protestant Militancy: France, 1555–1563' in Benedict *et al.*, *Reformation, Revolt and Civil War*, p. 41; Roberts, 'Most Crucial Battle', 254–5.

[24] Roberts, 'Most Crucial Battle', 254. Just such an arrangement was carried out at Condom: see G. Baum, E. Cuntz and R. Reuss (eds.), *Histoire Ecclésiastique des Églises réformées*, 3 vols. (Paris, 1883–9), I, p. 878. P. Serres, *Abrégé de l'histoire du Calvinisme de la ville de Montpellier*, ed. by M. Barral and M. Péronnet (Montpellier, 1977), pp. 81–2.

[25] Benedict, '*Un roi, une loi, deux fois*', pp. 77–8. On the situation in Orléans, for example, see A. Spicer, 'Continental Calvinism and its Churches – An Overview', *Aberdeen University Review* 58 (2000), 302.

[26] F. Garrisson, *Essai sur les commissions d'application de l'Édit de Nantes* (Paris, 1951), p. 205; F. Moisy, 'Le Rétablissement des Structures catholiques après le Siège de La Rochelle (1628–1648)', *Revue du Bas-Poitou et des Provins de l'Ouest* (1973), 15–16.

[27] Stegmann, *Édits des guerres de religion*, pp. 10, 34, 70, 87, 97–8, 132–3.

[28] Laurent, *Promenade à travers*, pp. 182–3.

[29] See Cabanel, *Itinéraires protestants en Languedoc*, I, pp. 170, 202–3, 319, II, pp. 39–40, 71, 119, 145, 222, 408–9, 411.

In their adaptation of the existing religious buildings for Reformed worship, the Huguenots mirrored what was happening in Scotland and the northern provinces of the Netherlands (and closer to home in the enclaves of Béarn, Orange and Sedan) where Calvinism became the established religion.[30] Although to some these buildings might have seemed tainted by their association with the celebration of the Mass, the waves of iconoclasm that accompanied the takeovers at the beginning of the religious wars represented a cleansing and purification of the churches. In some cases the iconoclasts argued that they were assuming the duty of the authorities in purging the churches of idolatry.[31] While the Huguenots were keen to eradicate the pollution and trappings of Catholicism, their willingness to adapt these purged churches for Reformed worship also reflects a different attitude towards the role and sanctity of religious buildings.

In his *Institutes* Calvin had identified the church of God as being 'where we see the Word of God purely preached and heard, where we see the sacraments administered according to Christ's institution'.[32] While this definition characterized Calvinist worship in general, it was a definition that applied to the Reformed community as a whole rather than to a specific building or temple. There was not an attempt to re-create a temple in the biblical sense.[33] Calvin rejected the notion that a temple, like a Catholic church, was consecrated for worship and possessed a sanctity or holiness of its own. He wrote:

public places have been appointed which we call 'temples'. These do not by any secret sanctity of their own make prayers more holy, or cause them to be heard by God. But they are intended to receive the congregation of believers more conveniently when they gather to pray, to hear the preaching of the Word, and at the same time to partake of the sacraments. Otherwise (as Paul says) . . . we

---

[30] Spicer, 'Continental Calvinism and its Churches', 303–4; A. Spicer, 'Architecture' in A. Pettegree (ed.), *The Reformation World* (London, 2000), pp. 513–14; A. Spicer, 'Destruction and Adaptation: The Experience of Scotland and the Netherlands' in D. Gaimster and R. Gilchrist (eds.), *The Archaeology of the Reformation* (forthcoming, 2002). See also G. Hay, *The Architecture of Scottish Post-Reformation Churches, 1560–1843* (Oxford, 1957); C. A. van Swigchem, T. Brouwer and W. van Os (eds.), *Een huis voor het Woord. Het Protestantse kerkinterieur in Nederland tot 1900* (The Hague, 1984).

[31] Benedict, 'Dynamics of Protestant Militancy', pp. 45–6; R. A. Mentzer, 'The Reformed Churches of France and the Visual Arts' in Corby Finney, *Seeing beyond the Word*, p. 205; N. Z. Davis, 'The Rites of Violence' in her *Society and Culture in Early Modern France* (Stanford, 1987), pp. 159, 163–4; O. Christin, *Une révolution symbolique. L'iconoclasme huguenot et la reconstruction catholique* (Paris, 1991), pp. 128–31.

[32] John Calvin, *Institutes of the Christian Religion*, ed. by F. L. Battles (Grand Rapids, 1975), pp. 62–3.

[33] See A. Spicer, 'Rebuilding Solomon's Temple? The Architecture of Calvinism' in R. N. Swanson (ed.), *The Holy Land, Holy Lands, and Christian History* (Studies in Church History, 36, 2000), pp. 275–87.

ourselves are the true temples of God . . . But those who suppose that God's ear has been brought closer to them in a temple, or consider their prayer more consecrated by the holiness of the place, are acting in this way according to the stupidity of the Jews and Gentiles. In physically worshipping God, they go against what has been commanded, that, without any consideration of place, we worship God in spirit and in truth.[34]

Calvin's emphasis on the importance of the correct form of worship rather than the place where services were held, helps to clarify why the Huguenots were prepared to utilize buildings that were initially designed to foster the sanctity and mystery of the Mass. Ultimately with the agreement of the Edict of Nantes, the Huguenots were obliged to restore to the Catholics the ecclesiastical property that they had occupied, and to construct their own places of worship.[35] Hand in hand with this restitution came the reintroduction of the Mass, which was met with strong opposition in the Huguenot strongholds.[36] In La Rochelle, the commissioners determined that the church of St Marguerite, which the Huguenots had seized at the beginning of the religious wars, should be returned to Catholic worship. The church had been adapted for Reformed services with the erection of galleries, benches and a pulpit, but on the eve of the church's return the temple was broken into and its furnishings vandalized by Calvinist rioters.[37] In this destruction of Protestant fittings, in a building that was to become again a Catholic church, one senses a degree of frustration and resentment amongst the Reformed community at the restitution of what had been a Huguenot temple.

Although the Huguenots possessed the legal means that permitted the construction of their own temples, it was only with the restitution of ecclesiastical property that the impetus to build became imperative. Some communities, particularly the villages of the Protestant south, were dispossessed of the buildings that they had occupied for a generation. In the principal Huguenot strongholds, the existing temples became overcrowded at the beginning of the seventeenth century, likely to have been

[34] Calvin, *Institutes*, p. 73.

[35] Garrisson, *L'Édit de Nantes*, pp. 29–30; Garrisson, *Essai sur les commissions d'application*, pp. 189–91.

[36] S. A. Finley-Croswhite, *Henry IV and the Towns. The Pursuit of Legitimacy in French Urban Society, 1589–1610* (Cambridge, 1999), pp. 106–9.

[37] The church had been used for Catholic worship between 1577 and 1585. La Rochelle, Médiathèque, MSS 164 No. 172, 'Proces verbal par Messieurs Parabel et Langlois Commissaires nommez par sa Majesté en l'année 1599 en Juillet et Aoust', pp. 12, 24, 25; 'Diaire de Jacques Merlin ou "Receuil des choses [les] plus mémorables qui sont passées en ceste ville" [de La Rochelle] de 1589 à 1620', ed. by C. Dangibeaud, *Archives historiques de la Saintonge et de l'Aunis* 5 (1878), 97–100; K. C. Robbins, *City on the Ocean Sea: La Rochelle, 1530–1650. Urban Society, Religion, and Politics on the French Atlantic Frontier* (Leiden, 1997), pp. 156–7, 248.

the result of their attempt to accommodate the ejected congregations.[38] In La Rochelle, the community resumed its project to build a new temple, which had languished since 1577, and the Grand Temple was inaugurated in 1603.[39] At Montpellier and Montauban, respectively, the Petit Temple (inaugurated 1603) and the Temple Neuf (1617) were erected.[40] The position was more difficult for the smaller communities in the Protestant heartlands; at Pouzages in Bas-Poitou, for example, the congregation was ousted from the choir of the parish church and was obliged to seek temporary accommodation under the market hall before it was able to build a temple in 1617.[41]

The Edict of Nantes also enabled the re-establishment of communities that had been suppressed during the course of the religious wars, particularly in the northern cities. At Rouen, the Huguenots began to worship secretly following Henri IV's defeat of the League in 1594. A royal brevet of 1599 granted them freedom of worship and construction on their temple at Quévilly began in the same year.[42] At Bionne, the Reformed community of Orléans constructed a temple within two months and it was inaugurated on Christmas Day 1599.[43] The most important of these temples was erected at Ablon near Fontainebleau by the Reformed congregation of Paris in 1601, although the community was given permission by the king to move their exercise to Charenton on the outskirts of the city in 1606.[44]

The late sixteenth and early seventeenth centuries therefore witnessed a dramatic expansion in construction, as the Huguenots, empowered by the terms of the Edict of Nantes, erected new temples across France. Unlike the Catholic churches that they had previously occupied, these new

---

[38] Garrisson, *Commissions d'application*, pp. 190–1; Chareyre, 'Le consistoire de Nîmes', I, p. 309; H. Guicharnaud, *Montauban au XVIIe. Urbanisme et architecture* (Paris, 1991), p. 92.

[39] AD Charente-Maritime, 17 3E 201, fos. 236v–238; Médiathèque, La Rochelle, MSS 58 P. Mervault, 'Receuil de la Naissance, Progrez…de La Rochelle', fos. 136, 138; MSS 153 R. Colin, 'Annales de La Rochelle', pp. 9, 21, 23; MSS 161 'Diaire de Jacques Merlin', p. 388.

[40] The actual date for the completion of the Petit Temple is variously given as early as 1601 or as late as 1605. Corbière, *Histoire de l'Église réformée de Montpellier*, pp. 130–1. On Montauban, see Guicharnaud, *Montauban au XVIIe*, pp. 92–9.

[41] P. Romane-Musculus, 'L'Église réformée de Pouzages de l'Édit de Nantes à sa Révocation', *BSHPF* 125 (1979), 9, 12. See also Benoist, *Histoire de l'Édit de Nantes*, II, p. 545; Chabrol, *La Cévenne au village*, p. 175; Cabanel, *Itinéraires protestantes en Languedoc*, I, pp. 170–1, 203, 319, II, p. 40.

[42] P. Benedict, *Rouen during the Wars of Religion* (Cambridge, 1981), pp. 228–9; P. Legendre, *Histoire de la persécution faite à l'Église de Rouen sur la fin du dernier siècle* (Rotterdam, 1704), pp. 1–2.

[43] L. Madeline, 'Histoire du Temple de l'Église réformée d'Orléans', *Bulletin de la Société Archéologique et Historique de l'Orléanais* (new series, 13, 1995), 44; L. Madeline, 'La communauté protestante' in *A l'ombre des Rois. Le grand siècle d'Orléans – catalogue* (Orléans, 2000), p. 102.

[44] J. Pannier, *Histoire de l'Église réformée de Paris sous Henri IV* (Paris, 1911), pp. 95–101, 435–8.

temples reflected the liturgical demands of Protestant worship, break-ing away from an architectural style which had fostered the mystery and sanctity of the Mass. In a number of places they adopted a polyg-onal design, reflecting the models of the proto-temples of the 1560s. These buildings were better suited to preaching the Word of God, ensuring that the minister was both visible and audible to the whole congregation.

The more prosperous and affluent Reformed communities employ-ed leading architects – such as Jacques II du Cerceau at Ablon and Charenton and later Salomon de Brosse at Charenton, and Pierre Levesville at Montauban – to design temples which reflected the latest architectural style; the decoration and use of high-quality materials sought to emphasize further the status of these buildings.[45] As a result these new temples made an important visual statement about Protestant worship and its apparent permanence. In fact, in Sully's new town of Henrichemont it was intended that the Catholic church and Protestant temple should be built on an equal footing and to a similar design.[46] Fur-thermore, with architects such as de Brosse and Levesville also involved in the programme of Catholic rebuilding and restoration after the de-struction of the religious wars, these new temples served to underscore the religious pluralism of France in the early seventeenth century.[47] Clearly the architectural projects of the major Huguenot strongholds could not be matched by the smaller congregations, but even here the erection of a temple served as an alternative religious focus for the community. An ex-ample of this can be seen in the Cévennes, where a temple was erected in the village of Vialas rather than the religious and administrative centre

---

[45] M. Prestwich, 'Patronage and Protestants in France, 1598–1661: Architects and Painters' in R. Mousnier and J. Mesnard (eds.), *L'Âge d'or du Mécénat* (Paris, 1985), pp. 79–80; R. Coope, *Salomon de Brosse and the Development of the Classical Style in French Architecture from 1565 to 1630* (Oxford, 1972), pp. 183–7; Guicharnaud, *Montauban au XVIIe*, pp. 94–6. Attempts to link the Grand Temple at La Rochelle with Philibert de l'Orme are less than conclusive. Although the projected temple dates back to 1569, construction did not begin until 1577, seven years after de l'Orme's death, and was then completely abandoned until work began again from scratch in 1600. Guicharnaud, 'Introduction to the Architecture of Protestant Temples', p. 147; J.-M. Pérouse de Montclos, *Philibert de l'Orme: architecte du roi (1514–1570)* (Paris, 2000), p. 326. On the design and construction of temples, see Mentzer, 'Reformed Churches of France', pp. 200–20 and Guicharnaud, 'Introduction to the Architecture of Protestant Temples'.

[46] Y. Guéneau, 'Le Protestantisme dans la Principauté de Boibelle et d'Henrichemont du XVIIe au XVIIIe siècles', *Cahiers d'Archéologie et d'Histoire du Berry* 48 (1977), 6; Coope, *Salomon de Brosse*, pp. 44–6.

[47] Coope, *Salomon de Brosse*, pp. 135–46, 235–7; Koch, 'Calvinism and the Visual Arts', p. 182. See A. Spicer, 'Huguenots, Jesuits and French Religious Architecture in Early Seventeenth-century France' in K. Cameron, M. Greengrass and P. Roberts (eds.), *The Adventure of Religious Pluralism in Early Modern France* (Berne, 2000), pp. 245–59.

of the parish at Castagnols, thereby creating two contrasting liturgical focal points.[48]

The construction of Huguenot temples was not, however, confined to the early seventeenth century; construction continued until the Revocation of the Edict of Nantes in 1685. Some temples were rebuilt after natural disasters befell them; the temple at Dieppe was blown down in 1606, while at Mens-en-Trièvres the temple was destroyed when fire engulfed the town in 1650.[49] As has already been indicated, temples such as that at Cleuné were rebuilt after being destroyed by Catholic opponents.[50] More positively, further impetus for the construction of new temples or the extension of the existing buildings during the seventeenth century resulted from overcrowding within the temples, which had contributed to the fractious disputes over seating.[51]

The continued construction of temples during the course of the seventeenth century ironically owed much to the policies of the crown towards the Huguenots. During the conflicts of the 1620s, a number of temples were severely damaged or destroyed by their Catholic opponents. The temple at Layrac, for example, was smashed by Catholic troops occupying the town in March 1622; the temple at Romorantin was burned to the ground the following year.[52] However, while Louis XIII might be portrayed as trampling down the forces of heresy, forcing the Protestant strongholds into obedience and destroying their fortifications, the crown permitted the reconstruction of temples. An edict was issued ordering that temples in the Cévennes, Foix, Gévaudan, Guyenne and Languedoc that had been seized or demolished during the conflicts of the 1620s should be restored, where they were still required.[53] Even where the king wished to make a clear statement about the submission of Protestantism to royal authority, the crown was prepared to make concessions for Reformed worship. Following the fall of La Rochelle in 1628, the king ordered that the Grand Temple should be granted to the Catholics, to

---

48 P. Dombre, J.-C. Schmitt, P. Schmitt Pantel and J. Verney, *Vialas en Cévennes et son temple depuis 1612* (Montpellier, 1997), pp. 22, 27–9.
49 Guicharnaud, 'Introduction to the Architecture of Protestant Temples', pp. 140, 142; P. Bolle, 'Religion et Vie quotidienne à Mens-en-Trièvres' in P. Bolle (ed.), *Le Protestantisme en Dauphiné au XVIIe siècle: Religion et vie quotidienne à Mens-en-Trièvres, Die et Gap (1650–1685)* (Poet-Laval, 1983), p. 42.
50 See above, note 5.
51 Mentzer, 'Reformed Churches of France', pp. 208–9; Bolle, 'Religion et Vie quotidienne', p. 43; Benoist, *Histoire de l'Édit de Nantes*, III, pt 3, p. 59.
52 G. Hanlon, *Confession and Community in Seventeenth-century France: Catholic and Protestant Coexistence in Aquitaine* (Philadelphia, 1993), p. 51; Benoist, *Histoire de l'Édit de Nantes*, II, p. 418.
53 *Édit du roy sur la grace et pardon qu'il a pleu à sa Majesté donner, tant au duc de Rohan & sieur de Soubise* (Paris, 1644), p. 11.

be a cathedral at the centre of a new diocese. Louis XIII also directed that the Huguenots should be granted a new site in the suburbs for their temple and they were assigned 6,000 *livres* for its construction.[54] Work on the new temple of Villeneuve began in 1630 while the Grand Temple was converted into a Catholic church.[55] It seems that the king also intended that the temple at Privas would have been similarly dealt with, becoming a Capuchin house, but it was destroyed by fire in the reduction of the town by the crown.[56] The king's actions in demonstrating the triumph of the forces of Catholicism also served to emphasize the importance of the temple as a symbol of the Reformed church.

Building continued into the reign of Louis XIV. In 1650 the archbishop of Embrun complained that nearly sixty temples had been rebuilt; the Catholic clergy complained to the Estates of Languedoc in 1648 that the Huguenots were establishing new places of worship and protested again two years later that they were opening new temples. To an extent some of these protests were disingenuous, for as Elie Benoist hastened to point out the temples had been erected with royal permission.[57] As the crown began to enforce more rigorously the Edict of Nantes, a number of temples were identified as having contravened its terms. This included places where there was no evidence that Reformed worship had been established in 1577 or had been practised in 1596 and 1597. Temples erected on property belonging to the church or which disturbed the celebration of the Mass also violated the edict.[58] The terms of the edict were more closely defined; for example, 'temples could not be so close to churches that the divine service could be interrupted by the singing of psalms, the sound of bells'. In such circumstances the temple was to be demolished but those of the Religion Prétendue Réformée were permitted to build another in a more suitable location at their own expense.[59] The temple in the village of Barre-des-Cevennes was demolished in 1668 for this

---

[54] AN TT 263/B/1/56 *Articles accordés par sa Majesté à ceux de la religion de la ville de La Rochelle le 10 Febvrier 1630* (s.l., 1643), p. 4.

[55] *Histoire des Reformés de La Rochelle depuis l'Année 1685 en laquelle l'Édit de Nantes a été revoqué* (Leiden, 1688), p. 313; J.-B.-E. Jourdan, *Éphémérides historiques de La Rochelle*, 2 vols. (La Rochelle, 1861–71), II, pp. 126–7. For engravings and plans of the converted Grand Temple and the temple of Villeneuve, see Claude Masse, *Receuil des plans de La Rochelle* (La Rochelle, 1979), plate 76.

[56] V. Chareton, *La Réforme et les guerres civiles en Vivarais particulièrement dans la region de Privas (Valentinois) 1544–1632* (Paris, 1913), p. 302.

[57] S. Deyon, 'La Destruction des Temples' in R. Zuber and L. Theis (eds.), *La Révocation de l'Édit de Nantes et le protestantisme français en 1685* (Paris, 1986), pp. 242–3; Benoist, *Histoire de l'Édit de Nantes*, III, pt 1, pp. 42, 148, 204.

[58] Garrisson, *L'Édit de Nantes*, pp. 30, 33; Deyon, 'La Destruction des Temples', p. 243.

[59] P. Bernard, *Explication de l'Édict de Nantes par les autres edicts de pacification, declarations & arrests de reglement* (Paris, 1666), pp. 86–7.

reason but a new temple on an alternative site had been completed by
1675.[60] This seems to have reflected the general policy of the crown in
interpreting the edict. Temples that had been built on sites that conflicted
with the terms of the edict were to be demolished, but where the community could prove their existence in 1596–7 they were permitted to
build anew in a more suitable location. When the smaller temples were
demolished in Montauban and Montpellier for contravening the terms
of the edict, the crown granted permission for the older existing temples
to be extended to accommodate the displaced congregation.[61] The differing approach towards these communities can be seen in the various
arrêts issued by the crown concerning the demolition of temples.[62] As late
July 1685, an *arrêt* ordered the demolition of the temples at Raucourt and
Givonne but the temple at Sedan was to be handed over to the Catholics
and another site found for a replacement in the suburbs.[63]

Even where the temple was deemed to contravene the edict, its demolition was not always immediate. In fact in the Protestant stronghold
of Uzès, where the chanting of psalms was considered to disturb the
celebration of the Mass, the community managed to evade demolition.
The congregation minimized the 'disturbance' by blocking the windows
and the main entrance to the temple, which faced the Catholic church,
and entered from the other side of the temple.[64] In situations where the
Huguenots could not avoid demolition, some were able to delay the implementation of the *arrêts*. In Alençon, where Elie Benoist was minister,
the temple occupied a central position within the town. An attempt was
made in 1661 to outlaw Protestantism in the town. Yet the Huguenots
were able to secure permission to construct a new temple a mere 600
metres from the town. Furthermore, even though the old temple was to

---

[60] Cabanel, *Itinéraires protestantes en Languedoc*, I, pp. 170–1.

[61] Benoist, *Histoire de l'Édit de Nantes*, III, pt I, pp. 171–2, pt 3, p. 54.

[62] For example, compare two edicts issued within a month of each other in 1663: *Arrest du conseil d'estat du roy, portant que les temples de la religion pretendue reformée de Lants, La Coste, Gignac, d'Ongles, d'Oppedettes, Signargues, Ioucquars, Gordes, La Bastide de Gros, La Breoule & Souliers, du pais de Provence, seront demolis suiuant les ordres de Monsieur de Saran Champigni intendant de justice des generalitez de Lyon & Dauphiné: Et l'exercice public de la Religion pretendue reformée interdit esdits lieux* (Paris, 1664) and *Arrest du conseil privé du roy portant que le temple de ceux de la R.P.R. de Montagnac en Languedoc au Diocese d'Agde, sera demoly dans un mois du jour de la signification du present arrest, à leurs dépens; & ils pourront en bastir un autre dans les faux-bourgs de ladite ville* (Paris 1664). The first edict ordered that no trace of a temple should remain after demolition whereas at Montagnac, where the existence of a temple could be proved as far back as 1585, a replacement was permitted in the suburbs.

[63] *Arrest du conseil d'estat qui interdit pour toujours l'exercice de la R.P.R. en la ville de Sedan, & la démolition des temples dans les lieux de Raucourt & Givonne* (Paris, 1685), pp. 4–5; D. McKee, 'Les Protestants de Sedan et la Révocation de l'Édit de Nantes: Opposition, Fuites et Résistance', *BSHPF* 127 (1981), 224–5.

[64] Cabanel, *Itinéraires protestantes en Languedoc*, II, pp. 265, 287.

be demolished within a month, the community was able to delay this for two years, until the completion of their new building.[65]

A further example of how communities circumvented and withstood the onslaught against the temples is worth citing, because it reveals the resilience and militancy of the Huguenots as well as the limited effectiveness of royal policy. The temple at Gercy near Soissons was demolished in 1665, but the community took the wood and other materials from the site and erected another temple at the château of Villiers-les-Guise, the home of the local seigneur, Jean du Vez, who possessed rights of *haute justice*. Although the case was investigated in 1670 and du Vez's rights of *haute justice* had been disputed even earlier, the temple continued to attract a considerable congregation and was still standing in November 1685.[66] Such examples represent pyrrhic victories in the face of what was a sustained campaign directed against the Reformed church in France. In the years between the start of Louis XIV's personal rule in 1661 and the Revocation, an estimated 650–700 temples were demolished.[67]

The temple represented a powerful visual symbol of the existence of a minority church within the midst of the Catholic community. With the suppression of the Huguenot congregations, the crown and local community sought to emphasize the triumph of Catholicism over heresy. Following the Revocation, the materials from the temples were frequently reused in the repair or construction of Catholic churches or chapels; their fittings, and in particular their bells, were appropriated, and in some cases the site of the temple was marked by a cross.[68] A small number of temples were appropriated for Catholic worship or more secular purposes, such as a school, and thereby served also to demonstrate the defeat of Protestantism.[69] The scale of this attempt to erase all traces of Protestantism from France further underscores the significance with

---

[65] Benoist, *Histoire de l'Edit de Nantes*, III, pt 1, pp. 597–9; B. Robert, 'La Réforme à Alençon', *BSHPF* 83 (1934), 93–5. The *arrêt* concerning the temple at Sedan granted the community permission to use the building for another six months until the completion of the new temple: *Arrest du Conseil d'Estat qui interdit pour toujours l'Exercice de la R.P.R. en la ville de Sedan*, p. 5.

[66] AN TT 276/A/7/42, 45, 47; *Arrest du Conseil d'Estat, pourtant reglement sur plusieurs entreprises de ceux de la Religion pretendue réformée dans la Generalité de Soissons et Diocese de Laon* (Paris, 1664), pp. 3–5; O. Douen, 'La Révocation de l'Édit de Nantes en Thiérache', *BSHPF* 27 (1878), 289.

[67] Deyon, 'La Destruction des temples', pp. 241–2.

[68] *Ibid.*, pp. 251–5. See also above, plate II, p. 177.

[69] Benoist, *Histoire de l'Édit de Nantes*, III, pt 1, p. 290, pt 2, pp. 580, 581, 582, pt 3, pp. 739–40. An interesting comparison can be made with the consecration of former synagogues in the Holy Roman Empire during the later middle ages: see J. M. Minty, '*Judengasse* to Christian Quarter: The Phenomenon of the Converted Synagogue in the Later Medieval and Early Modern Holy Roman Empire' in B. Scribner and T. Johnson (eds.), *Popular Religion in Germany and Central Europe, 1400–1800* (Basingstoke, 1996), pp. 76–9.

which the Catholics imbued the temple. For the Huguenots themselves, the building had from as early as the 1560s been a statement of defiance, of the permanence of their religion, which of course became a reality following the Edict of Nantes. While these buildings may initially have been a place of shelter, few congregations were still worshipping in barns by the later seventeenth century. They had built temples that reflected the status and importance of their congregation, as well as creating a fitting place in which to assemble for worship. The buildings were not sacred places, for the holiness of the temple should rest within the individuals themselves; the structure was merely a place where the Huguenots could with common voice rejoice, worship and pray to God.[70]

70 Calvin, *Institutes*, pp. 73–4. See also Spicer, 'Rebuilding Solomon's Temple?', pp. 282–3.

12. 'Ensevelir honnestement les corps': funeral corteges and Huguenot culture

Bernard Roussel

One hundred thousand years ago, modern human beings, people possessed of a skeletal structure similar to ours, lived in Palestine and perhaps in Ethiopia and North Africa. Not only did they resemble us anatomically, but they buried their dead in tombs and oriented the bodies. Pollen from flowers and offerings to the deceased can also be found in the graves. In short, they observed religious rites.[1]

Millennia later, around 1560, the men and women who were members of the first Reformed churches of the kingdom of France appeared to do considerably less for their dead. Even by the late eighteenth century, their ways had changed little. Still, it is not as if they did nothing. On the occasion of a death, they thought it enough, circumstances permitting, to proceed in a simple procession to 'bury properly the body of the deceased'.[2] Historians often explain this reserve by pointing to the extreme anti-Catholicism of the earliest adherents to the Reformed movement, and/or to their indifference toward the body, or even to the repression of emotion among the mourners. Yet these suggestions fail to explain fully the comportment adopted upon the death of between 600,000 and 800,000 Huguenots, generation upon generation of men and women. As this essay explores the issues surrounding death and burial in the Huguenot world, keep in mind that death, as much as gender, age group and social position, is a cultural construction. The 'death' of French Protestants as well as Catholics in the sixteenth century was not necessarily 'death' as it is now understood in contemporary discussions about hospice care or euthanasia.[3] Indeed, Reformed funeral practices present the historian with a representation of death, of the association

[1] A. Langaney, 'Les Bases génétiques de l'Évolution humaine' in Y. W. Michaud (ed.), *Université de tous les savoirs. Qu'est ce que la vie?* (Paris, 2000), p. 129.
[2] Pierre Viret, *L'Office des mortz fait par dialogues en maniere de devis . . . 1. L'enterrement* (Geneva, 1552), p. 31.
[3] C. M. Koslofsky, *The Reformation of the Dead. Death and Ritual in Early Modern Germany, 1450–1700* (London, 2000), p. 5.

of body and soul, of the individual and his membership in the community, of the living and the dead. All are elements of a specific culture, 'Christian' naturally enough, but one which the scholar must be careful to respect as unfamiliar.

This essay seeks to demonstrate that when Protestants followed the path that led from the deceased's home to the burial place, they publicly expressed an essential trait within their culture. The speed with which it was established, its spread and durability invite the historian to seek an explanation tied to the coherence of a system of Reformed representations and practices, and to position it, furthermore, in conjunction with the rite of the Lord's Supper. This rite was unquestionably an integral part of the religion of the men and women who broke with the customs of their fathers, mothers, neighbours and fellow parishioners for many different reasons, about which historians may never be certain.[4]

The discussion that follows has artificially isolated, for editorial and methodological purposes, the brief interval between the moment of death and the burial of the body. The time amounted to no more than twenty-four hours, except for nobles who died while travelling.[5] Without disregarding the horrible conditions in which so many people died, the scholar must, in the interests of focusing the present inquiry, look past these terrible circumstances. Let us finally understand that, for analytical clarity, we will address that which was done for the mortal remains of the deceased at his home, under circumstances where close relatives, friends and neighbours moved about and acted in what might be called the normal course of events. We will observe the way in which they followed a path, which led to a pit, hollowed out in the earth. The countless people who had taken this path before them and even many contemporaries believed that their destination was a dangerous and perilous place. Yet

---

4 See B. Roussel, '"Faire la Cène" dans les Églises réformées du Royaume de France au seizième siècle (ca. 1555–ca. 1575)', *Archives de Sciences Sociales des Religions* 85 (1994), 99–119.

5 Discipline de l'Église de Saint Lô (1563), 'De la sépulture, art. 2: On ne se hastera de les enterrer pour éviter les inconvénients [i.e. in the case of mistaken death], et aussi on les laissera trop longtemps sans les inhumer de peur de corruption [i.e. for reasons of hygiene; no allusion is being made to possible ritual uncleanliness through contact with a cadaver]': M. Reulos, 'Les Débuts des communautés réformées dans l'actuel Département de la Manche (Cotentin et Avranchin)', in *Réforme et Contre-réforme en Normandie*, special issue of *Revue du Département de la Manche* 24 (1982, fascicules 93-94-95), 54. For an example of a noble woman's request to be buried elsewhere: Antoinette d'Aubeterre, Dame de Soubise, du Parc et de Mouchamps. 'Testament', *BSHPF* 13 (1864), 306–13, 16 June 1570: '[Aujourd'hui à La Rochelle], veulx néantmoins, s'il plaist à nostre dieu faire sa volunté de moy, que mon corps soit porté et inhumé au temple dudict Mouchamps, auprès de la sépulture de feu mondit sieur et mary', 311.

for the Huguenots, the tomb was a 'lit de repos', a bed in which to sleep, a resting place offered by mother-earth. It was no longer an underground gallery leading to an inferno, nor was it an opening from which the 'disappeared' escaped to torment the living.

Several short yet illustrative accounts of Huguenot burial suggest its essential features. In 1553, Marie de Montsaujon, wife of Antoine de Villemor, a notary and attorney at Troyes and 'a woman who feared God and attended religious services', stipulated in her will that 'her body be buried at night, by lantern light, without torches or funerary pomp, rejecting the showy displays customary among papists'. Upon deliberation, the local ecclesiastical magistrate allowed 'her mortal remains to be interred without objection'.[6]

Philippe de Luns, a young woman from Périgord, provides another example, one possessed of more provocative and tragic consequences. No more than 'twenty-three years old or thereabout', she was imprisoned in the wake of the hysteria that followed discovery of a secret meeting of Huguenots in the rue Saint Jacques (4 September 1557). Suspected of having buried her husband, who died in May 1558, in her garden, she responded 'no, on the contrary, he had been taken to the Hôtel Dieu [the Poor House] to be buried with the other poor [she offered an affidavit of proof] and without any other superstitious ceremonies'.[7]

Later, in June 1569, during one of the many periods of armed conflict, the Catholic 'Dame de Brassac' (Brassac is a town near Castres) was killed by a Protestant soldier. Fire soon engulfed the building which was the scene of the drama and 'they had to carry her body down to save it from the flames. It remained exposed until Jacques Gaches, a local resident and member of the Religion [thus a Protestant], having taken a shroud, wrapped the body, and despite the disorderly conduct of the soldiers, carried it into the church where he interred her as honourably as he could, in so far as the circumstances of the moment allowed.'[8] This is a wonderful example of a Huguenot who, in his own fashion, paid final tribute to a Catholic woman whom he evidently respected. The expression 'he interred her as honourably as he could' is especially revealing.

Moving forward into the seventeenth century, the simplicity of the funeral cortege was maintained, as attested by 'interment invitations',

---

[6] Nicolas Pithou de Chamgobert, *Chroniques de Troyes et de la Champagne durant les guerres de religion (1524–1594)*, ed. by P.-E. Leroy and I. Palasi, 2 vols. (Reims, 1998–2000), I, pp. 131–2.

[7] Jean Crespin, *Histoire des martyrs*, ed. by Daniel Benoît, 3 vols. (Toulouse, 1887), II, pp. 565–6.

[8] *Mémoires de Jacques Gaches sur les guerres de religion à Castres et dans le Languedoc (1555–1610)*, ed. by Charles Pradel (Paris, 1879), p. 88.

which Huguenot artisans of Paris sent to family and friends.[9] If, in the social disruption, which characterized much of the Huguenot community during the years immediately following the Revocation of the Edict of Nantes, worry over 'obligations' due the dead is absent from the *Mémoires* of Jean Cavalier,[10] under other circumstances the desire was to see everything done in orderly fashion, indeed 'honourably', as shown by some mid-eighteenth-century examples. On 1 February 1757, Gaspard Le Vasseur, an attorney attached to the *parlement* and a man 'of Protestant sentiment, died at the age of seventy-eight'. According to the burial permit signed by Bricogne, police commissioner of the Châtelet, 'he is to be buried without commotion, scandal or pomp on the grounds belonging to a certain Moreau at Port-au-Plâtre [near Bercy]. The police are ordered to assist [provide protection] if necessary.'[11] Here, concern over public order joined Reformed custom, except that the conditions were imposed in wholly sordid fashion. Nearly seventy years after the Revocation, the administrative rules remained harsh and pitiless.

Taken together, these spare narratives announce the principal components of longstanding Huguenot practice.[12] Following the probable comforting of the dying, when the situation lent itself to such,[13] those in attendance confirmed death's arrival. Later, at the appropriate moment, friends and relatives accompanied the body to a preselected location – the choice of burial site is dealt with further below – for interment. The pastor, the official minister of God's Word, took no part in the cortege, unless he participated in a wholly private capacity, and the troupe that escorted the remains was never understood to be a congregation to whom

---

9 L. Raulet, 'Les Billets d'enterrement d'artistes huguenots de l'Ancienne Académie royale de Peinture et de Sculpture (1653–1712)', *BSHPF* 56 (1907), 53–69. As an example: 'Monsieur, vous êtes priez d'assister à l'enterrement de Monsieur Lans, vivant, peintre ordinaire du Roy en son academie, – décédé en sa maison sur le quai de la Mégisserie – qui se fera dimanche 20 novembre 1661, à cinq heures du soir, au cimetières du faubourg St Germain, où la Compagnie aura agréable de se trouver.' I wish to thank Raymond Mentzer for bringing this article to my attention.

10 Jean Cavalier, *Mémoires sur la guerre des Camisards* (Dublin, 1726).

11 According to an anonymous note discovered in the Archives of the Châtelet by a nineteenth-century scholar. It is obviously but one of many examples.

12 Additional examples can be found in the classic studies: P. de Félice, *Les protestants d'autrefois. Vie intérieure des Églises, mœurs et usages. Les temples – Les services religieux – Les actes pastoraux* (Paris, 1897), pp. 248–72; B. Faivre, 'La Mort à travers la littérature protestante aux 16e et 17e siècles', Mémoire de maîtrise, Université de Paris IV (1973); P. Ariès, *L'Homme devant la mort* (Paris, 1977); M. Vovelle, *La Mort et l'Occident, de 1300 à nos jours* (Paris, 1983).

13 See M. Carbonnier-Burkard, 'L'Art de mourir réformé. Les récits des "dernières heures" chez les réformés français aux XVIIe et XVIIIe siècles', in *Homo religiosus. Autour de J. Delumeau* (Paris, 1997), pp. 99–107; M. Carbonnier-Burkard, 'Les Manuels réformés de préparation à la mort', *Revue de l'Histoire des Religions* 217 (2000), 363–80.

he might address a sermon. This conduct was particular to the faithful within the Reformed churches of France.[14] Behaviour among French Protestants did not follow the evolution found at Geneva or in the English and Lutheran worlds toward funeral practices. Outside France, Protestants accentuated social differences or, as in the case of Lutheran Germany, funerals became veritable nocturnal Baroque festivals.[15]

In all of this, it is important to realize that these burial reports accord with the succinct instructions contained in the *Disciplines*, frequently updated regulations governing the French Reformed churches. Early, strikingly similar local *Disciplines* issued by the churches of Bayeux and Saint-Lô prescribed the burial of the dead 'decently and without pomp'. In each case, the article entitled 'De la sépulture' was explicit. 'The dead should be buried decently and without pomp; they should be accompanied to the cemetery by the elder or deacon and the faithful of their neighbourhood; and to avoid all superstition, they should be placed in the ground without sermons or prayers.'[16] Other articles of the *Disciplines* treated the fabrication and carrying of the bier, the acquisition of the shroud and the elders' comforting of the bereaved. On a question where the weight of local and family custom was so fundamental, it is hardly surprising that the *Discipline* developed and disseminated by the national synods was extremely guarded. The compilation of 1563, prepared after the national synod of Lyon, stated in the final article of the title concerning ministers: 'To avoid all superstition, ministers will offer neither prayers nor sermons at the interment of the dead.' Little

---

[14] Though extensive comparison is not possible here, see the suggestion of Koslofsky, *Reformation of the Dead*, p. 93: 'Anabaptist communities simplified the funeral to an unadorned burial service; the Reformed tradition reduced clerical participation to an absolute minimum. But Lutheran reformers did not proceed with this extreme simplification or elimination of the funeral ritual . . . The Lutheran understanding of the funeral attached a fundamental doctrine, the promise of the resurrection as a consequence of salvation *sola fide*, with a ritual directed to the consolation of the living and the display of honour.'

[15] Max Engammarre is presently studying this question for Geneva. Meanwhile, see U. Rohner-Baumberger, *Das Begräbniswesen im calvinistischen Genf* (Basel, 1975). The documentation is abundant for England and Lutheran Germany. Three recent studies are: C. Gitting, *Death, Burial and the Individual in Early Modern England* (London, 1984); S. C. Karant-Nunn, *The Reformation of Ritual. An Interpretation of Early Modern Germany* (London, 1997); Koslofsky, *Reformation of the Dead*. Also see B. Roussel, 'Des Rituels luthériens à la Liturgie réformée' in M.-C. Pitassi (ed.), *Edifier ou instruire? Les avatars de la liturgie réformée du XVIe au XVIIIe siècle* (Paris, 2000), pp. 15–31; M. Vénard and B. Vogler, *Histoire du Christianisme. VIII. Le Temps des Confessions (1530–1620)* (n.p., 1992), p. 948 underscores, better than Vovelle, *La Mort et l'Occident*, pp. 229–36, the differences between Reformed and Lutheran, but they only discuss the former in terms of bans and abstentions.

[16] For the church of Bayeux (1563), see R. M. Kingdon, M. Reulos and R. A. Mentzer, '"Disciplines" Réformées françaises du XVIe siècle: une découverte faite aux États Unis', *BSHPF* 130 (1984), 81; and for the church of Saint-Lô (1563), Reulos, 'Les débuts des communautés réformées', 54.

would be added later, despite occasional requests for more solemn funeral observances.[17] The *Forme des Prières et Chantz ecclesiastiques*, which regulated worship, made no suggestions at all,[18] and for good reason.

Within theological circles, Jean Calvin was remarkably discreet. Pierre Viret, on the other hand, wrote a dialogue entitled *L'Enterrement*, which, in many ways, better satisfies the historian's needs. The roles in the dialogue are distributed among Théophile and Hilaire, who are Reformed Protestants, the Catholic Thomas, and Eusèbe, the pious man who must be converted.[19] Viret compares, with eloquence and erudition, the funeral rites of antiquity, the Jewish world and early Christianity, and critically evaluates – without the slightest concession – contemporary customs. Viret was, at the time, living at Lausanne, but the validity of his comments extends well beyond the frontiers of the canton of Vaud. Consideration of a few of his salient remarks discloses their value.

Emotion: The grief of those who are witness to death must be able to express itself, but not to excess. '[Jesus Christ] did not say: Do not trouble yourself over the deceased and do not be saddened. That would be overly stoic and thereby turn men into stones or trees, lacking all feeling. This is not the message of Evangelical truth.'[20] Viret insisted upon appropriate bearing and moderate conduct which affirm that the faithful 'do not grieve like the pagans and infidels, who have no hope of resurrection [1 Th. 4:5]'.[21] Restraint is proper and fitting deportment.

Simplicity: 'We can render no greater honour and service to the deceased than to bury them decently in the ground, according to the Word of God, who said: You are dust, and to dust you shall return [Gen. 3:19].'[22] The burial of Jesus was, for Viret, one of the perfectly clear biblical foundations of such decency. On this point, Viret severely criticized certain unidentified Franciscans who, according to persistent rumour, had but scorn for human remains. Rather, the believer has the sense of

---

[17] See the *Discipline* edited by Isaac Huisseau in 1666, chap. x, 'Des exercices sacrés de l'assemblée des fidèles' in F. Méjan, *Discipline de l'Église réformée de France* (Paris, 1947), pp. 260–1. Article V ended in restrictive fashion the open discussion at the national synods held at Gap (1603), Charenton (1631) and Alençon (1637): 'Il ne se fera aucune prière, ou prédication, ni aumônes publiques aux enterrements, pour obvier à toutes superstitions: et seront exhortés ceux qui accompagnent les corps de se comporter avec modestie durant le convoi, méditant selon l'objet qui se présente, tant les misères et brièveté de cette vie, que l'espérance de la vie bien-heureuse.' Article VI prescribed mourning, not in 'dress' but 'in the heart'.

[18] John Calvin, *Opera selecta*, ed. by P. Barth and G. Niesel, 4 vols. (Munich, 1970), II, pp. 11–58.

[19] This is the first *Dialogue* in a group of five that constitute *L'Office des Mortz fait par dialogues en manière de devis*, third part of the *Disputations chrétiennes*. The edition cited here is that published at Geneva in 1552.

[20] Viret, *L'Office des mortz*, p. 30 (Théophile).   [21] *Ibid.*, p. 31 (Théophile).   [22] *Ibid.*, p. 26 (Hilaire).

being close to the simple 'virtue' (*honnesteté*) of Diogenes in Cicero's *Tusculanae Disputationes*, who, 'although he was not much concerned about the details of his burial, none the less ordered that his body not be left for the dogs'.[23]

The cemetery: In the words of Théophile, 'Consequently, it is enough for us to bury the bodies of the dead decently and to place them in the ground, as in a bed, to await the coming of Jesus and the general resurrection of the dead.' If possible, burial should be in a

cemetery, a place designated [by Christians] for their interment, because it is like a bed or resting place, or even the lodging of deceased believers . . . We would do great injury to our [deceased] bodies, which were the temple of the Lord in which God dwelled, and which have been consecrated by the blood of Jesus Christ, to His honour and glory, and dedicated to the eternal glory of His kingdom, if we threw them to the dogs, vultures, or other wild beasts and carrion feeders, who will not live on after death and participate in immortality.[24]

Then Viret adds, speaking of the nature of cemeteries:

It is both a great superstition and idolatry to think that the ground itself confers some sort of sanctity upon the dead. Sanctity does not come from the ground, whatever its nature, but from the saints who rest there. This is why the place where the saints are buried is sanctified. With true Christians, this is the case, even if it happens to be in Turkey. By the same token, if infidels are buried there, it is polluted, even if it happens to be in the earthly paradise.[25]

Altogether, these passages from Viret constitute a veritable gold mine for the historical anthropologist.

This dramatic break with long-established traditions inevitably distressed, shocked and disturbed the 'unreformed', the Catholic community. In this regard, it is critical to note the determination of French Protestants to maintain their beliefs and worship without leaving the kingdom or abandoning their social position and all that it entailed. It was this claim to a division of symbolic and ritual 'space', within the same territory, that led to difficulties both before and after the Edict of Nantes.

Already in the early 1560s, upon the death of François II, whose funeral was perhaps less majestic than usual, some observed that he had been buried 'à la luthérienne'.[26] Later, Florimond de Raemond, a

---

[23] *Ibid.*, p. 28 (Hilaire).   [24] *Ibid.*, pp. 31 ff. (Théophile).   [25] *Ibid.*, p. 33 (Théophile).
[26] On 22 January 1561 Theodore Beza wrote to Bullinger of the king's funeral without the customary pomp, 'adeo ut nunc vulgato proverbio jactetur Lutherano more sepultus Lutheranorum hostis' [People have coined a derisive saying: bury '*à la luthérienne*' the scourge of the Lutherans]. See H. Aubert, F. Aubert, H. Meylan *et al.* (eds.), *Correspondance de Théodore de Bèze* (Geneva, 1960–), III, pp. 71–2.

well-informed Catholic observer, offered some polemical thoughts on Huguenot funeral practices:

> After one of them passes beyond the threshold of this life, he is placed in a coffin and carried out by servants without pomp, ceremony, or prayer; and in the case of ordinary people, the body is carried by carcass haulers from the local slaughterhouse to some field or profane spot that the authorities have designated for the burial of those of his religion. The body is, of course, followed by friends and relatives, but without any sign of mourning, indeed without any sign of Christian faith. The pastor does not even attend, unless the deceased is someone of great standing and even then he attends as a private person rather than as pastor. The entire group moves in silence, for no one would dare even to mutter a prayer to God, lest he or she be taken for a papist. You see how far their impiety extends. It is certainly tearful to see, along with this miserable treatment of the dead, the loss of their souls.[27]

His commentary is caustic and has engendered a polemical and mis-leading historiographic tradition. According to Florimond de Raemond, Reformed Protestants blaspheme against the Creator, because they have no respect for the deceased's remains. They contradict biblical models by their failure to pray for the dead, thereby endangering the dead as well as the living, who do nothing to ease their situation. The absence of an elaborate funerary display has much to do with a refusal to restore the social order, which the irruption of death has disturbed. The offence against God goes hand in hand with the endangerment of the social order.[28]

Others evidently shared these views and thoughts. The passage of Reformed funeral processions frequently provoked riots. People sought to prevent the burial of the deceased Protestant and treated the remains no better than a rotting animal carcass. They burned, drowned and dismembered corpses; they exhumed bodies and threw them on the garbage heap. As early as 1558, Claude Portesain, an imprisoned goldsmith from Troyes, was beaten to death by his fellow prisoners for 'failing to remove his hat in passing by the church of Notre-Dame' de Troyes. He was given anything but a decent burial in the cemetery. Dogs soon dug up the corpse. 'Having noticed this, a group of Catholics removed the body from the cemetery and reburied it in a place where people habitually piss and shit.'[29]

---

[27] Florimond de Raemond, *L'Histoire de la naissance, progrèz et decadence de l'heresie divisée en huict livres* (Rouen, 1623), bk 8, chap. 18: 'De la Sepulture des Calvinistes, et comment ils ont désiré d'estre ensevelis dans les Églises catholiques', pp. 1052–65 (citation p. 1056).

[28] *Ibid.*, pp. 1057–8. The tenor of the argument and Florimond de Raemond's references suggest that this Catholic polemicist may have read Pierre Viret even though he never cites him in this passage.

[29] Pithou, *Chroniques de Troyes*, I, pp. 191–3.

Niggling obstructionist laws can lead to burials that some would consider dishonourable. These vindictive measures sometimes become the rule and, as such, they support the recognition that the desecration of cadavers and tombs is an effective and horrible way to insult adversaries, whether living or dead. At the same time, it allows mentally disturbed souls to express themselves in times of great social tension.[30]

Thus, it would be wrong to say that there is nothing more to be said on the question of Reformed 'funerary rites' and thereby invite historians to move toward examination of other topics. Quite the opposite. An entire research field exists in looking for, within the system of representations and rites among Reformed Protestants, the reasons behind the surprising conjunction between, on the one hand, the abandonment of Catholic imagery and practices – purgatory and the exhortation to pray for the dead – and, on the other, the permanent adoption of very unusual behaviour, which an overriding concern for 'humanity' fails to explain.

Hence the thesis of this essay, which is neither speculation about the emotions of those who witnessed death, nor a study of the attitudes of Reformed Protestants in the presence of death, but comes closer to historical anthropology: Reformed funerary practices are a ritual sequence dependent on the rite of the Lord's Supper.

This ritual sequence brought to fruition the representations inculcated through regular sermons and catechism lessons, and to whose appropriation the Lord's Supper contributed. These representations were in the forefront of the memory and imagination of the faithful as they confronted liminal situations such as death. This ritual sequence associated the death, which the faithful witnessed, with words and actions that they had experienced and internalized over the course of their lives. It concluded a journey in which Reformed Protestants organized their representations of 'life', 'dying', 'death' and the consequences.

The description and analysis of the rituals of the Lord's Supper and of the burial prompt two observations. The first, which is hardly insignificant, centres on the domain of gesture. In both cases, a procession takes place. When French Protestants celebrated the Lord's Supper, they moved toward the pastor in an orderly procession. Another orderly

---

[30] For this point, there are extensive accounts of 'spontaneous' or 'legal' desecration of Calvinist corpses as well as many studies of the question. Two useful analyses are H. Gelin, 'Cent cadavres de Huguenots sur la Claie et à la voirie sous Louis-le-Grand', *BSHPF* 52 (1903), 385–456 and M. Lindemann, 'Armen- und Eselbegräbnis in der europäischen Frühneuzeit, eine Methode spezialler Kontrolle' in P. R. Blum (ed.), *Studien zur Thematik des Todes im 16. Jahrhundert* (Wolfenbüttel, 1983), pp. 125–39. Various studies of the profanation of Jewish cemeteries in Western Europe are equally illuminating.

procession was that by which people proceeded toward the burial site. In each instance, the procession lent a communal character to a highly individual event: the reception of the bread and wine, and the funeral cortege and subsequent burial.

The second observation involves a precise examination of the elementary attitudes and words associated with the Eucharistic rite and of analogous elements in the funeral cortege. At the celebration of the Lord's Supper, the men and women who received the bread and wine heard the words: 'Let us lift our spirits and hearts to heaven and to Jesus Christ, and let us not be distracted by these terrestrial and corruptible elements, which we see with our eyes and touch with our hands.'[31] Indeed, there is nothing here – neither finely worked chalice and paten, nor elevation of a host – which would be capable of captivating the senses. Within the context of 'ritual-play', this is an invitation to disassociate the body from the soul, to elicit a ritual death, since death, as we will see, was defined at this time and within this milieu by their disassociation. The soul was then invited to absorb itself in the knowledge and contemplation of a saviour who is clearly stated to be in heaven. Similarly, along the route which leads to the grave, no one was distracted by the terrestrial elements 'which we see with our eyes and touch with our hands': the corpse was not manipulated, or placed in the ground with a particular orientation or posture; those in attendance remained silent and their demeanour was restrained.

At this point, it is important to recall a basic theme of Reformed anthropology which is inserted into the economy of the rite. The human soul is immortal. After death, it ascends to its celestial saviour to await eventual reunion with the body from which it has been separated.[32] This representation of death as the separation of the body from the soul

---

[31] The text of the liturgy of the Lord's Supper, found in *La Forme des Prières . . .*, is extensively examined and explained in B. Roussel, 'Comment faire la Cène? Rite et retour aux Écritures dans les Églises réformées du royaume de France au XVIe siècle' in E. Patlagean and A. Le Boulluec (eds.), *Les retours aux Écritures. Fondamentalismes présents et passés* (Louvain, 1993), pp. 195–216 and B. Roussel '"Faire la Cène" dans les Églises réformées du Royaume de France au seizième siècle', *Archives de Sciences Sociales des Religions* 85 (1994), 99–119.

[32] Remember that Calvin denounced, beginning with the introduction to his *Psychopannychia* of 1534, those who denied the immortality of the soul: *CO*, v, cols. 170–1. Elements of eschatology were taught in the *Catéchisme de l'Église de Genève*, which was also used, though not exclusively, in the French kingdom: see, the seventeenth 'Sunday', questions cols. 106–10. This message was received. In his last will and testament of 23 March 1566, shortly before his Genevan 'friends' executed him, Jacques Spifame wrote (speaking in the third person): 'Qu'il playse [à Dieu] recepvoir aujourd'huy son ame au repos eternel . . . s'assurant, quant à son corps, que la terre et le sepulchre en vouldra compter au jour de la resurrection generalle': A. Delmas, 'Procès et mort de Jacques Spifame', *BHR* 5 (1944), 105–37.

has paramount importance. Texts attributed to Protestant martyrs evoke the concept with particular precision.[33] Imprisoned, deprived of the opportunity to worship, tortured and knowing that they will not escape the stake, many martyrs speak of the progressive disassociation of their suffering body, weak because it is also flesh, from the soul. This is a disassociation which they speak of having experienced or wish to experience, although none committed suicide. 'My desire is to die rather than live. I wish that the fight were over and that the nut was cracked.'[34] 'I would like to move on, to be with Christ.'[35] Note that here, as in numerous model prayers from the sixteenth and seventeenth centuries, the personal pronoun or name designated the 'soul'. Let us try to imagine! The meditation, possibly grief, of the participants in the funeral cortege may, in theory, only be the lifting of their 'soul' to heaven, where the soul of the deceased dwells. And since this essay began by suggesting that these people are unfamiliar or alien to us, it is obvious that, in this milieu, a person does not call out to the corpse in invoking the name of the deceased as often happens nowadays. Friends and relatives have not carried 'anyone' to the burial spot.

I would like to play a little with the words. The 'death' (*le décès*) of a member of the Reformed faithful is not the 'death' (*la mort*) of his soul. In connection with this point, allow me to explain how the funeral rite and the Lord's Supper are connected the one to the other.

For those whom the consistory allows to participate, the Lord's Supper offers a 'fruit' clearly identified by the prayers and words that are read before each communicant goes forward to receive the bread and wine. It is worth quoting them in disassociating intentionally the two expressions that draw them to a close.[36] The distribution and ingestion of the bread and wine are understood to be signs of a communion with the 'saviour' who 'truly wished us to be participants in His body and blood so that we wholly possess Him in such a manner *that He lives in us ...*'[37] This, then, is a proposal of mystical union. Thus, the faithful's existence is marked by the sacrificial signs of a saviour to whom he or she is united through faith. This conjunction is here below, the heart of a struggle. Although

---

[33] As an example among many, in 1558, Jean Morel, described 'a young man', within the context of a long discussion over the Lord's Supper (itself significant), who said: 'Et quant à mon ame, j'ai bon besoin d'en avoir le soin; car c'est une chose tant precieuse, qu'encores que nostre corps soit le temple du S. csprit, si est-ce que nostre Seigneur met autant de différence entre le corps et l'ame qu'il y a entre le corps et le vestement': Crespin, *Histoire des Martyrs*, II, p. 627a.

[34] '...que la noix fut cassee'. The martyr's unusual expression conveys a sense of breaking open the skin and allowing the soul to escape. *Ibid.*, III, p. 454b (Antwerp, 1564).

[35] *Ibid.*, III, p. 455a.   [36] *La Forme des prières ...*, p. 48.   [37] See John 13:20.

fragile, it is frequently re-established through repeated participation in the Lord's Supper.

The faithful then hear the words that it is the will of the saviour that '*we* [*live*] *in Him*'. The analogy of the meal is no longer adequate for the movement evoked by this expression. It refers to the total and definitive union of the faithful 'with his saviour'. Observe the suggestion of movement. The site for the union's realization is in 'heaven', the place where the deceased's soul goes. Here it is worth quoting Archambaut Seraphon's account of the martyrdom of Philippe Cene and his companion Jacques, who were jailed with him. Seraphon wrote that on 'the first Saturday of September [1557], it was with wonderful constancy [that they] went to participate in the Lord's Supper with Jesus Christ and His angels'.[38]

Historians of religion are thoroughly familiar with this situation, one in which the complete attainment of the fruits of a rite is deferred. Thus, the complete union of the soul with its celestial saviour, promised by the celebration of the Lord's Supper, will only be realized after death. The words of the officiating pastor and the language of the ritual disclose the metaphorical order, on the one hand, and the reality, on the other. The soul, really separated from the body by death, departs to live in heaven, outside of the flesh, which uses the body as an instrument. Time and again, Pierre Viret, along with numerous other authors of religiously edifying essays that appeared during the second half of the sixteenth century, wrote that it is not that the body is 'dead'. Rather, it 'sleeps' in a bed provided by 'mother-earth'. Jean de l'Espine went so far as to assert that the 'dead' body retains a germ of life – an element of continuity between death and resurrection – much like the egg that the chicken has laid.[39] Out of this was born the requirement for a simple, decent burial,

---

38 Crespin, *Histoire des martyrs*, II, p. 479a. Note here the re-emergence of the theme of the Lord's Supper.

39 Jean de l'Espine was, in the years after 1561, an eminent Reformed minister: '[La mort] met le corps et l'âme en repos bien heureux...A parler proprement, la separation du corps et de l'âme en l'homme fidele ne doibt point estre appelee mort...[La mort] met l'âme hors de prison et l'envoye en liberté au Ciel, pour estre là recueillie au sein de Jesus Christ, et jouir avec luy et tous les esprits bien heureux des consolations eternelles qui y sont promises et reservees aux elus...Et le corps d'autre costé, en la terre comme en un lict, pour dormir et reposer à son aise, sans que son somme soit plus interrompu ou troublé, ny par songes fascheux...ny par craintes, ny par alarmes et bruits violents...et ce jusques au jour de la resurrection...[Ce corps] n'est point privé de vie, lors mesme qu'il est pourri en la terre, d'autant qu'il est tousjours accompagné de la grace de Dieu et compris aussi bien qu'est l'âme en l'alliance eternelle qu'il a faicte avec son peuple.' These lines have been excerpted from various passages of the *Excellens discours...touchant le repos et contentement de l'Esprit...* (Geneva, 1587) and the *Consolations et Instruction aux malades*, in *Opuscules théologiques* (Geneva, 1598). L'Espine and his contemporaries broke with Calvin's restraint on all these questions. See, on this question, B. Roussel, 'Jean de l'Espine (c. 1505–97): Écrire au Temps des Troubles' in

one in keeping, as Viret indicates, with that of Jesus of Nazareth. At the moment of death, then, body and soul separate. Subsequently, it would be erroneous to say that the soul 'sleeps' or that the body is 'dead'. The soul 'lives' and the body 'sleeps'. There is nothing more to be done or said about this 'body'. Finally, after the dying person has been piously edified in her or his final hours, the soul truly lacks nothing.

The notion of deferred attainment of the happiness of salvation binds then the rite of the Lord's Supper to the funeral procession. The cortege is a sign of the absence of the soul by this time and of the fate that it experiences henceforth in heaven. The Lord's Supper 'creates' the possibility for adopting a disposition and inclination to break with other, often less elevating, practices. It probably provides the necessary courage as well. Yet much of this eludes the historian. Here, death belongs to the biological order and it cannot be understood as the interruption of the history of the faithful with their God. It is not a 'death'. The rite of the Lord's Supper superimposes on the immediate experience another vision of life. The 'real' of the empirical experience and the 'metaphoric' of discourse and of religious rite are substituted one for the other. As Calvin put it, 'We are all born dead and live as dead, until we are made participants in the life of Christ.'[40] From the moment of baptism, the believer 'dies' to sin and to the world in order to 'live' for God. His death completes entry to life, the true and the eternal. Thus, the Lord's Supper makes the participants in the funeral procession the true *faux-vivants* who accompany the body of a true *faux-mort* to the grave.

This resounds upon the sociability of the living and the dead who, from a religious point of view, are not distant from one another. All are more or less participants in the same life. How far must this then go to revise the best received ideas? The representation of purgatory implies a greater distance between the living and the dead, because the soul of the deceased is elsewhere in the third place, where the living can do something for it.

A. Pettegree, P. Nelles and P. Conner (eds.), *The Sixteenth-century French Religious Book* (Aldershot, 2001), pp. 139–56.

[40] 'Nam quum spiritualis mors nihil aliud sit quam alienatio animae a deo, omnes mortui nascimur, et mortui vivimus, donec efficiamur vitae Christi participes': Calvin, *Commentarii in . . . [Epistolam] ad Ephesios*, in *Ioannis Calvini Opera Exegetica* (Geneva, 1992), XVI (ed. by H. Feld), p. 177, lines 15–17, ad Eph. 2:1 ff. Theodore Beza annotated this text in similar fashion in his *Novum Testamentum* (1st edn 1598), p. 266: 'Mortem spiritualem intelligit: unde et mors illa, quam primam vocant, sequuta est (ut Rom. 5:12) et secunda quae et aeterna dicitur. Ideo dicuntur mortui quicunque non sunt renati, quia sicut immortalitas damnatorum non est vita, sed mors quaedam perennis, nempe cum aeterno exitio conjuncta: sic etiam haec animi et corporis coniunctio, vita proprie non est, sed mors in iis qui Christi Spiritu non aguntur, ut Es. 9:1; et Ioan. 5:28; Rom. 6:2 et 13; et 7:10; et 1 Tim. 5:6, et passim in Scripturis.'

The Reformed funeral cortege clearly relates back to communal representations for Protestants. God alone saves us and Reformed Protestants do nothing for their dead. The body – the body of Christ, the body of the church – gathered for the celebration of the Lord's Supper is not disrupted by the death of one or another among the faithful whom God has drawn to Himself, to use language which is frequently employed in the consistory registers of local Reformed churches.[41]

In addition, this funeral rite, through the representations that it evokes, reinforces the remarkable function of the consistory. After all, the consistory decided who was permitted to join the Eucharistic procession, and who was barred. If it had not been preceded by regular participation in the Lord's Supper, dying would again become 'death' and not access to life. As early as 1557, Reformed ecclesiastical leaders, meeting in the Assembly of Poitiers, declared that 'if a member of the congregation has been ... barred from the table of the Lord, [the elders and deacons] will admonish him diligently to repent ... reminding [him] that outside the church there is no salvation, much as it was at the time of the flood outside Noah's ark; [they will] also remind them that if they die in this world in such a state [excommunicated], they will be miserably endangered'.[42]

The Reformed break with traditional Catholic practices is unmistakable and, beginning in the 1560s, contributed to the construction of a specific culture. Protestant funerary practices were one of the elements of it, and they were integrated into the others. Certainly, Reformed Christians could be found among the participants in Catholic funerals. But the historian ought not to pass 'consistorial' – namely severe – judgment on activities, which are likely an example of the compartmentalization of conduct under the pressure of social constraint.

None the less, the Reformed Protestants of the kingdom of France were not Anabaptists who resigned themselves to living outside of history. Nor were they similar to the Puritans who agreed to live 'in their own element' within the Church of England or those who expatriated, certainly 'to catch fish', but also according to the statements of their pastors to establish a society based on their principles. On the whole, Reformed Protestants early on adopted specific religious practices and representations (rejection of ecclesiastical hierarchies, congregations without clerics,

---

41 See, for instance, F. Francillon (ed.), *Livre des délibérations de l'Église réformée de L'Albenc (1606–1682)* (Paris, 1998), pp. 192–3: deaths are recorded by phrases such as 'Dieu a retiré à soi...'; 'M ... est allée à Dieu'; 'Anne ... a esté appelée de Dieu'; all are alternatives to the usual '... est décédé(e)'.

42 'Articles polytiques pour l'eglise reformee Selon le S. Evangile, fait a Poictiers, 1557', art. 2, in E. Arnaud, *Documents protestants inédits du XVIe siècle* (Paris, 1872), pp. 9–10.

and consistorial authority, for instance).[43] Their culture, together with Huguenot political ideas and resistance, contributed to making them an indomitable minority. Still, as noted earlier, they sought not to compromise their integration into French society. They wished to create their own spaces in a world where Catholics thought of themselves as possessing a territorial right. The resulting conflicts were numerous and included, for instance, clashes over cemeteries.[44]

Although the date of acquisition of the cemetery varied from one locality to another, the Reformed funeral cortege frequently ended at a cemetery, which the faithful had been able to obtain in one fashion or another. For them, it was not sacred ground. They believed, like Monica, the mother of Saint Augustine, who died at Ostia, that 'no place is distant for God and I have no fear that God will be unable to find and raise me from the dead at the end of the world'.[45] Still, possessing a place to bury the dead is a condition of 'virtue and decency'.

A specific culture, an unfailing loyalty, the demand for the exercise of a right to the burial ground which they zealously guarded lest anyone take it from them – all of these elements figured in the cemetery that a group of Protestants were able to acquire at Le Puy in 1566. It was an enclosed field. Above the entrance 'were the arms of the king in blue and gold' and an inscription, which read 'Blessed are those who die in Jesus Christ.' To bury one of their dead, 'they carried the body on their arms; a black cloth with the royal arms was draped over it'. The chronicler Jean Burel, who recorded the episode, commented through Catholic eyes that it was a 'very strange thing and [was] scandalous to watch'.[46] This is the same concern over social conformity that led to the displacement of other customs – wakes, funeral meals and the like – within an arena of civility that Reformed Protestants had no intention of deserting, but which had no precise tie to religious ritual.[47] For the very same reason, Huguenot aristocrats could be buried in family chapels or could build funerary monuments, which conferred honour upon the descendants of their noble lineage.

---

[43] See B. Roussel, 'Les premières *Disciplines* et la construction d'une culture réformée', *Actes du Colloque de Haïfa, Mai 2000* (forthcoming).

[44] See P. Roberts, 'Contesting Sacred Space: Burial Disputes in Sixteenth-century France' in B. Gordon and P. Marshall (eds.), *The Place of the Dead. Death and Remembrance in Late Medieval and Early Modern Europe* (Cambridge, 2000), pp. 131–48.

[45] See Augustine, *Confessions*, bk 9, chap. 28.

[46] Jean Burel, *Mémoires de Jean Burel. Journal d'un bourgeois du Puy à l'époque des Guerres de religion*, ed. by A. Chassaney (Saint-Vidal, 1983), pp. 19–20.

[47] On the emergence of new customs amongst the Reformed, see J. Garrisson, *Protestants du Midi, 1559–1598* (Toulouse, 1991), p. 250.

The Lord's Supper is the scene of a conversion, but not a conversion of the Eucharistic species into the body and blood of Christ. Rather, it is the conversion of the faithful who, having consumed the bread and wine, signs of the sacrifice of their saviour, are called to live henceforth as under the cross, that is, to endure a life of unending persecution and struggle. They are exhorted to be 'dead' to themselves and to the world. Their actual biological death brings the struggle to a conclusion. The soul will 'live' better and no longer exist under the cross, while the body 'sleeps'. Continuity is established between the Lord's Supper that is celebrated here below and that which the faithful imagine occurs in heaven above, as all await the eventual reunion of body and soul.

Who would not perceive here a paradox, much as in every organized religion? Reformed Protestants existed in a world that they had disenchanted more thoroughly than had other Christians and in which they actively intervened. This disenchantment occurred precisely at the moment of the Lord's Supper by demonstrating that there is nothing 'divine' here below, even in the Eucharistic elements. At the same time, and for the best reasons, they appeared to turn away from earthly concerns to attain, as soon as possible, 'true life'. The paradox in this is not difficult to comprehend, and the Lord's Supper along with funerary practices allow the believer to come to terms with it. There is a time for everything. This paradox is constitutive of the complex identity of French Reformed Protestants, which is based on a specific culture. It is possible to live within the paradox. The danger is that it might be transformed into a contradiction, for then the individual would be forced to choose between two mutually exclusive propositions, to choose this earth over heaven or vice versa. This would be destructive to the system of representations initiated by Reformed Protestants. And, of course, it goes to the heart of the difficulty that Reformed Christians experienced during the sixteenth and seventeenth centuries.

This essay opened with an invitation that scholars pay close attention to the suggestions of historical anthropology. One must avoid burying important characteristics of Reformed culture. French Protestants did less for their deceased brethren than did their ancestors some 100,000 years earlier. But they engaged in an innovative discourse on 'life' as they lowered silently, 'honestly', and without any other ceremony the remains of a fellow believer into the grave.

13. *Huguenot militancy and the seventeenth-century wars of religion*

Alan James

Jean Guiton, La Rochelle's former admiral and mayor during the fateful royal siege of 1628, died in 1654. Among the personal possessions listed in his will were portraits of both Louis XIII and Cardinal Richelieu, the two men most directly responsible for the downfall of the city and, by extension, of the Huguenot movement in France. This curious detail is brought to our attention by historians as a damning indictment of the military spirit and life of the Huguenots in the seventeenth century. It seems that the firebrand, who is said to have once stabbed the table of the municipal council with his knife threatening to do the same to anyone who spoke of surrender to the crown and whose statue today stands in the main square as a symbol of the city's independent spirit and proud history, actually harboured royalist sympathies. The implication is that the Huguenots of the seventeenth century no longer had sufficient moral conviction, nor the ideological will, to oppose their rightful monarch.[1] Indeed, soon after the fall of the city, Guiton joined the ranks of the growing royal navy, just as the duc de Rohan, the last of a line of noble, Calvinist military leaders, later accepted a command in the army. For its part, the crown was happy to accept these defections. In 1626, Richelieu had suggested accepting requests previously made by Rohan and by his younger brother, the duc de Soubise, for posts in the army and navy respectively as a means of undermining Huguenot military resistance.[2] This conjuncture of royal interests with those of the remaining Calvinist nobility, upon whom the Huguenots depended for their military and political strength, suggests that the era of confessional conflict was well and truly over.[3]

---

[1] D. Parker, *La Rochelle and the French Monarchy: Conflict and Order in Seventeenth-century France* (London, 1980), pp. 145, 169.

[2] P. Grillon (ed.), *Les papiers de Richelieu. Section politique intérieur. Correspondance et papiers d'État. Lettres de Richelieu*, 5 vols. (Paris, 1975–80), I, pp. 191–2, 'Advis sur la rébellion du sieur de Soubise', June 1626. Soubise had initially demanded a command in the royal navy in the aftermath of the Peace of Montpellier of 1622: Public Record Office, London, SP78/75, fo. 125.

[3] M. P. Holt, *The French Wars of Religion, 1562–1629* (Cambridge, 1995), p. 189.

The history of the Huguenots from the Edict of Nantes of 1598 to the siege of La Rochelle of 1628 is indeed largely one of internal division, impotence and futility. Thus accounts of their decline tend to reflect on the changing attitude of the crown to confessional diversity and its motives for going to war with its subjects. Accordingly, the enormity of the royal military operations around La Rochelle speaks more eloquently to historians on the nature of the emerging absolutist state than on the Huguenot community itself. Their ongoing military struggle and the appalling deprivations suffered during the siege appear simply to have resulted from external circumstances and the efforts of an increasingly isolated, anachronistic and ultimately self-interested military leadership. Already, in the events leading up to the settlement of 1598, the religious struggle had been effectively derailed by the personal agendas of individual, ambitious, Calvinist nobles such as the duc de Bouillon.[4] Many individual communities were reluctant, therefore, to act in concert and to jeopardize their existing, tenuous privileges, and military resistance by the wider Huguenot community was becoming increasingly rare as a result. When the duc de Soubise tried to rally his co-religionists against the crown prior to the siege, for example, the city council at La Rochelle was initially quick to dissociate itself from the wayward adventurer. Even as the ships of the duke of Buckingham hove into sight in support against the crown's growing military pressure in 1627, there was a marked reluctance to heed Soubise's advice to embrace them.

Attempts to look beyond the influence of the nobility and to locate the impetus for continued armed resistance within the Reformed community identify a minority of 'radicals' who led the others down the reckless path of rebellion. The delegates of the Huguenot national assemblies have been viewed as the disaffected elements of their community who vainly attempted to co-ordinate their reluctant constituents across France.[5] Studies of La Rochelle similarly reveal dangerous divisions within the urban political environment, which allowed a minority of militants temporarily to influence the municipal government. The civic rebellion of 1614 has been seen as a turning point that brought to the fore the conflict between a closed, ruling, Calvinist oligarchy of 'moderate' mercantile interests, who had a stake in preserving the status quo and who thus protested their obedience to the crown, and 'extremists', or disenfranchised radicals, who violently sought a local

---

4 N. M. Sutherland, *The Huguenot Struggle for Recognition* (New Haven, CT, 1980).
5 J. S. Valone, *Huguenot Politics, 1601–1622* (Lewiston, NY, 1994).

political voice.[6] Nevertheless, whether it was due to the misguided ambitions of two noble brothers, the miscalculation of an aggressive national assembly or the irresponsible actions of a peculiarly militant city, it appears that an unrepresentative minority element within Huguenot society invited the crown's military intervention and, therefore, their community's eventual demise.

Yet Huguenot militancy (defined for the purposes of this essay as a willingness to take up arms against the crown) provides more than an insight into the political fringe of the community. From its inception in the 1550s, one of the most striking features of the movement was its capacity for political organization and for military action against the crown, and the sheer scale of their military activity in the sixteenth century has much to teach about the organization and character of Huguenot society.[7] Despite the peace imposed by the Edict of Nantes in 1598, this militancy remained an ongoing reflection of the commitment, ambitions and beliefs of the wider community in the seventeenth century. After all, from 1620, the Huguenots still had the wherewithal to fight three wars, which preoccupied the crown for nearly a full decade. Acknowledging this in his recent survey of the sixteenth-century wars of religion, Mack Holt successfully extended his coverage beyond the traditional end point of 1598 to 1629. He did so, not by attempting to assess the implications of the siege of 1628 in the light of growing royal authority, but by drawing attention to the earlier, 'heroic' resistance of the Huguenots, especially during the first war from 1620 to the Peace of Montpellier of 1622.[8]

This war was shaped by three successive royal campaigns to the west and south of the country. The first, in the summer of 1620, met little resistance from the Huguenots and led to the re-establishment of Catholicism

---

[6] K. B. Robbins, *City on the Ocean Sea: La Rochelle, 1530–1650* (Leiden, 1997).

[7] No full-sized study of the Huguenot military effort exists, although Mark Greengrass offers a useful, brief survey providing relevant printed sources: M. Greengrass, 'Financing the Cause: Protestant Mobilization and Accountability in France (1562–1589)' in P. Benedict, G. Marnef, H. van Nierop and M. Venard (eds.), *Reformation, Revolt and Civil War in France and the Netherlands, 1555–1585* (Amsterdam, 1999), pp. 233–54. Although J. B. Wood has begun the important work of addressing the military strength of the crown, *The King's Army: Warfare, Soldiers, and Society during the Wars of Religion in France, 1562–1576* (Cambridge, 1996), there remains very little about the Huguenot military. But see J. de Pablo, 'L'Armée huguenote pendant la troisième Guerre de Religion', *ARG* 47 (1956), 64–76. For a useful overview of military affairs, see R. J. Knecht, *The French Civil Wars, 1562–1598* (London, 2000).

[8] Holt, *Wars of Religion*, p. 182. This period of conflict is comprehensively covered by A. D. Lublinskaya, *French Absolutism: The Crucial Phase, 1620–1629* (Cambridge, 1968), pp. 146–219. For the military affairs of the Huguenots, see M.-E. Richard, *La vie des protestants français de l'Édit de Nantes à la Révolution (1598–1789)* (Paris, 1994), pp. 85–101.

at Pau and the union of Béarn with France.[9] Though, legally, this was not an infringement of the Edict of Nantes, many saw this action by Louis XIII as a serious threat to the corporate existence of the Huguenots elsewhere. In response, a general assembly was called (gathering illegally on Christmas Day in 1620 at La Rochelle) that would direct the war effort across the country over the next two years. The second royal campaign, of 1621, which aimed to put a stop to any such open disobedience, was also largely successful. The majority of Huguenot towns simply opened their doors or put up only token resistance. Nevertheless, there were also a number of remarkable instances of effective defiance that year which should not be overlooked. For a month, Soubise successfully defended St Jean-d'Angély, which was strategically significant, providing protection from the landward to nearby La Rochelle. Though the larger royal army prevailed, in this way Soubise provided Rohan with the opportunity to organize the military resources of the Midi and to prepare the Huguenots' main defence at Montauban, the largest and most significant Huguenot city beyond La Rochelle. In general accounts of the war, the siege of Montauban of 1621 is one of the most celebrated demonstrations of latent Huguenot defiance. Agrippa d'Aubigné, for one, stressed the bravery and determination of the inhabitants, which he symbolized, in particular, through his portrayal of the women who participated, one of whom continued to hurl stones at the city's attackers after losing an arm to a cannon ball.[10]

It should be noted that such episodes provide more than an opportunity to celebrate individual feats of bravery in the midst of inexorable, overall decline. The royal army was forced to abandon the siege in November and to put off for the next year the military subjugation of the Huguenots. Thus despite the many losses suffered, the Huguenots had managed to stop a determined royal effort in 1621 and denied the crown an opportunity to impose new terms on their political organization. This achievement is remarkable on its own. Yet it also belongs as part of a much wider military effort, for at the same time, a Huguenot navy was taking the initiative along the Atlantic coast. Under the command of Soubise himself, a fleet from La Rochelle defeated a royal force off the nearby Île de Ré and blockaded it through the winter at Brouage. On land and at sea, the Huguenots were proving themselves capable of being formidable opponents.

9 C. Desplat, 'Louis XIII and the Union of Béarn to France' in M. Greengrass (ed.), *Conquest and Coalescence* (London, 1991), pp. 68–83.
10 Agrippa d'Aubigné, *Histoire universelle*, ed. by A. Thierry, 10 vols. (Geneva, 1999), X, p. 126.

The effectiveness of the Huguenots' resistance at this time is often overshadowed by the efforts of the crown to undermine their military capacity which, under the terms of the Edict of Nantes, was legally defined by their security towns alone. They were allowed to keep some 200, which were to have Protestant governors and about half of which were to be garrisoned at the crown's expense.[11] As is often pointed out, however, this was only a temporary concession by the king, granted by renewable royal brevets. This dependence on the goodwill of the monarch had the effect of dividing the Huguenot community between those eager to court his favour and those willing to challenge him. Indeed according to d'Aubigné, in those provinces where they enjoyed any protection at all, the Huguenots had two sorts of security towns. One sort was only 'artificially pegged' to the community by their status as security towns. Dominated by the garrison or by the individual local lord, these places were easily infiltrated or influenced by royal agents. As often as not, the garrisons were also poorly maintained. In other words, the military leadership of these security towns was too closely linked to royal authority to be of any effective use to the wider Huguenot church. Since they could be manipulated, when Louis XIII set out on his campaign in 1621 he had every reason to expect, ahead of time, the capitulation of most Huguenot towns.[12] In the end, the vast majority had nothing to gain from open disobedience, and the noble leadership of the Huguenot movement effectively collapsed.

Yet to focus attention on the series of towns that simply opened their doors to the king is, according to d'Aubigné, to ignore the situation in the other sort of town, the genuine Huguenot centres, which he defined as those with a significantly large Protestant population that could defend itself. Among these, d'Aubigné numbered Sancerre, La Rochelle, St Jean-d'Angély, Montauban and Montpellier. Here the pattern was different, resistance much more common. Recently, Philippe Chareyre has followed the same logic, insisting that the Huguenots' military security was not provided by the Edict of Nantes, nor indeed by the security towns at all, but in effect simply by their own population density.[13] It is perhaps not a startling revelation that the Huguenots were strongest where they were most numerous, but it is useful none the less, for by restricting our view somewhat we can see their military activity, not in terms of a series of capitulations by the majority of the Huguenot leadership, but of the

[11] Holt, *Wars of Religion*, p. 166.   [12] D'Aubigné, *Histoire*, x, pp. 30–2.

[13] P. Chareyre, 'Les places de sûreté' in J.-P. Babelon, A.-M. Cocula, C. Desplat and J. Garrisson (eds.), *L'Édit de Nantes* (Nantes, 1998), pp. 51–62.

active resistance of the few in those places that are more representative of the wider Huguenot church.[14]

In this light, during the early seventeenth century the activities of individual Huguenot nobles in particular appear somewhat less significant. The positions they adopted are often said to betray an overall sense of fatigue, indifference and underlying royalism within the movement, tempered only by the personalities and private agendas of a few bellicose individuals. Taken as a whole, however, they reflect both the attitudes that were dictated by the different circumstances in which Huguenot towns found themselves and the wide range of personal reactions that one might expect to find within the movement after many years of peace. Some cooperated with the crown; some abjured Protestantism altogether, but those such as Rohan and Soubise who did fight represented a militancy that was evident in areas with significant Protestant populations. They might not have been universally revered by their co-religionists, but their ambitions had to have been based on a reasonable expectation that they would receive support. In short, they were responding to, as well as trying to initiate, Huguenot militancy.

As such, the relative eagerness of the Calvinist nobility to go to war, which has long been considered the main source of Huguenot militancy and its clearest expression, is perhaps better seen as simply a barometer of a more widespread defiance. Building on recent work on religious violence during the wars, Philip Benedict has suggested that the swiftness with which 'a para-military system' grew out of the organization of Reformed churches in the 1550s was a reflection of the values of the movement as a whole. When the crown proved unwilling to satisfy them, the Huguenots were ultimately prepared to resort to violence to advance the cause of Christ. Huguenot militancy, in other words, was more than the sum of the current stock of noble leaders who directed it. It was, Benedict suggests, a defining feature of the community and something which could not be easily hijacked and directed toward personal ends or narrow class interests.[15]

As crucial as the nobility undoubtedly remained, they were never the only expression of Huguenot militancy. In the intermittent periods of warfare after 1572, truly national, independent Huguenot institutions

---

[14] J. Garrisson similarly describes a 'regroupement de forces et . . . une consolidation de la huguenoterie dans ses bastions traditionels' prior to the war. J. Garrisson, *L'Édit de Nantes et sa Révocation* (Paris, 1985), p. 49.

[15] P. Benedict, 'The Dynamics of Protestant Militancy: France, 1555–1563' in Benedict *et al. Reformation, Revolt and Civil War*, pp. 35–50.

failed to develop, and military resistance continued in a localized fashion, organized in particular by the towns of the Midi. Yet as Mark Greengrass has suggested, this still required some national co-ordination and an ongoing commitment to organized resistance.[16] Huguenot assemblies were thus also an essential feature of the Huguenots' political and military survival, whose success depended on maintaining the delicate, shifting balance between noble leadership and expressions of local militancy. Indeed, in light of Benedict's particular assertion that, from its inception, 'The movement would never have developed without its willingness to disobey laws prohibiting its assembly',[17] we might profitably consider the assemblies, even those of the seventeenth century, not just as a playground for renegade radicals, but as the legitimate, if not unanimous, expression of ongoing Huguenot militancy, binding and focusing the energy of the remaining nobility and those towns with a significant Protestant population.

The Saumur assembly of 1611, which met in the aftermath of the assassination of Henri IV and the resignation of the Huguenot duc de Sully from court, politicized the movement and exacerbated tensions within the Huguenot elite. Philippe Duplessis-Mornay's aim of reconciling the needs of the church with obedience to the crown began to give way to a new, more confrontational political discourse in the provinces, expressed by the likes of d'Aubigné and Rohan. In their hands, the language of faithful obedience and loyalty gave way to the defence of the interests of the community and of the faith. They recognized that to be successful the Huguenots could not rely exclusively on the nobility who, with divided loyalties between the crown and the church, could be easily bought off and corrupted by a monarch determined to divide the movement.[18] These were not lone voices. Indeed, this perspective informs the nature of Huguenot politics over the next decades, which focused on defending the privilege of holding national assemblies.

Generally speaking, the crown's aim was to limit the duration of Huguenot assemblies and to restrict their role to the nomination of candidates for the two Huguenot deputies-general to the court agreed under the terms of the Edict of Nantes. The Huguenots, for their part, saw them as an opportunity to petition the crown, to interpret the edict, and, it should be said, to maintain almost surreptitiously some form of national,

---

[16] Greengrass, 'Financing the Cause', pp. 248–53.   [17] Benedict, 'Dynamics', p. 50.
[18] A. Herman, 'The Saumur Assembly, 1611: Huguenot Political Belief and Action in the Age of Marie de Medici', Ph.D. thesis, Johns Hopkins University (1984).

political body.[19] By negotiating Huguenot involvement in the noble rebellion against the crown by Condé in 1615, for example, the assembly at Nîmes firmly established a reputation for militancy that even worried some of its own members.[20] Accordingly, at the heart of the Huguenot military resistance which followed the royal campaign to Béarn in 1620 and which sparked the renewal of war was the assembly at La Rochelle. According to Valone's analysis of the membership, the most influential of the delegates came from Poitou, Saintonge and Guyenne. In this respect, Huguenot militancy radiated from the western provinces. But rather than suggesting that the assembly, therefore, represented the militant political fringe of the community, it could equally be said to have represented its geographic, militant heartland.

The assembly issued a *règlement* on 10 May 1621 governing Huguenot military organization.[21] A few articles touched on finances, including providing support for Reformed pastors and those made homeless by the fighting. Measures were also taken to ensure military discipline, but above all the ruling that was issued elaborated a national, Huguenot, military structure. The country was divided into eight departments and assigned to prominent Calvinist nobles with extensive authority. By this time, however, the commitment of many of these people to the cause was questionable, though the important areas of upper Languedoc and upper Guyenne were reserved for Rohan, whose militancy was clear, whilst the western department of Brittany and Poitou (and later Saintonge) was confirmed as Soubise's. Thus, from the outset, the assembly hoped to provide the leadership for this renewed period of open conflict, with a central role in the organization and co-ordination of military resistance for itself. To this end, it reserved considerable direct authority that superseded that of the military leaders themselves, including the nomination of some officers. Above all, it reinforced the principle that no peace could be signed without its consent. Thus, this was something more than the process of parcelling out the kingdom or assigning spheres of influence. The assembly was the outward expression of Huguenot militancy which it intended to co-ordinate.

For years, assemblies had taken the lead in making legal demands of the crown and, now, in levying taxes and in organizing military resistance.

[19] N. M. Sutherland, 'The Crown, the Huguenots, and the Edict of Nantes' in R. M. Golden (ed.), *The Huguenot Connection: The Edict of Nantes and its Revocation, and Early French Migration to South Carolina* (Dordrecht, 1988), p. 48.
[20] Valone, *Huguenot Politics*, pp. 101–24.
[21] BN, Dupuy 100, fos. 14–30, 'Règlement général fait par les depputés de l'assemblé général de La Rochelle, 1621'.

In doing so, it is true that the latest assembly had crossed the line from loyal, if disgruntled, subjects to rebels. Yet it was not acting in an arbitrary, autocratic manner, pushing the community into an illegal, belligerent position.[22] Indeed, this perception – that the Huguenot community was led astray by militant elements within the assembly, or elsewhere – may very well have its origin in the crown's desire to isolate a culpable faction. By blaming the assembly, for example, the crown could continue to make serious offers of clemency to the nobility and to the 'loyal' Huguenot population and in this way avoid a general religious war. Yet, for historians, it is not a straightforward exercise to isolate the source of Huguenot militancy in this way. Defiance, in one form or another, came from a number of directions. Clearly, this war operated in the interests, and under the authority, of different elements of Huguenot society: individual nobles, national and provincial assemblies, and also municipalities.

The assembly, for example, did not so much coerce as depend on the towns for its success. Indeed, by working together toward common goals, however briefly, the nobility, the assemblies and the municipal authorities demonstrated that defiance was still largely characteristic of an otherwise divided community. In the conduct of naval affairs, in particular, this combination of militant impulses and the union of national and municipal interests is most clear. Whilst maintaining the pretence of a national organization, the assembly recognized its political strength in the west and south of France. For this reason alone, it saw control of the sea lanes of the Atlantic as essential, both for the defence of the strategic port city of La Rochelle and for the projection of Huguenot military strength afar.[23] Thus from 1620, the assembly and city worked closely together to this end. A fund was created to maintain a fleet, and an admiral and vice-admiral were chosen from the city's council. In June 1621, an admiralty court was created, and in the name of both 'assembly and city', letters of marque were issued to privateers permitting them to attack enemies of the religion.[24] This was an important legal development which firmly established the Huguenots' willingness to adopt an overtly illegal military

[22] Lublinskaya, *French Absolutism*, p. 173.
[23] Naval forces were seen as necessary not just against royal forces but against the duc d'Épernon who, as governor of Guyenne, claimed La Rochelle in his jurisdiction. Médiathèque, La Rochelle (henceforth MLR), MS 58, 'Recueil de la naissance, progrez, accroissement, et décadence de la ville de la Rochelle', fo. 165v. Many of the observations for this chapter were based on this retrospective account by Pierre Mervault who sympathized with the council and blamed the radicals for the city's downfall.
[24] BN, Duchesne 100, fo. 43.

posture against the crown, representing a militancy that permeated beyond the confines of the assembly. Though the Huguenots generally continued to protest their obedience to the king and defended the legality of
the assembly (and even the military leaders were formally to command
'under the authority of His Majesty'),[25] there could be no possible legal
justification for creating an independent naval authority. This was an un-
ambiguous expression of open defiance and, legally, there had been no
equivalent since the council of Jeanne d'Albret oversaw the independent
organization of Huguenot military forces in La Rochelle from 1568.[26]

Quite apart from the legal implications, these naval preparations were
also effective militarily. Within two months, it is claimed, as much as
20,000 *écus* in revenue was brought in from privateering, and a fleet of
fifteen warships was gathered which easily matched the numeric strength
of the royal fleet. In the words of the diarist Pierre Mervault, 'Posterity
will marvel at how a little city like La Rochelle, without support or help
from anyone, was able within three days to put together a navy strong
enough to beat back a royal force gathered from all over France for over
a million *livres*.'[27] In addition to defeating a fleet commanded by the duc
de Guise in 1621, Soubise also occupied the strategic Île d'Oléron and
policed commerce in and out of the Gironde, imposing tariffs to help
finance the greater cause. By 1622, he reportedly had twenty warships,
of which he furnished eight from those he had captured the previous
year at the Sables d'Olonne and including a ship lent by the king of
England.[28] These successes are not only noteworthy for their own sake,
but also for the fleeting co-ordination of otherwise potentially disparate
interests they represent and as a symbol of the momentary return to the
militancy that characterized the movement in the 1560s.

The co-operation necessary to co-ordinate naval resources effectively
suggests that militancy was not the private reserve of any single con-
stituent element of the community. Neither the nobility (in the form of
Soubise) nor the national assembly was imposing an expensive, aggressive naval agenda on La Rochelle. Rather, they were trying to capital-
ize on, and to control, existing energies. According to Kevin Robbins,
the bourgeois uprising in the city in 1614 which radicalized municipal

---

[25] BN, Dupuy 100, fo. 27.
[26] A. James, 'Between "Huguenot" and "Royal": Maritime Affairs during the French Wars of
Religion' in K. Cameron, M. Greengrass and P. Roberts (eds.), *The Adventure of Religious Pluralism
in Early Modern France* (Berne, 2000), pp. 101–12.
[27] MLR, MS 58, fo. 173v. For a detailed account of the naval developments of 1621, see *ibid.*,
fos. 165v–176.
[28] Archives des Affaires Étrangères, Paris, France 777, fo. 108.

government was the story of an 'unenfranchised', 'restive' bourgeoisie hoping to gain political emancipation from a traditional, Calvinist, oligarchy.[29] Yet there were clearly military interests involved as well. Previous gatherings, including a Huguenot assembly of the 'circle' of Brittany, Aunis, Anjou and Saintonge in November 1612, met 'out of the fear they felt that the crown was about to mount a surprise attack'.[30] Indeed, this fear was fully justified as five armed warships sent by Marie de Medici appeared menacingly off La Rochelle the following year. Though nothing came of this particular incident, the city council's determined efforts to prevent any such assemblies, and the mayor's protestations of loyalty to the crown, led to the drawing up of a petition and the subsequent rebellion of 1614. Thus, whatever other local political pressures motivated the uprising, it appears also, in part, to have been a contest between conflicting interpretations of the city's military interests.

Thereafter, naval affairs remained a priority. The former 'judge of the admiralty of Guyenne' at La Rochelle, Jean de Mirande, had been a high-profile, and especially hated, target for the anger of the bourgeois during the rebellion of 1614. His displacement and the subsequent creation of a new admiralty in 1621 were, therefore, important steps in the political enfranchisement of the more militant elements of Rochelais society. Jean de Tharay, the leading figure of the radical bourgeois, exploited his support in the harbour area of the city and by 1618 was already in control issuing passports.[31] As with so much else in the early modern period, it is difficult to divorce purely political motivations from religious issues. Robbins argues that La Rochelle's long history of ambivalence to Geneva and its anti-clerical tendencies led to a natural 'political' volatility and that, despite the ruling oligarchy's strong ties to local Calvinist ministers, the radicals left the institutions of the church largely untouched out of 'indifference'. Yet this does not fit entirely comfortably with his assertion that the rebellion was motivated in part by a desire for greater 'congregational control'.[32] Moreover, since the representatives of the clergy in the assembly itself were increasingly numerous and united in their militancy, it seems that any expressions of the radicals' militancy, such as La Rochelle's aggression at sea by 1622, was more than a local political issue, just as it represents more than the vain ambitions of Soubise or the agenda of an out-of-touch assembly.

[29] Robbins, *City on the Ocean Sea*, pp. 253–73.   [30] MLR, MS 58, fos. 147v–149.
[31] Robbins, *City on the Ocean Sea*, p. 338.   [32] *Ibid.*, pp. 271, 298.

The militant direction of naval strength was something rather more fundamentally characteristic of the confessional identity of the Huguenot movement.

Accordingly, the Huguenots' successes in 1621 and 1622 reignited Catholic fears over their capacity for causing widespread disorder. Even in distant and land-locked Lyon, for example, where there was a marked decline in the anxiety caused by the local Protestant minority from 1618, news of the events of the war threatened to unleash furious reprisals against them.[33] However, any fear of a national Huguenot military revival was premature. An army led by Soubise was routed in April 1622 at the Île de Riez, a spit of land on the coast north of La Rochelle, by royal forces ultimately on their way to Montpellier. This effectively turned the military tide, and the peace that followed the siege of Montpellier made explicit what had previously been implied by the Edict of Nantes: there were to be no assemblies of any kind by which the Huguenots might articulate political grievances or organize military resistance. Moreover, the royal brevets guaranteeing Huguenot security towns would be allowed to lapse in 1625. Not only did this legally and militarily emasculate the movement, but it revealed deep divisions, not just within the noble leadership, but between the assembly and Rohan himself, who negotiated the treaty.[34]

The first war, therefore, brought mixed results for the Huguenots. Nevertheless, in many ways, the navy had been the jewel in their military crown, and it symbolized perhaps most clearly the effective coalition of militant energies. In contrast to the relatively unhappy turn of events on land, at the time the peace of Montpellier was being signed in October 1622, the Huguenot navy, under Jean Guiton, was putting up an heroic resistance against royal forces near La Rochelle. Subsequently, the navy would take on even greater strategic significance as the crown focused more specifically on La Rochelle itself, which was now the principal source of Huguenot militancy. Yet problems had already begun to emerge. The city and the assembly had been fighting over revenue from prizes taken at sea,[35] and soon after Soubise had taken the Île d'Oléron in 1621 the radical bourgeois of the city challenged his jurisdiction over the island, wishing to govern it themselves and to extract contributions

33 T. Boffard, 'L'Application de l'Édit de Nantes à Lyon, 1598–1685', *BSHPF* 145 (1999), 288, 299–300.

34 'Discours sur les raisons de la paix faite devant Montpellier, 1622', *Mémoires relatifs à l'histoire de France*, ed. by J. F. Michaud and J. J. F. Poujoulat, 33 vols. (Paris, 1857), XIX, pp. 539–42.

35 Valone, *Huguenot Politics*, pp. 174–5.

from the Catholic population. Later, they pressed for the aggressive occupation and military preparation of the island, which was judged by
some as unnecessary provocation of the crown and one of the causes of
further conflict.[36] In this competition for the direction of naval affairs,
there was a range of voices articulating different approaches: Soubise,
the assembly, the conservative ranks in the city, and the radicals. Thus
the conflict was not yet the simple bipartite one between 'moderates'
and 'radicals' that historians often employ. In predominantly Protestant
places such as La Rochelle, not only was there a greater determination
by some to defy the crown but an array of different militant stances.

Increasing military pressure by the crown, however, began to create
the appearance of a clear polarity within the community. With the king's
growing determination to achieve a military resolution, the co-ordination
of these different expressions of militancy became more difficult to sustain. Indeed, as the military initiative passed to the crown over the final
two wars of 1625–6 and 1627–9, the Huguenots' military fortunes turned
sour. In September 1625, admiral Montmorency won a decisive victory
at sea over Soubise, whose exploits in the Atlantic represented the bulk
of Huguenot military activity by this time. The third and final confronta-
tion had, to a large extent, been prompted by English intervention in
1627. Once the forces of the duke of Buckingham were defeated and
they retreated from the Île de Ré, the full force of the crown's military
energy was focused on La Rochelle and the final, complete destruction
of the last major bastion of Huguenot resistance. In these conditions,
it was impossible to sustain any diversity. Huguenot militancy had been
reduced, of necessity, either to resigned capitulation or fanatic, desperate
resistance.

It is useful to accept the identification between the 'prudents' and
'fermes' in d'Aubigné's writings, distinguishing between those who identified Huguenot interests with obedience to the crown and those who
stood by their principles and were willing to fight for the community
and the faith. Yet it, too, muffles the range of discordant militant voices
prior to the final political settlement of 1629. Within the ranks of those
who would count themselves among the 'fermes', there were a number
of distinctions to be made. The problem for the Huguenots was thus
not a lack of militancy, as such, but that of a single focus or definition of
the preferred form this militancy should take. Rohan himself, who was
scathing of those who submitted to the crown with little or no struggle

---

[36] Robbins, *City on the Ocean Sea*, p. 347.

and who held himself up as the pinnacle of integrity and Huguenot resistance, was in many ways isolated.[37] He had developed a reputation for recklessness within the assembly as early as 1615 by putting forces into the field without its authorization. He had also disapproved of calling another assembly in 1620. By meeting illegally and by attempting to resolve the 'unresolvable' problem of Béarn, Rohan claimed, the assembly had simply invited the king's retribution. According to his memoirs, he felt the Reformed community should maintain the moral, and legal, high ground by resorting to arms only when threatened or when the crown was in clear breach of its agreements. For this reason, he singled out another noble for opprobrium, Jean de Favas, vicomte de Castets. Favas, like Rohan, was prepared to lead forces against the crown, but having been one of the prime movers behind the assembly of 1620 and later associating himself with La Rochelle in its conflict with both the assembly over admiralty revenues and Soubise over the Île d'Oléron, his extremism was seen by Rohan as one of the principal causes of the movement's downfall.

Even amongst the active Calvinist nobility, then, there were divisions which arose from the fundamental contradiction between their role as servants of the crown and protectors of the faith. That Jean Guiton himself, perhaps the most active and inspirational militant, could come to serve and even to admire the crown simply serves as a powerful symbol of the difficult balance of loyalties that the Huguenot community as a whole had to strike. Yet this was not new to the seventeenth century. From its inception, the relationship between the Huguenot church and the monarchy was fluid and complex. As a result, this ambivalent role of the military leadership, the debilitating divisions within the wider movement, and indeed even the predominantly provincial, or local, outlook of the Huguenot population, in particular that of La Rochelle, had all long been familiar characteristics of the community. Though they contributed to the Huguenots' ultimate demise, they should not, therefore, necessarily be allowed to obscure the significance of their continuing military effort in the early decades of the seventeenth century.

However briefly, during the first war from 1620 to 1622, the many disparate militant interests of the Huguenots translated once again into unity and strength. This was not the initiative of a few nobles, nor of any other single element of their society, but the coalescence of different impulses, for a residual resilience and willingness to defend themselves

---

[37] 'Apologie du duc de Rohan sur les derniers troubles de la France à cause de la religion', *Mémoires*, XIX, p. 605.

still permeated the community. For this reason alone, it is not enough to explain the determination of the crown to defeat the Huguenots simply in terms of a growing authoritarian trend in government, even less by analysing local political conflicts. This simply does not do credit to the Huguenots' historical agency, their willingness to take decisive, effective action, and the strength of their confessional identity.

The peace imposed by the Edict of Nantes allowed a range of different perspectives and strategies for defending Huguenot privileges to flourish. In particular, many felt, not unreasonably, that quiet co-operation with the crown was the best way to guarantee their preservation in the new century. In this way, the settlement did much to undermine the Huguenots' commitment to resistance, exacerbate existing tensions and divide loyalties, but it could not eliminate their dangerous predilection for defiance. Thus, although the crown combined a number of strategies to weaken the Huguenots, only through military pressure could they fatally reduce the Huguenots' freedom of action. Even in the aftermath of the final Peace of Alès of 1629, the Huguenots still maintained a tenacious instinct for survival, but as a direct consequence of the defeat their political survival henceforth depended incontestably on only one possible strategy, that of demonstrating their collective loyalty.[38] In many ways, then, Huguenot militancy provides convenient thematic bookends to the French wars of religion, making the final, comprehensive military victory by the crown in 1628–9 their only possible resolution.

[38] E. Labrousse, *Conscience et conviction. Études sur le XVIIe siècle* (Paris, 1996), pp. 71–95.

14. Epilogue

Raymond A. Mentzer and Andrew Spicer

The Revocation of the Edict of Nantes in 1685 profoundly disturbed and transformed the Huguenot world. The repercussions were broad and enduring, permeating every domain from the religious and cultural to the demographic and economic. French Protestants found themselves enmeshed in a tragic experience, which ran far deeper and lasted much longer than anyone might have expected. Although the developments were not entirely unexpected and the Huguenot community had been under increasing constraint for decades, few might have predicted that the anti-Protestant measures would be so severe and the campaign to eradicate the Reformed churches and their followers so relentless. In the end, modern French Protestantism is indelibly marked by the lengthy period of the *Désert*, the difficult century of proscription and persecution that followed 1685. The ordeal concluded only with the Edict of the Toleration in 1787 and the beginnings of the Revolution two years later. This time of suffering became the heroic age, which ultimately eclipsed the formative era of the sixteenth-century religious wars and the brilliant cultural achievements that occurred during the first half of the seventeenth century.

Although estimates vary, when Louis XIV issued the Edict of Fontainebleau in mid-October 1685, abrogating the Nantes legislation of the previous century, French Reformed society totalled some 800,000 to 1,000,000 persons.[1] The Huguenot presence was strongest and densest in Dauphiné, across the Midi, and toward the west in Poitou and Saintonge. Lesser concentrations of Reformed Protestants were scattered through Normandy, the Paris basin and the Loire valley.[2] These demographic features would change dramatically in the years that followed.

---

[1] P. Benedict, *The Huguenot Population of France, 1600–1685: The Demographic Fate and Customs of a Religious Minority* (Transactions of the American Philosophical Society, 81, 1991), pp. 7–10; J. McManners, *Church and Society in Eighteenth-century France*, 2 vols. (Oxford, 1998), II, p. 565.

[2] S. Mours, *Essai sommaire de géographie du protestantisme réformé français au XVIIe siècle* (Paris, 1966).

The Revocation did not eradicate Protestantism in France, but it did alter the community in powerful ways. The overall Huguenot population unquestionably declined as people defected to the majority religion. On the other hand, those who persevered were far more dedicated. Indeed, several historians have argued that the Revocation reinvigorated a moribund church whose followers were being gradually assimilated into Catholic society. According to this view, confessionally mixed marriages, enticements toward conversion, and a variety of other pressures were taking their inexorable toll. The Revocation and events thereafter rekindled Huguenot determination and, in this sense, proved counterproductive.[3] Did these grave circumstances trigger a reawakening of the earlier process of 'confessionalization' proposed by Philip Benedict? Although the heyday of the so-called 'confessional age' had passed, the fierce rivalry and escalating violence 'defined and reinforced' religious solidarity and cultural distinctiveness with unprecedented intensity.

The choices that Huguenots faced in 1685 were few and unpleasant. As Philippe Joutard has pointed out, they could abandon their Reformed faith, go into exile, pretend to convert, or resist.[4] Some Protestants were, of course, celebrated in their defiance. They took refuge in the mountains and forests, or the anonymity of large cities; many among them were eventually arrested and punished.[5] For most people, however, overt resistance and the prospect of dragonnades, prison, the galleys or execution held little appeal. The bulk of the great aristocratic protectors and military leaders of the sixteenth and early seventeenth centuries had long made an accommodation with the Catholic monarchy. Lesser provincial nobles drifted away after the collapse of Rohan's revolt and the Peace of Alès in 1629. As is evident in Amanda Eurich's analysis of Huguenot magistrates at Castres and Pau, Protestant office-holders, both noble and bourgeois, clung to preferments in the royal judicial and fiscal bureaucracy, yet were under intense pressure to convert in the decades leading up to 1685. Most buckled. Leadership in 1685 rested consequently with the financial and commercial bourgeoisie, persons with business and professional interests. In the immediate, however, they voiced but ineffective objections and organized little opposition to the

---

[3] G. Hanlon, *Confession and Community in Seventeenth-century France: Catholic and Protestant Coexistence in Aquitaine* (Philadelphia, 1993), pp. 102–11, 207–19. P. Joutard, 'The Revocation of the Edict of Nantes: End or Renewal of French Protestantism?' in M. Prestwich (ed.), *International Calvinism, 1541–1715* (Oxford, 1985), pp. 339, 366–8.

[4] Joutard, 'End or Renewal?', pp. 339–41.

[5] S. Mours and D. Robert, *Le protestantisme en France du XVIIIe siècle à nos jours* (Paris, 1972), pp. 12–13.

king's act.[6] Had the Huguenots made a grievous error in adopting after 1598 a posture that Alan James characterizes as 'quiet co-operation with the crown', along with demonstrations of 'collective loyalty', in hopes of safeguarding their status and insuring their continuance? Was, moreover, passive resistance, which so many Huguenots counselled, in the eighteenth century, simply the logical extension of the earlier stance? After 1715, Reformed ecclesiastical leaders renounced armed resistance and even prayed for the king in their clandestine worship assemblies.

The crown had already coerced, perhaps most dramatically through its employ of intimidating dragonnades, the vast majority of Huguenots into abjuring by the eve of the Revocation. Hence, Louis XIV and his advisors could offer the fiction that the Edict of Nantes was no longer needed. 96 per cent of Protestants at the Huguenot stronghold of Montauban converted in August 1685. At Marsillargues, a small solidly Huguenot town near Nîmes, 95 per cent of the Reformed population abjured.[7] Yet these conversions were hardly sincere. Catholics certainly recognized the reality, but hoped that within a generation or two the old ways would be forgotten. In the ensuing years, Protestants generally persevered in towns and regions where they were the majority and, accordingly, possessed sufficient density for mutual assistance and collective endurance. They had long experience with pulling together and providing mutual aid when threatened. Witness the Reformed community of Bordeaux analysed by Martin Dinges. Conversely, the Huguenots drifted toward assimilation or quit regions where they were the distinct minority.[8]

In the late 1680s, for instance, royal officials in the diocese of Alès, north of Nîmes, counted 17,902 'old Catholics' as compared to 41,736 *nouveaux convertis* or *nouveaux catholiques*. The latter complied with the obligatory gestures such as attending Mass or having the priest perform baptisms and marriages, but little more. Only half of the 'new converts' at Alès even bothered to take Catholic Communion. Similarly, Catholic priests at the nearby Huguenot bastion of Anduze reported than only 10 per cent of 'new Catholics' received Communion at Easter 1689. At the same time, Protestants from these areas of concentrated strength were reluctant to flee; only slightly more than 3 per cent of those from

[6] E. G. Léonard, *Histoire générale du protestantisme*, 3 vols. (Paris, 1961), II, pp. 345–7 offers a stinging critique of Reformed leadership, especially among the pastorate, at the time of the Revocation.

[7] J.-M. Daumas, *Marsillargues en Languedoc, fief de Guillaume de Nogaret, petite Genève* (Marsillargues, 1984), pp. 71–6; McManners, *Church and Society*, II, p. 568.

[8] Joutard, 'End or Renewal?', pp. 347–8.

Alès emigrated.[9] Altogether, the blatant coercion and mistreatment of the late-seventeenth and eighteenth centuries frequently fortified the Protestant zeal of 'new Catholics'. Huguenots, particularly those who lived and worked in substantial Protestant communities, played a double game, carefully conforming to the legal requirements imposed by the monarchical state, all the while resisting Catholic practices in small ways, and collectively perpetuating their Protestant beliefs and traditions.[10]

In contrast, Protestants at Aubusson, a hub for tapestry production in central France, found it difficult to persevere in cohesive and enduring fashion. They were only some 18 per cent of the population, roughly 550 persons in a total of 3,000. About 200 Huguenots, more than a third, departed around 1685; 150 went abroad, another 50 moved to other parts of France. Of the 350 who stayed at Aubusson, 200 appear to have assimilated into the religious majority, while 150 were converts to Catholicism in name only. Not unexpectedly, the exodus of so many Huguenot artisans dealt the tapestry industry a deathblow.[11] These demographic and economic patterns, which were replicated in their broad outlines throughout Berry, the region surrounding Aubusson, were devastating. Members of the scattered and minority Huguenot congregations assimilated, fled the kingdom or migrated to larger towns such as Orléans and, above all, Paris where they sought to benefit from a measure of urban concealment. Over the course of the eighteenth century, what once had been more than a dozen Protestant communities in Berry shrank to three.[12]

A fifth or more – 150,000 to 200,000 – of all French Protestants went into exile to the Swiss cantons, various German principalities, the Netherlands, the British Isles and eventually to North America, South Africa, Scandinavia and Russia.[13] They, of course, carried their religious and cultural perspectives to these lands. At the same time, the departure

---

[9] M. Carbonnier-Burkard and P. Cabanel, *Une histoire des protestants en France* (Paris, 1998), p. 81; F. Puaux, 'Statistique des opinions religieuses du diocèse d'Alès', *BSHPF* 61 (1912), 184–5.
[10] R. A. Mentzer, *Blood and Belief: Family Survival and Confessional Identity among the Provincial Huguenot Nobility* (West Lafayette, IN, 1994), pp. 162–83.
[11] J.-L. Broilliard, 'La population protestante d'Aubusson 1685', *Mémoires de la Société des Sciences naturelles et archéologiques de la Creuse* 42 (1986), 3e fasc., xl.
[12] D. Boisson, *Les Protestants de l'ancien Colloque du Berry de la Révocation de l'Édit de Nantes à la fin de l'Ancien Régime (1679–1789), ou l'inégale résistance de minorités religieuses* (Paris, 1999); Mours and Robert, *Protestantisme du XVIIIe Siècle*, pp. 12–13.
[13] E. Labrousse, 'Le XVIIe siècle' in H. Dubief and J. Poujol (eds.), *La France protestante: histoire et lieux de mémoire* (Paris, 1996), pp. 71–3. Joutard, 'End or Renewal?', pp. 346–7, follows S. Mours, *Les galériens protestants* (Paris, 1970), p. 58 in proposing a figure of 200,000 or more *émigrés*. In general, see M. Yardeni, *Le refuge protestant* (Paris, 1985) and R. D. Gwynn, *Huguenot Heritage. The History and Contribution of the Huguenots in Britain* (Brighton, 2001).

of many members of the social and intellectual elite, people who had traditionally led the Huguenot community, had a stunning effect on those who remained in France. The overwhelming majority – roughly 80 per cent – of the 873 pastors in place at the moment of the Revocation went into exile.[14] A substantial number of intellectuals also fled abroad. The pastor and historian Philippe Le Noir de Crevain, for example, had already emigrated to Holland in March 1685. The former minister at Alençon, Elie Benoist, settled in Delft where he wrote his monumental *Histoire de l'Édit de Nantes* between 1687 and 1695.[15] Members of the petty nobility, merchants and skilled artisans left as well. They certainly possessed greater mobility than Protestant peasants of the Midi, who were tied to the land. Not surprisingly, during the next decades, worship became more familial and private or, when communal, occurred secretly and sporadically. French Protestantism also became less structured, and those who rose to positions of leadership tended to be less educated, as well as rustic, proletarian and female.[16]

The Revocation meant, of course, the destruction of Huguenot temples and the cessation of Reformed services. Hundreds of temples, built at enormous financial sacrifice and emotional commitment by Huguenot communities large and small, were pulled down. In its own way, each was, according to Andrew Spicer, an appropriate visual expression of Huguenot theological perspectives and corresponding aesthetic sensitivities. The campaign to raze the temples had been in progress for several decades, at least since the strict application of the Edict of Nantes in the 1660s. The end of formal services initially shifted the locus of Huguenot religious culture to the domestic sphere. Although household worship had always been an important element in Reformed piety, it now assumed primacy. Fathers led their families in prayer, readings from Scripture and the singing of psalms; mothers taught children basic prayers and may have given rudimentary catechism instruction.

At the same time, the faithful began to assemble clandestinely and illicitly in the *Désert* or wilderness, a strong biblical image that underscored

---

[14] Joutard, 'End or Renewal?', p. 343, utilizing figures from S. Mours, 'Les Pasteurs à la Révocation de l'Édit de Nantes', *BSHPF* 144 (1968), 67–105, 292–316, 521–4. According to Carbonnier-Burkard and Cabanel, *Protestants en France*, p. 78, there were 780 Reformed pastors, of whom 160 abjured (130 definitively) and 620 went into exile.

[15] P. Benedict, 'La Chouette de Minerve au Crépuscule, Philippe Le Noir de Crevain, pasteur sous Louis XIV', *BSHPF* 146 (2000), 335–66; C. Johnston, 'Elie Benoist, Historian of the Edict of Nantes', *Church History* 55 (1986), 468, 472–3.

[16] See generally the comments of M. E. Wiesner, *Women and Gender in Early Modern Europe* (Cambridge, 1993), pp. 203–10.

Huguenot determination. A population that time and again had striven to demonstrate its obedience and loyalty to the crown now gathered for worship in defiance of the law. Rural artisans and others of lesser social and economic status dominated the earliest assemblies. Women, in particular, assumed a stronger, more conspicuous presence than they had previously enjoyed. Anne Montjoye travelled throughout Périgord for two years, conducting religious services in secluded woods and private homes. She directed the assembled faithful as they prayed, read passages from Holy Writ and sang psalms. Royal authorities finally surprised and captured her and several dozen worshippers in 1688. Adamantly refusing to abjure, she went straightaway to the gallows. Over the next dozen or so years, assemblies in Poitou, to take another example, were occasionally led by returning pastors, equally often by unlettered farmers, artisans and women. One woman was popularly known as the 'prêcheuse'.[17]

Although the Reformation in France as elsewhere had reinforced patriarchy and restricted women's religious roles, the uncertainty and turmoil, maltreatment and disruption after 1685 allowed for a resurgence of their leadership and action. Men, especially publicly prominent individuals, found it difficult to avoid conversion, however half-hearted. The Revocation devastated those Huguenots who held positions in the judicial or financial administration. All of the judges associated with the *chambre de l'Édit* of Castres, for instance, converted by 1685. Still, many couples appear to have pursued a strategy common among early modern religious minorities: husbands outwardly conformed, while wives guarded the family's religious traditions. Pressure to convert was initially stronger for men, who tended to represent the family in the public sphere, than for women. Wives and mothers remained quietly and privately the family conduit for Reformed beliefs and practices. The tactic appears consonant with the fundamental role assigned to women in the religious upbringing of children. Women frequently displayed greater constancy. Husbands abjured to preserve the family's hard-won economic resources, while wives remained Protestant. Families thereby hoped to preserve discreetly and unobtrusively their Reformed faith for themselves and successive generations.[18]

The Revocation ultimately became an occasion for profound spiritual introspection and female prophecy. As noted, within weeks of Louis XIV's banning of the Reformed churches, Protestants began to

[17] Mours and Robert, *Protestantisme du XVIIIe siècle*, pp. 59, 80.
[18] McManners, *Church and Society*, II, p. 628; Wiesner, *Women and Gender*, p. 202; Mentzer, *Blood and Belief*, pp. 169–72.

gather clandestinely in the countryside for worship. These meetings grew rapidly in size and frequency. The presiding preachers were frequently unschooled and inexperienced laymen, often from artisan ranks. Most pastors had, after all, fled or converted. Their devout yet untrained successors, perhaps inspired by notions of the priesthood of all believers, conducted worship, gave sermons, baptized infants and administered the Lord's Supper. Most worshippers came from simple backgrounds as well; they were predominately rural craft workers, many among them women.

The influential presence of female preachers and worshippers suggests the manner whereby the ordeal of the *Désert* dissolved established relationships and offered critical leadership roles to persons who had previously been relegated to subservience. Here, Huguenot women could draw upon the example of strong female figures from the Old Testament. They became primary conveyers of religious traditions within the household and led their families to secret services in the woods and mountains. Many were willing to suffer long and painful incarceration. Those caught attending illegal religious assemblies or engaging in other dissenting and insubordinate acts were placed in Catholic hospitals and nunneries, where they sometimes inscribed defiant words and phrases on walls and attic beams.[19] Women whose offences royal authorities judged particularly egregious went to prison. Some remained there half-forgotten for years. The most celebrated among these courageous female resisters were the several dozen who were imprisoned for decades in the Tour de Constance at Aigues-Mortes. Marie Durand, for example, was confined at the age of fifteen and passed thirty-eight years in the tower prison until her release in 1768. Others died without the slightest expectation of release. Finally, a number of young women became prophetesses and protested the oppression of Protestants in a less confrontational but unconventional and highly effective manner.

Prophesying was likely the most startling development associated with the Revocation and the disappearance of an educated pastorate as well as established ecclesiastical structures. The movement began in February 1688 when an illiterate teenage shepherdess from the rural Dauphiné began to sing psalms and preach in her sleep. Though previously unable to converse in anything other than the local dialect, she offered sermons in 'perfect French' during her trance-like state. Other young women and men soon followed suit, giving voice to their apocalyptic inspiration

---

[19] Perhaps the most famous phrase is 'register' (i.e. *résister* in the local dialect), which Marie Durand etched into the stone of her prison at Aigues-Mortes. Women held at the convent of the Sisters of Saint Clare at Montauban carved similar phrases into wooden attic timbers.

and spiritual visions. In a series of illicit prophesying assemblies, they shook violently, wept and cried out for repentance. Both the adolescent visionaries and those who witnessed their activities were undoubtedly familiar with the prophet Joel's words in the midst of catastrophe: 'Your sons and your daughters shall prophesy.' Later, on the first Pentecost, the apostle Peter had quoted this passage in his sermon to the Jews.[20]

Although explanations vary, these prophets and prophetesses appear to have taken psychological refuge in acting out biblical texts, thereby expressing their anguish over the disaster that had befallen their religion and culture. Their parents' seemingly facile surrender to Catholicism deprived them of normal verbal expression for their discontent. Instead, they convulsed and raved, all the while attracting a substantial following.[21] The message of protest was unmistakable. It further angered Catholic authorities and even troubled some Huguenots. If, finally, the prophesying proved subversive, it soon prompted related activities that were openly rebellious.

The prophesying movement spread across the Midi and eventually turned violent as the more zealous sought to wreak God's retribution upon their oppressors. The murderous, protracted revolt of the Camisards – so designated for the white shirts that the insurgents typically wore – began with the assassination of the abbé du Chaila, a much-detested 'inspector of missions' and royal agent in the Cévennes. In early 1702, for instance, he had hung a young prophetess, who, among other things, had predicted his approaching death. When, in July, he arrested a group of seven adolescent Protestants, three girls and four boys, who were fleeing to Switzerland, reaction was swift and furious. Du Chaila sent the girls to a convent at Mende and held the boys at Pont-de-Montvert. Events reached a crisis after the 'Spirit' commanded the woolcomber and prophet Abraham Mazel to gather fifty or more followers and liberate the young boy prisoners. In the ensuing mêlée, the abbé and three of his companions were killed. The act touched raw, exposed nerves on both sides of the bitter confessional struggle. Some Protestants turned to similar acts of vengeance, such as murdering priests and burning churches. Others waged better-organized, more lasting and initially successful guerrilla warfare. Royal troops responded predictably with further repression and reprisals.

The war dragged on for eight years and led to the death of numerous Protestants as well as Catholics. Although various groups of Huguenot

---

[20] Joel 3:28; Acts 2:17.   [21] Joutard, 'End or Renewal?', pp. 363–4.

artisans and peasants at first operated independently, they soon coa-
lesced around the military leadership of Jean Cavalier, an apprentice
baker, and the celebrated Rolland, nom de guerre for Pierre Laporte.
Cavalier led them in a succession of military victories in the Cévennes
mountains and eastern Languedoc. Their guerrilla campaigns benefited
from material support from the local Protestant populace and a confidence borne of the prophesying movement. Over time, however, Louis
XIV's armies wore down and subdued the rebels. Cavalier surrendered,
Rolland was killed and other leaders negotiated separate truces. The
principal fighting ended by October 1704, and while more ardent and
steadfast Camisards revived the conflict in 1705 and continued until
1710, the revolt had effectively collapsed.[22] In any event, much as Luc
Racaut indicates for the sixteenth century, 'armed rebellion' did not accord well with the 'image of the Huguenot martyr', whether it was outlawed pastors despatched to the gallows, modest artisans suffering on the
galleys, or steadfast mothers and daughters languishing in convents and
prisons. French Protestants would now proceed in an altogether different
direction.

In late August 1715, just weeks prior to the death of their persecutor,
Louis XIV, a handful of Huguenot ecclesiastical leaders and several laymen gathered near Nîmes with twenty-year-old Antoine Court to begin
the reorganization of the French Reformed church. Court disapproved
of both armed resistance and prophesying. He had personal experience
with the latter; as a young boy, he had attended prophetic assemblies with
his mother, and had subsequently served as a guard for the prophetess
Claire. Court possessed tremendous organizing talent and energetically
set about reconstituting the church.

The group of pastors and laymen over which Court presided sought
to restore Reformed identity, along with discipline and respectability.
They re-established a systematic federative structure for the churches of
the *Désert*. Pastors were given formal training, typically in Switzerland,
and despatched to clandestine churches in France; they and lay elders
were assigned specific responsibilities; secret consistories and synods con-
vened regularly; disciplinary forms for ecclesiastical censure and fraternal correction were created. At the same time, women were barred from
preaching, and prophesying was firmly repudiated. Court ushered in the
explicit return to an 'orthodox' church polity and the orderliness that it

---

[22] For a detailed account, see P. Joutard, *Les Camisards* (Paris, 1976); also his *La légende des Camisards*
(Paris, 1977).

represented. The reinstitution of this highly structured and traditional approach spread rapidly through the covert world of Huguenot worship. On the other hand, a number of important traditional features of French Protestantism – poor-relief systems, for example – could not be easily resuscitated.

Court followed his success in reconstituting the provincial structure of the Reformed churches by organizing the provinces into a national network. The first national synod in nearly seventy years met in Vivarais in 1726. The following year, Court established a seminary at Lausanne to prepare pastors. The project may not have possessed the academic breadth and intellectual sparkle that Karin Maag details for the sixteenth- and seventeenth-century Huguenot academies. Still, the Lausanne seminary owed much to the earlier tradition and ongoing notions of the fundamental importance of well-educated pastors and stable institutions for their preparation.

Although Court withdrew to Lausanne by 1729, he continued to direct developments in France by correspondence. At the sixth national synod *au Désert* in 1756, the thirty-three deputies represented Protestants from every region of the kingdom. Local congregations, isolated and fragmented by the Revocation and attendant abuse, had come together under difficult circumstances. Rebuilt through the efforts of Court and others, the churches of the *Désert* often proclaimed themselves 'sous la croix', and they endured despite continuing hardship and intimidation. Indeed, by the mid-eighteenth century, they felt sufficiently strong to contemplate a dialogue with a regime that had long sought to eradicate them. The political value of 'negotiation with the crown', which Penny Roberts identifies as an essential feature of the sixteenth-century Huguenot movement, reasserted itself. Once again, to borrow Timothy Watson's language, the principals in the Huguenot movement set about transforming themselves from 'subversive' to 'respectable'. Reintegration of the French Protestants had begun as both sides gradually entered into discussions over the terms for reinstatement of coexistence.

One unexpected effect of the Revocation, at least from the Catholic viewpoint, was that Huguenots enjoyed a measure of restored political influence on the local level. Raymond Mentzer points out that they had been progressively barred from municipal offices during the latter years of the regime of the Edict of Nantes. Now, as 'new Catholics', they could reclaim positions of power and authority in local government affairs.[23]

---

[23] Joutard, 'End or Renewal?', p. 360.

These meagre gains, however, were generally confined to specific localities where 'new Catholics' were a majority. They were, moreover, little recompense for pervasive mistreatment.

Protestants observers both contemporary and subsequent have reproached Huguenot society, or at least some within it, for failure to respond adequately to the crisis of the Revocation and its sombre aftermath. The Methodist minister Mathieu Lelièvre and the Reformed historian Emile Léonard, the former writing in the early twentieth century, the latter in the 1960s, had harsh words for the pastors. Both cited Claude Brousson, a celebrated attorney, pastor and martyr, who accused the men who served as pastors on the eve of the Revocation of scandal and indecency, intemperance and buffoonery; they were deceitful and quarrelsome, vain and malicious; they shirked their duties and failed to minister to their congregations.[24] Certainly, the last national synod before the Revocation, meeting at Loudon from November 1659 until January 1660, expressed doubts regarding the behaviour of some pastors. Had the academies, as Léonard later charged, become incapable of training students properly for their future task? Other grievances focused on lay leadership. Paul Rabaut, the leading pastor in France after Court's departure for Lausanne, voiced concern in the 1740s about the temerity of the bourgeoisie, from whose ranks the elders had traditionally come. On the other hand, he took enormous pride in the steadfast faith of ordinary folk.[25]

In reality, it was probably easier for individuals without significant economic resources or social status to shun, for instance, official Catholic marriages and baptisms. For religious reasons, they preferred to have these rites performed secretly and illegally by Protestant pastors. Those with wealth and position, however, could rarely afford to risk the validity of their civil status. They required legally recognized marriages and legitimate heirs in order to maintain family bonds, strengthen parental influence and assure the orderly, unchallenged transmission of property from one generation to the next. Thus, prominent Protestants often conformed outwardly for the sake of their children's future. The family's economic and social requirements tempered resistance and promoted the need to be at least officially Catholic.

Rabaut's observations, however, were not without value and prompt other interpretative possibilities. Whatever the merits of the various

---

[24] M. Lelièvre, *De la Révocation à la Révolution. 1. 1685–1715* (Paris, 1911), p. 6, as cited by Léonard, *Histoire générale*, II, p. 346.

[25] McManners, *Church and Society*, II, p. 594.

complaints against pastoral and lay leadership, the harsh indictment of the Reformed churches and their followers can be turned on its head. Hadn't ordinary people risen to the challenge? Didn't prophets, for example, demonstrate knowledge of Scripture or women the literacy necessary to inscribe moving and evocative words on the walls where they were unwillingly detained? The evidence speaks to the fundamental place of the text and its systematic dissemination within Huguenot culture.

A related consequence of the eighteenth-century harassment of Protestants was, in some observers' opinion, a profound scepticism and anticlericalism. A number of Huguenots who grew up after 1685 had scant knowledge of or access to their parents' and grandparents' religion, and no taste or respect for what they regarded as an oppressive Catholicism. When coupled with the traditional regard for learning and erudition among the Protestant minority, the developments could lead to an affinity for the emerging Enlightenment and its secular approach.

For those Huguenots who led a double life – outward conformity to Catholicism, inner faithfulness to Protestantism – accommodation meant seeking out the *curé* for baptism of infants, and marrying before a priest. These actions could be rationalized in term of the need to establish civil identity. Curiously, death was often one of the tensest moments for 'new Catholics' and their families. Deathbed refusal of the last sacraments – confession, the host and extreme unction – could mean confiscation of family property, and prison or the galleys if a sick person rallied. Sometimes *curés* looked the other way; often families claimed a 'sudden death', which would have given them no opportunity to summon a priest. A few 'new converts' welcomed the opportunity to renounce their earlier forced abjuration. Deemed relapsed, their bodies were ignominiously dragged through the streets on a litter and eventually tossed upon the local garbage heap. Yet the penalty could backfire. When the corpses of three Huguenots from Metz were so treated, their co-religionists, far from feeling shame, 'glorified' the victims.[26]

As Bernard Roussel indicates in his discussion of burial rituals, Reformed Protestants, while not indifferent to the treatment of the corpse, had 'disenchanted' the ceremonies surrounding its burial. Did this sense of metaphysical detachment extend, albeit in lesser fashion, to other Catholic rites? Calvin and his followers emphasized sacred transcendence and, accordingly, located Christian religiosity in a spiritual

[26] Mours and Robert, *Protestantisme du XVIIIe siècle*, p. 31.

universe independent of time and the material world. Would this view have made it less onerous for 'new Catholics' to assist at Mass and receive communion 'without any devotion', even pretending that the host was 'a morsel of apple'?[27] Early Protestants found elaborate Catholic rituals and their stress upon the immanent character of the liturgy offensive and idolatrous. Had some of their 'new Catholic' descendants ceased to regard these rites as abhorrent? Were they simply taken to be devoid of meaning?

What finally do we make of these perspectives on the Huguenot world? This is, after all, the narrative of a religious minority that created a unique and enduring culture. How, to pose an obvious question, is the issue of Huguenot culture related to tenacious perseverance? Indeed, what were the essential elements of the culture experience that accompanied the Reformation in France? How are we to interpret the difficulties that the situation posed for the construction and internalization of religious and social identity? What were the wider reverberations? How generally do the circumstances help us better understand the status and nature of religious minorities in the early modern age?

As Mark Greengrass aptly remarks, the Huguenots were 'never more than a minority'; a situation which inevitably shaped a mentality that was defensive, stoic and collective. Not surprisingly, this was a close, highly integrated community. Its members worshipped together in the temple and joined in common religious rites. They shared similar political objectives, constantly exchanged letters and ideas, and together pressed the crown through formal petitions as well as the court system to respect their civil status. The elite despatched their sons to municipal *collèges* and regional academies; they engaged in intellectual pursuits that added lustre to the entire community. Above all, they collectively suffered unrelenting persecution. Some yielded, at different moments and for a variety of reasons. Others offered fiery resistance. More than a few sought ways for accommodation and quiet survival. Even today, the memory of Huguenot society and culture is, for French people of every hue and stripe, one of intellectual achievement, communal solidarity and religious suffering.

While for many people today, the century of the *Désert* has overshadowed the events of the sixteenth and seventeenth centuries, the resilience of the movement and its survival owed much to the values and character traits formed during the wars of religion and the years under the Edict of

---

[27] *Ibid.*, p. 23.

Nantes. Although the Huguenots fell victim to an intolerant opposition as well as the *raison d'état* of an absolute monarch in 1685, their struggle, achievement and continuance of religious coexistence within such a powerful nation state should not be diminished. The Edict of Nantes was not a panacea and represented but the shadow of what the movement had hoped for in 1562. It was none the less a remarkable accomplishment for a numerically small and geographically confined sector of French society in an era of confessional conflict.

Index

Lightning Source UK Ltd.
Milton Keynes UK
UKHW011949171118

332535UK00001B/80/P